PLAY IT AGAIN:
COVER SONGS IN POPULAR MUSIC

always,
for Julie, Anaïs, and Rivers…
three Originals

Play it Again:
Cover Songs in Popular Music

GEORGE PLASKETES
Auburn University, USA

ASHGATE

Published by
Ashgate Publishing Limited
Wey Court East
Union Road
Farnham
Surrey, GU9 7PT
England

Ashgate Publishing Company
Suite 420
101 Cherry Street
Burlington
VT 05401-4405
USA

www.ashgate.com

British Library Cataloguing in Publication Data
Plasketes, George.
    Play it again : cover songs in popular music. – (Ashgate popular and folk music series)
    1. Cover versions.
    I. Title II. Series
    782.4'2164–dc22

Library of Congress Cataloging-in-Publication Data
Plasketes, George.
    Play it again : cover songs in popular music / George Plasketes.
        p. cm.—(Ashgate popular and folk music series)
    Includes bibliographical references and index.
    ISBN 978-0-7546-6809-1 (hardcover : alk. paper)
    1. Popular music—History and criticism. 2. Cover versions—History and criticism.
I. Title.

    ML3470.P58 2009
    781.6309—dc22

                                                            2009035084

ISBN 9780754668091 (hbk)
ISBN 9780754699910 (ebk)

Mixed Sources
Product group from well-managed
forests and other controlled sources
www.fsc.org Cert no. SA-COC-1565
© 1996 Forest Stewardship Council
FSC

Printed and bound in Great Britain by
MPG Books Group, UK

Contents

LOOK WHAT THEY'VE DONE TO MY SONG: GENDER, IDENTITY, MEDIA MAKEOVERS

DON'T FORGET TO DANCE: TECHNIQUE AND TECHNO TRANSFORMATIONS

CONTEMPLATING COVERS

BACK COVER: EPILOGUE

Notes on Contributors

Lee Barron is Professor of Media Culture and Society at University of Northumbria. He has published extensively in journals such as *Body & Culture*, *The Journal of Popular Culture*, *Chapter and Verse*, *International Review of the Aesthetics* and *Sociology of Music*, and in a range of edited collections on popular music and film.

B. Lee Cooper is the author of 15 books on various aspects of popular music, including the three volume series *Rock Music in American Culture* (Haworth, 1995–99), and more than 400 articles and book/record reviews. One of his recent publications is an anthology of essays on *New Orleans Music: Legacy and Survival* (2008).

Don Cusic is Professor of Music Business at Belmont University in Nashville, Tennessee. He is the author of 12 books on popular music, including a biography on Eddy Arnold and gospel music.

Andrew G. Davis recently completed his MA thesis on political satirist Bill Hicks in the Department of Communication & Journalism at Auburn University in Alabama. Davis is the co-founder and Executive Director of the Feathered Serpent Collective, a multi media arts management firm. He is host of *Grown Folks'Show*, a weekly public radio broadcast WEGL/Alabama specializing in funk, R & B, soul, groove and blues.

Joshua S. Duchan is a Mellon Post-Doctoral Fellow in the Music Department at Bowling Green State University in Ohio. He has published several articles on various dimensions of college a cappella.

Stuart Lenig is a professor of Theatre at Columbia State Community College in Tennessee. He is completing a book on Glam Rock to be published by Praeger Press.

Greg Metcalf is a lecturer at the Smithsonian and an adjunct professor at the Smithsonian University of Maryland, the Maryland Institute College of Art and Johns Hopkins University in departments of American Studies, Art History, Comparative Literature, English and Humanities. He has published works on film, art, popular culture and celebrity identity in the work of Andy Warhol. He is currently working on a book on the DVD novel for Praeger Press.

Remy Miller is Professor of Art, Memphis College of the Arts in Tennessee and fronts the band the Remainders. His paintings, drawings and sculptures have been exhibited in art galleries and museums regionally and nationally.

George Plasketes is Professor of Radio-Television-Film and Popular Culture at Auburn University in Alabama. He has authored two books on Elvis Presley images and fanaticism, and various other works on music, media and popular culture. His most recent book is *B-Sides, Undercurrents and Overtones: Peripheries to Popular in Music, 1960 to the Present* (Ashgate, 2009).

Russell Reising, Professor of American Literature & Culture, University of Toledo, recently was selected to deliver the opening address at the Rock and Roll Hall of Fame and museum for its special show on psychedelic music, "I Want to Take You Higher." He has published two books for Ashgate's "Popular and Folk Music Series"—one, an award-winning volume on The Beatles' *Revolver*, and another on Pink Floyd's *Dark Side of the Moon.*

Sheldon Schiffer is an Associate Professor of Film at Georgia State University in Atlanta. His interests are in subcultures and their appearance and expressions in film, music, and media. His films include *The Rise and Fall of Black Velvet Flag*, a documentary on the 1990s lounge-punk band. His new works examine American appropriation of Afro-Brazilian martial art, *Capoeira* in cinema, music and popular culture.

Erik Steinskog is an Associate Professor in Musicology at the Grieg-Academy, Department of Music, University of Bergen. His articles on queer pop, opera and aura have been published in *Trickster*, *Studia Musicolgica Norvegica*, and *The Actualities of Aura: Twelve Studies on Walter Benjamin*, a volume which he co-edited.

David Tough is Assistant Professor of Audio Engineering Technology at Belmont University in Nashville. He has worked for Capitol Records, Warner Chappell and BMI Music Publishing, and WEA Distribution, and as a producer, engineer and writer for several independent artists in Los Angeles and Nashville.

Deena Weinstein, Professor of Sociology, DePaul University in Chicago, is author of *Heavy Metal: The Music and its Culture* (De Capo, 2000), several sociology texts, and countless articles on postmodernism, media, celebrity, youth culture and rock.

Christine R. Yano is Professor of Anthropology, University of Hawaii and author of *Tears of Longing: Nostalgia and the Nation in Japanese Popular Song* (Harvard. 2002).

General Editor's Preface

The upheaval that occurred in musicology during the last two decades of the twentieth century has created a new urgency for the study of popular music alongside the development of new critical and theoretical models. A relativistic outlook has replaced the universal perspective of modernism (the international ambitions of the 12-note style); the grand narrative of the evolution and dissolution of tonality has been challenged, and emphasis has shifted to cultural context, reception and subject position. Together, these have conspired to eat away at the status of canonical composers and categories of high and low in music. A need has arisen, also, to recognize and address the emergence of crossovers, mixed and new genres, to engage in debates concerning the vexed problem of what constitutes authenticity in music and to offer a critique of musical practice as the product of free, individual expression.

Popular musicology is now a vital and exciting area of scholarship, and the *Ashgate Popular and Folk Music Series* presents some of the best research in the field. Authors are concerned with locating musical practices, values and meanings in cultural context, and may draw upon methodologies and theories developed in cultural studies, semiotics, poststructuralism, psychology and sociology. The series focuses on popular musics of the twentieth and twenty-first centuries. It is designed to embrace the world's popular musics from Acid Jazz to Zydeco, whether high tech or low tech, commercial or non-commercial, contemporary or traditional.

Derek B. Scott,
Professor of Critical Musicology,
University of Leeds, UK

Acknowledgments

While sketching out this appreciation with the telly on, the new "We Are the World" video aired during the NBC network's broadcast of the opening ceremonies of the Winter Olympic Games in Vancouver. The premiere seemed a fitting punctuation mark for this project. After all, the charity anthem represented yet another strand of the cover song. The current Haiti Relief rendition is an encore twenty-five years after the Hunger for Africa original, with Quincy Jones orchestrating both. The only repeat artist in the new version was Michael Jackson, posthumously digitized in duet with sister Janet. And wasn't that actor Vince Vaughn choir crashing in the back row? I'll take the 1985 original.

The "We Are the World" gathering struck me as being slightly analogous with *Play It Again*, though this leans more toward "With A Little Help From My Friends." I'm grateful and honored to have the opportunity to continue my relationship with the fine front row folks at Ashgate, and to be a part of the press's *Popular and Folk Music Series*. Praise on high to Editor Extraordinaires Heidi Bishop, Professor Derek Scott, and Sarah Charters for nurturing this manuscript from proposal to publication, and for indulging the excessive word count. We're so sorry (Uncle) Albert Stewart for the copy flaws, but your painstaking proofing thankfully doesn't miss much. As for the Heartbeat of this collection, it has been both privilege and pleasure working with the Fab Fourteen authors who comprise the chorus of this Cover Cause. Your varied perspectives sing so soulfully on these pages; every word rings true. And thanks for not taking me up on the Boxed Set bribe that I initially offered for your writing contribution.

I can always count on steadfast background vocalists Gary Burns and *Popular Music and Society*, George Lewis, Gary Edgerton and Bill Kolar. Thanks pals.

At Auburn University, my Department of Communication & Journalism Chairs, Mary Helen Brown and Margaret Fitch Hauser, are continually supportive and resourceful, as are my colleagues, and Deans Anne Katrine Gramberg and Paula Bobrowski in the College of Liberal Arts. Much gratitude to Shannon Solomon for the manuscript manicure and Microsoft management.

Let's close with "Family Affair." My wife Julie, our daughter Anaïs, son Rivers, and dog Lulu are the Best Versions Ever, providing daily inspiration, clarity, purpose and amazing grace. Endless thanks. And love.

Introduction

Like A Version

George Plasketes

These are the ways of Providence, of which all art is but a little imitation.

—Charles Dickens

The arts have always borrowed from, commented on, and been judged by their past. The time-honored use of quotation as homage, apprenticeship, allusion, and parody appear in literature, film, and the visual and performing arts. Music, too, has its equivalents of quotation, borrowing, and interpretive works. Perhaps never before has this been more apparent than during the postmodern era. By the late 1980s and into the 1990s, popular music was undergoing a qualitative change, and the lines between authenticity and imitation, borrowing and artistic plagiarism, grew increasingly blurred. At the center of this musical market and cultural movement were cover songs.

Covering—the musical practice of one artist recording or performing another composer's song—has always been a significant attribute of popular music. In 2009, the Internet database Second Hand Songs estimates that there are 40,000 songs with at least one cover version. Some of the more common variations of this "appropriationist" method of musical quotation include traditional tunes such as "Take Me Out to the Ball Game" (a celebrity sing-along cover during the seventh inning stretch of every Chicago Cubs home game), patriotic anthems, religious hymns such as "Amazing Grace," work songs, a cappella renditions, Muzak's instrumental interpretations, marching bands, Christmas classics, and children's songs. Novelty and comic collections from parodists such as Weird Al Yankovic also align in the cover category, as does the "larcenous art" of sampling, and technological variations in dance remixes and mashups. Film and television soundtracks and advertisers increasingly rely on versions of familiar pop tunes to assist in marketing their narratives, images, brands and products. By the mid-1990s, cover compilations and multi-artist tribute records saturated the marketplace to the point that they transcended trendy and became established as a viable subgenre. The exhaustion prompted *Musician Magazine*'s Dave DiMartino to observe, "Most interesting in the world of trendy tributes is the simple question, 'Who's left?'" Ten years after, tributaries continue to flow and cover variations abound. Duets, concert commemorations, live, intimate *Unplugged* performances popularized by MTV, impersonators and *American Idol* contestants are among the sing-along, star making, microphone machinery that comprises the collective karaoke craze of additional cover fragments and fallout.

The cover phenomenon in popular culture may be viewed as a postmodern manifestation of rampant recontextualization in music as artists revisit, reinterpret and re-examine a significant cross section of musical styles, periods, genres, individual records and other artists and their catalogs of works. Covering also embraces, cultural, commercial and creative contexts. Critical discussions explore issues such as contextualization, authenticity, repetition, ownership, originality, cultural exhaustion, homage, and conflicts between commodity and concept. Defenders of the song adaptations counter with the importance of a historical context, preservation, and the value in exposing new and unknown artists and listeners to timeless tunes. In the process, a new set of song standards is emerging. One of the simplest views within this musical milieu might be that the process of covering, whether considered within the conceptual or commercial context, is about favorite songs and about great songs. Classics and standards. In the process, no matter the artistic or commercial intent, these musical artifacts are kept culturally alive, repeating as echoes and historical duets.

The cover complex, with its multiple variations, issues, and contexts, comprises an important and rich popular culture text. These re-recordings represent aural artifacts which embody artistic, social, cultural, historical, commercial, biographical, and novel meanings. Through homage, allusion, apprenticeship, and parody, among other performance modes, these diverse musical quotations express, preserve, and distribute popular culture, popular music and their intersecting historical narratives.

Coverage

There has been a curious void in literature devoted to the critical inquiry on cover songs, particularly when considering the pervasiveness of covers in the music marketplace. The published works remain sparse, at best, with a smattering of scholarly articles, essays, and book chapters. The few book length treatments, such as Joseph Lanza's *Elevator Music: A Surreal History of Muzak Easy Listening and Other Moodsong* (1995) and *Merry Christmas, Baby: Holiday Music From Bing to Sting* by Dave Marsh and Steve Propes (1993), are specialized, not to mention somewhat dated.

Two studies are framed by specific genres. Singer-songwriter Nanci Griffith's and Joe Jackson's *Other Voices: A Personal History of Folk Music* (1998) provides a musicological song-by-song companion piece to Griffith's two recorded volumes of collaborative contemporary covers *Other Voices, Other Rooms* (1993) and *Other Voices Too: A Trip to Bountiful* (1997). Michael Awkward's *Soul Covers: Rhythm and Blues Remakes and the Struggle for Artistic Identity* (2007) explores how Aretha Franklin, Al Green and Phoebe Snow used covers to negotiate questions of artistic, racial and personal identity.

A few sources provide in depth case studies of individual songs, among them Dave Marsh's *Louie, Louie* lineage (1993), Jody Rosen's *White Christmas* (2002) tome and Bill Moyers's documentary *Amazing Grace* (1992). All of these sources demonstrate the complex biographical, social, political, artistic and cultural heritage contained in songs.

Little by little, covers are shifting from being uncovered toward being discovered. Among the articles in print in the popular press is Tom Bligh's "A Treatise on Cover Songs" in the *Oxford American Magazine*'s 2006 music issue. The most varied assemblage of articles on cover songs is located in the seven essays that comprise a special issue of *Popular Music and Society* (Volume 28, Number 2) in May 2005. Remastered versions of some of those essays have been expanded, updated and adapted into these pages. In April 2009, the International Association for the Study of Popular Music (IASPM) solicited submissions for a similar special issue of *Copyright Volume!* designed to focus on the multidisciplinary approach to cover songs. An increasing number of resourceful online sites and data bases are devoted to compiling, categorizing and considering cover songs, among the dot-coms are Coverville, CoversProject, SecondHandSongs and artist sites such as DylanCoverAlbums, which archives the voluminous Bob Dylan interpretive discography.

This collection of essays represents the first scholarly volume of critical perspectives on cover songs. The eclectic group of contributors are artists, scholars, writers and professionals who represent an array of musical tastes and interests, academic interdisciplines and expertise, and walks of life that span the visual arts, filmmaking, music, history, music business, literature, sociology, anthropology, journalism, media arts, theatre and audio engineering. Their approaches to their subject matter reflect the polysemic nature of cover songs as a text. In addition to comparative case studies of individual songs, the chapters address genres, gender and generation, artists, audience and industry, ideology and identity, and creative and commercial contrasts and issues within theoretical, critical, cultural, historical and global contexts.

From Cover to Cover

The fifteen essays in this collection are organized into several thematic sections which are more overlapping than they are mutually exclusive. The groupings are intended to provide some sense of structure for the assortment of readings. The "Front Cover" initiates the cover song quest with a sprawling survey of "The Cover Age," a characterization of the past quarter century's predominant "Re" mode of cultural production. The chapter serves as a treatise that chronicles and collages cases of the vast, continuous "coverage" within the music and mass media marketplace. The discussion presents issues such as authenticity, intertextuality, ownership, apprenticeship, repetition, and preservation as they relate to cover songs and its many variations and the re-performance processes in popular music and culture.

Historical, ideological and global perspectives follow, beginning with Lee Cooper's study of early song assimilation through cover recording. The essay utilizes two weekly popular music charts, *Billboard* and *Cash Box*, to track expanding commercial interest in new music, whether performed by traditional stylists or by new artists. Cooper chronicles how American musical culture shifted dramatically at mid century (1953–57) due to the cross pollination of singing and instrumental styles exhibited in multiple performance of new songs.

Sheldon Schiffer presents the cover song as a historical marker and force that reshapes ideology. With particular emphasis on Mod, Punk and post-Punk texts, the discussion reaches beyond musical and lyrical content to characterize the cover song as a complex form of sociocultural expression that includes politics, race, fashion, style, subculture, generation and class.

Christine Yano expands the cover cartography to a world view by way of the Japanese sentimental ballad form, *enka*. The multiple performance practices in the song genre are not only enterprise driven, but also embedded within cultural values, aesthetics, sociality, respect and hierarchy. The universal cover triangulation between song, composer, and interpreter generates what Yano labels an "emergent authenticity" to characterize authority and validation accrued over time through processes of imitation, repetition and tribute.

The midsections of this volume focus on the recontextualization process through covering. The transformation case studies include individual songs and their various versions, albums, genres and artists' catalogs. Andrew Davis traces the genealogy of Hoyt Axton's "The Pusher" from a counterculture anthem of excess popularized by John Kay and Steppenwolf in the touchstone 1960s film *Easy Rider* to an anti-drug outcry of black empowerment (Nina Simone) to a pro-drug, anti-religion rejection of American values (Blind Melon). Each of these artists use the same lyrics to recontextualize the overall meaning of the song through a personal narrative of drug use. Stu Lenig visits the mod Brit scene of the 1960s via David Bowie's *Pin-Ups* (1973). The album is a statement of influences by the enigmatic artist featuring songs by faves such as the Who, Yardbirds, and Kinks. The record foreshadowed the album-length cover album and tribute trend that became prolific during the 1990s

The recontextualization theme continues in the section that follows, "Look What They've Done to My Song." As the title suggests, the focus shifts slightly, emphasizing the looking as well as the listening. These three chapters chronicle a variety of visual texts and voices interpreting the extensive songbooks of Leonard Cohen and Bob Dylan and their various adaptations into television and film presentations. There have been a number of Cohen cover projects, among them Jennifer Warnes's elegant *Famous Blue Raincoat* (1987) and the multi-artist tributes *I'm Your Fan* (1991) and *Tower of Song* (1995). Employing gender as a theoretical base, Erik Steinkosk uses the Liam Lunson's concert documentary of the Hal Willner produced tribute, *Leonard Cohen: I'm Your Man* (2005) and its soundtrack, to frame his discussion of repetition, identity and subversion in a variety of Cohen covers, including the transcendent Jeff Buckley and John Cale versions of the hymnlike "Hallelujah."

From the Byrds adaptations in the 1960s to the Todd Haynes Dylan bio *I'm Not There* and presentations between and beyond, the vast Dylan discography, rivals, if not surpasses, the Beatles catalog in volume and variation of interpretation. While Dylan covers merit a book length treatment, there are two chapters here which scratch the surface with depth and detail. Russell Reising documents one of Dylan's most frequently covered compositions, "All Along the Watchtower," with particular emphasis on the Jimi Hendrix classic electrified version, and its widespread presentation throughout scenes and soundtracks of television episodes and film. Greg Metcalf broadens the context, inventively connecting career and covers by outlining how Dylan's body of works reveals a series of variations on the idea of the cover. In a review of Dylan's 46th album, *Together Through Life* (2009), Joe Klein writes that Dylan "began as a tribute act: Woody Guthrie reinvented," from the way he pooched lips and held his guitar to singing mostly other people's songs on his first, eponymous album. (2009: 152) Metcalf pursues a similar path as Klein, tracing a narrative arc that outlines how Dylan has used covers, especially of his own songs and own personae, to recreate and reposition himself and his work. Dylan expands the concept of cover recordings, integrating them into his projects in music, radio, and film, and into the inescapable identity which is parodied, imitated, and ultimately explored in the film *I'm Not There*.

Technique and technology within different musical genres represent a significant, and evolving dimension of cover songs. Joshua Duchan veers from the musical mainstream to the margins, placing Imogen Heap's vocoder-vocal, Laurie Anderson-like, "Hide and Seek" within the unsung mimicry of collegiate a cappella. Duchan provides renewed attention to musical detail and technique within this unique musical setting. The concept "microcovering" highlights aspects of composition and arrangement that frequently lie at the margins of critical analysis.

"Mashup" is a relatively new variation of the cover song. David Tough provides an overview of the techno-process of mashup, which is usually created by combining an a cappella vocal from one song and the musical track from another. Technology and software programs have made the adaptation process cost and time efficient, not to mention immediate. Artists often utilize lesser known pop songs with alternative rhythm tracks, creating a contemporary sound with broader appeal. The mashup is part of a cover expansion into a subgenre of "found sound."

Rhythmic renditions and sound sampling in disco and dance remixes are cover precursors to the mashup. Lee Barron draws from literature on adaptation (from novel to film or television) and applies it to dance and its genres, particularly HI-NRG and Trance/Europop, because of its penchant for covering classic songs beyond mere sampling. The discussion addresses various song adaptations, and their audiences, in relation to their overtly camp sensibility and the postmodernist subversion of the tones and subjects of the original tracks.

The trio of essays that wind down the cover discussion are contemplative critical pieces that consider artist, audience, aesthetics, and of course, authenticity. The cover song inherently invites comparison and contrast as a duet between the original and its version(s). Don Cusic addresses the common perception that dismisses singers who cover songs as being less "legitimate" than the original artist. Cusic argues for the validation of artistic interpretation as a credible form that transcends mere copying.

The record replication that is the core of covering generates inevitable discussion about quality and originality. These themes emerge as Remy Miller integrates art criticism into the cover conversation while considering the qualities that distinguish a great cover version from lesser interpretations. Miller proposes three broadly subjective qualifications: 1) affection and commitment to the original; 2) intention of art; and 3) point of view or "something to say." Miller identifies these common qualities in four songs, contrasting originals by the Jackson Five, Carole King, Jimi Hendrix and Iggy and the Stooges with their cover versions recorded by Graham Parker, Nils Lofgren, Derek and the Dominoes and the Sex Pistols.

Deena Weinstein's "History of Rock's Pasts Through Rock's Covers" from 1998 is one of the seminal scholarly articles on covers songs. In the closing chapter, Weinstein provides an encore or sequel. Perhaps more than anything, the piece is a meditation on the essence of the cover song. In this case, the cover and its original are treated as "cultural siblings" whose rivalry and mutuality converge in a "stereophonic act" involving a listener's history, tastes, pleasure and appreciation. The nifty term—"stereophony"—may be as aptly inventive a characterization for cover songs in their purest form as there is. Simply dissected, "stereo" captures the mutuality and duality of covers, while "phony" suggests a fake, lacking originality or authenticity.

The chapter provides a fitting conclusion to this collection. The stereophonic premise reverberates, a ricochet that echoes through the previous pages, while promising the possibility of continuous coverage. As Weinstein concludes, ultimately, much of the meaning and value in the cover song lies in its ability to brings listeners to new places and positions, and to make possible the broadening, deepening, and enhancing of appreciative capacity. With apologies for giving away the ending, that critical view also serves as a punctuation mark for *Play It Again.*

The array of essays assembled here may fulfill a similar purpose with its audience by broadening, deepening, and enhancing their appreciation capacity, and perhaps even provide a measure of pleasure, on some critical or casual level. Whether interjecting "Re," "tributaries," "emergent authenticity," "found sound," "microcovering," or "stereophony," among other critical perspectives, into the cover song conversation, these re-flections exhibit the scope and depth, contrasts and complexities, and the abundant mutuality of this musical text.

As the initial scholarly volume on the subject, "groundbreaking" may be overstating the cover cause of this overdue collection. These chapters represent a foundation of fifteen, a significant sampling that lies at the forefront of the Cover Curve. The thoughts and words on these pages will hopefully contribute meaning and multiplicity to the body of works on cover songs that is certain to steadily accumulate, if not proliferate, in popular music literature. While *Play It Again* covers considerable ground, there remains an endless expanse of musical territory to uncover. The stereophonic act persists. Sibling songs, duets repeating in rivalry and reciprocity. Over and over. Again and again.

FRONT COVER: TREATISE

Chapter 1

Further Re-flections on "The Cover Age": A Collage and Chronicle[1]

George Plasketes

Songs are just songs and everyone should sing them.
—Rickie Lee Jones ("Beneath the Covers," 2000)

In 2005, Malvina Reynolds's "Little Boxes," a song from 1962 that satirized the sameness of suburbia, was revived as a soundtrack signature for the opening titles of the Showtime cable television series *Weeds*. During the course of the show's second and third seasons, in 2006 and 2007, the catchy, ticky-tack tune was transformed into a little box set of Reynolds's renditions.[2] Twenty-six artists were recruited to contribute their own interpretations of Reynolds's cookie cutter community commentary to announce each episode. Participants in the diverse cover chorus included Pete Seeger, who popularized the original in 1963, Elvis Costello, Randy Newman, Billy Bob Thornton, the Decemberists, Death Cab for Cutie, Donovan, Regina Spektor, Joan Baez, the Shins, the Individuals, Mates of State, Kate and Anna McGarrigle (*au France*), Jenny Lewis, Linkin Park, and Engelbert Humperdinck.

A comparable concentration of cover versions is prevalent in the Parisian velvet curtain cabaret setting of Baz Luhrman's musical spectacle *Moulin Rouge* (2002). The film's "Elephant Love Medley" scene alone fuses fragments of thirteen popular love songs and ballads from a range of artists that includes Sweet, the Beatles, Kiss, U2, Dolly Parton, David Bowie and Elton John. On a slightly smaller scale, there is the annual indie cover event at legendary free form radio station WFMU in Jersey City, New Jersey. Since 1996, Hoboken band Yo La Tengo has participated in the listener-supported station's fundraiser by appearing in the studio. Listeners who call in and pledge money are rewarded with the opportunity to request a favorite song—any song, from any artist or genre—which Yo La

[1] This chapter is a remastered and expanded edition of an essay that appeared in the special issue on cover songs in *Popular Music and Society* in 2005. Thanks always to the journal's editor extraordinaire Gary Burns.

[2] The show abandoned "Little Boxes" as an opening theme during its fourth season (2008) as the setting for the storyline crossed the border into Mexico from southern California suburbia.

Tengo then performs live. In 2006, an eclectic compilation culled from eight years of the WFMU fundraisers was released. The ample "best of/worst of" collection, *Yo La Tengo Is Murdering the Classics*, is a 70-minute set, consisting of 30 cover versions plus one seven-song cover medley.

Collectively, the inventive recycling of "Little Boxes" as the *Weeds* theme song, Luhrman's "poperatic" big screen extravaganza and the WFMU/Yo La Tengo annual call-in cover request epitomize the resourceful and rampant repetition of contemporary "coverage" in popular music.

Déjà Vu (All Over Again)

Since the 1980s, decades before Internet recycle bins and replay refuges such as You Tube, American culture has been operating on "Re" mode control. This cultural condition, identified by *Washington Post* television critic Tom Shales in his enduring essay, "The Re Decade" (1986), is an endless lifestyle loop of repeating, retrieving, reinventing, reincarnating, rewinding, recycling, reciting, redesigning and reprocessing. Reverse gear, rammed in maximum overdrive. Creators and audiences alike are revisionaries, infatuated with the familiar and wired with all access passes to the antecedent, reconsidering, reexamining, reinterpreting, revisiting, and rediscovering the world through replays and reissues, reruns and remakes. What goes around comes around. And 'round again. The Ecclesiastical Pete Seeger/Byrdsian chime "Turn, turn, turn" backmasks into "Re-turn, re-turn, re-turn" as history repeats. The past is prologue and preference, occupation and preoccupation, an orientation and value scale that is positively postmodern, with producers parasitical of predecessors, and consumers captivated by "previously played" packaging.

Popular music's backward spin accelerated and diversified dramatically during the Re Era. Whereas Shales branded the 1980s "The Re Decade," the past quarter century's "like a version" loop in music invites "The Cover Age" as a fitting characterization. Standardization, interpretation, incorporation, adaptation, appropriation and appreciation have been manifest in a multitude of manners and methods, including retrospectives and reissues, the emergence of rap and sampling as commercially dominant pop styles, karaoke, and a steady flow, if not wave, of cover compilations and tribute recordings which revisited a significant cross section of musical periods, styles, genres and artists and their catalogs of compositions. In the mid-to late 1970s, Bill Murray's lounge lizard lampooning as "Nick" the nightclub singer on *Saturday Night Live,* with unforgettable renditions such as the *Star Wars* theme that rivaled, if not foreshadowed *American Idol* loveable loser William Hung, was way ahead of popular culture's karaoke curve.

The continuous coverage cultivated a cluttered climate, re-mix mentality within the music, mass media and marketplace triad. Artists, producers, record companies and consumers were cohorts in the massive cover up. Everyone was running, and re-running, for covers.

Re-ality Row and Back to the Future Shock: "Reflections of the way life used to be..."

"Re" was not a trend that faded with other Big 80s phenomena. Re-forms ran rampant, having evolved symbiotically within the technospace, marketplace and collective consumer consciousness during the past 25 years. By the end of the millennium, nostalgia was well rooted as a permanent state of mind, soul, spirit and lifestyle. Objects in our collective cultural rear view mirror were closer than they appeared. The times were re-actionary, with hints of the strand of "nostalgia paralysis" Alvin Toffler predicted in 1970 in *Future Shock*. As Baby Boomers clung to their childhood as collectors and packrats—lost in the Mary Hopkins "Those Were the Days" lyric lament of never endingness—a new Generation Next emerged—the "Echo Boomers." This demographic of consumers rediscovered and appropriated the iconography, music, language and lifestyle of earlier eras as the basis for defining their own culture and perspective. ("Nostalgia," 2000)

"Repeat what you sow"—or what has already been sown by someone else—became the mantra, mode and mindset. VCR's and electronic replay—the most important invention since print, in the view of media theorist Tony Schwartz—empowered "time shifting" (Shales 1986). Sports coverage featured endless replays for fans clad in throwback jerseys and Puma gear to review action from every angle, speed and color analyst viewpoint, before being replayed on the stadium's Jumbotron or Diamond Vision scoreboard, and then edited for ESPN's *Sports Center* recycle stages, to be followed by distribution through its franchise fragments ESPN 2, News, Classic, and/or Desportes. Cheaper imitations, "knockoffs" and reproductions were plentiful, from clothing and accessories to pottery and house designs. Vintage was fashionable. The reconfigured Volkwagen Beetle and PT Cruiser were among retro road rulers. Reunions, career comebacks and retirement resurrections, from Michael Jordan to Celine Dion to the Eagles—warranted the line from the situation comedy *Grounded for Life* (FOX)—"We go to all their farewell concerts, you never know when it will be the last one." Reinventions seemed requisite. The mother of makeovers, Madonna, built a biographical cast of en vogue, in the groove, multiple personas— pop star, entrepreneur, provocateur, virgin, whore, material girl, mother, new age spiritualist, cowgirl, divorcee, diva, dominatrix, divorcee, actress, political activist, model, subject of coffee table sex book, children's book author, and Kabalist, starring "Esther," her *persona incarnata* for the perfectly titled 2004 "Reinvention Tour".

Another striking strand of "Re productions" reverberated in narratives which circulate beyond the pages of original literary sources to, from, and between stages and screens, often in the name of adaptation, nostalgia and exposing new generations to a work, rather than mention that familiarity breeds content and capital. Examples of "based on" border on the boundless beyond the bestseller list; the volume and variety was re-diculous. Reel remakes included recontextualized colorization of classics. Super heroes such as Batman, Spiderman, and X-Men adventure from comic strip to cartoon to cable to film to sequel. *Chicago* went from Broadway musical to Academy Award winning film while Mel Brooks's film *The Producers* (1967) achieved its greatest success on stage. Filmmakers continually excavated television series—*The Brady Bunch, Mission Impossible, The Flintstones, The Addams Family, The Avengers, My Favorite Martian, I Spy, Bewitched, Miami Vice, Get Smart*—into big screen "based on" bombs. *The Fugitive* went full circle from television to film (1993) and back to a short-lived television re-remake in 2000.

No genre was immune from imitation. Family fare such as *The Parent Trap* (1998), *Cheaper by the Dozen* (2003), *Please Don't Eat the Daisies* (2004) and *Bad News Bears* (2005) received Disney makeovers. *Psycho* (1998), *Texas Chainsaw Massacre* (2003) and *Dawn of the Dead* (2004) were recurring nightmares of the Hitchcock, Hooper and Romero forerunners, while *The Ring* (2003) and *The Grudge* (2005) had Japanese predecessors. *Ocean's Eleven* (2001), followed by *Twelve* (2004) and *Thirteen* (2007), were Rat Pack redux and counting. *The Cat in the Hat* (2003) was back, from page to Seussical on stage to big screen. The movie mirroring continued, among the more notable being Peter Jackson's re-epic *King Kong* in 2005, Willy Wonka melting into a dark chocolate Charlie, from Gene Wilder into Johnny Depp, and Steve Martin mimicking Peter Sellers *Pink Panther* in 2009.

Imports were also recast. *La Femme Nikita* (1990) was Americanized into *Point of No Return* (1993) then back to its original title as a cable television series on the USA Network. Similarly, George Sluizer directed both the French and American versions of his psychological thriller *The Vanishing* (1988; 1993). Cross cultural copping could be seen in television game and reality shows "borrowing" from British variations of *Who Wants to Be A Millionaire? Whose Line Is It Anyway?* and *Survivor.* Other adaptations were more subtle and seemingly sincere in their artistic intent, such as Cameron Crowe's *Vanilla Sky* (2001) version of the film *Abre Los Ojos.*

Nickelodeon cable network's *TV Land* was a microcosm of the reruns on television, while DVD represented syndication's second life with entire seasons of television series. Elsewhere on cable, neighbors were *Trading Spaces* in mindless makeovers and remodeling. In 2004, VH-1 launched a star search for the new Partridge Family, while TBS was casting for the *Real Gilligan's Island.* Among broadcast networks, NBC's *The Rerun Show* (NBC, 2002) featured improvisation actors recreating scenes from "Classic TV" such as *Diff'rent Strokes* and *Facts of Life*. It was deja view and déjà vu—all over again—all along Re-ality Row.

Re-Disc-covery: "Oh I believe in yesterday.."

> Someone has to stop these juvenile pretenders before they get to the Beatles.
> —critic Elysa Gardner, in review of A*Teens, *Pop 'til You Drop.* (2002)

Rewind has become the norm, the expectation in The Cover Age. Everything oldie is new again in radio's recycled rotations, from country, Top 40, adult contemporary and modern rock formats to the steady stream of acoustic and jazz interpretations on Sirius/XM satellite's *The Coffee House*. During the first four months of 2004, there were more than 20 covers receiving significant airplay on radio according to the data firm Mediabase. The Previous Playlist during the early 2000s included Uncle Kracker (Dobie Gray's "Drift Away,"), Dixie Chicks (Fleetwood Mac's "Landslide,"), Green Day (Sonny Curtis/Bobby Fuller Four's "I Fought the Law") Limp Bizkit (The Who's "Behind Blue Eyes"), No Doubt (Talk Talk's "It's My Life") Counting Crows and Vanessa Carlton (Joni Mitchell's "Big Yellow Taxi"), Foo Fighters (the artist formerly and currently known as Prince's "Darling Nikki"), and the Goo Goo Dolls (Supertramp's "Give A Little Bit"). From punky—Kelly Osbourne (Madonna's "Papa Don't Preach")—to pop princess—Hilary and Haylie Duff (Go Go's "Our Lips Are Sealed")—via single or soundtrack (*A Cinderella Story*, 2004), young performers relied on covers to propel their careers, musical and otherwise.

Some songs were in re-covery; it was not their first encore. Sheryl Crow's "The First Cut is The Deepest," culled as the single from her "Best of" collection in 2003, is an early Cat Stevens obscurity popularized by Rod Stewart. Dionne Warwick and Dusty Springfield covered the Burt Bacharach/Hal David composition, "I Just Don't Know What to Do With Myself," long before the White Stripes. Neil Diamond's "I'm A Believer" was a hit for the Monkees before becoming the *Shrek* soundtrack signature by Smash Mouth. Tim McGraw's twangy take on Elton John's "Tiny Dancer" was cover contrast to Lani Hall's earlier smooth jazzy rendition and the fictional band Stillwater and its entourage's live tour bus sing along in the film *Almost Famous*. There were minor modifications with many interpretations. Joss Stone changed the gender in her R & B version of the White Stripes "Fell in Love With A Boy." The Ataris saw a Black Flag, rather than Deadhead, sticker on the Cadillac in Don Henley's "The Boys of Summer."

That round of retreads was preceded by another cluster of covers: Shaggy (Chip Taylor's tune "Angel of the Morning" popularized by Merillee Rush), Eddie Vedder and Pearl Jam (J. Frank Wilson and the Cavaliers' "Last Kiss"), Lenny Kravitz (Guess Who's "American Woman"), Madonna (Don McLean's "American Pie"). Sampling sprinkled the soundscape, from Janet Jackson larcenous lifting of America's "Ventura Highway" opening guitar riff on "Someone to Call My Love," to chorus remixes such as Pras Michel's adaptation of U2's "Still Haven't Found What I'm Looking For" on "Haven't Found," and Nitty borrowing bubblegum from the Archies' "Sugar, Sugar" on "Nasty Girl," to Hollaback girl Gwen Stefani hauling back showtune classics "If I Were A Rich Man" from *Fiddler on the Roof* and *The Sound of Music* samples. The techno-ique was not exclusive to dance, rap, hip hop and R & B. Familiar riffs and verses also surfaced as samples on obscure album tracks, with the technology tempting surprising sources. Quirky Jill Sobule, perhaps best known for her tune "I Kissed a Girl," beds Chicago's "Saturday in the Park" throughout her "Cinnamon Park" on *Underdog Victorious*

(2004). And Jason Darling's title track from *Night Like My Head* (2003) features Beck-like borrowing of John Mellencamp's "Jack and Diane" chords, which had been previously integrated into Jessica Simpson's " I Think I'm in Love With You." Simpson's dumb down, 'ho down, slut pop *Coyote Ugly* version of Lee Hazelwood's "These Boots Are Made for Walkin'" disgraced Nancy Sinatra's 1960s hit, and subsequent credible covers of the classic kiss off recorded by Sam Phillips on the *Ready to Wear* soundtrack and Mellencamp violinist Lisa Germano. Similarly, in 2008, Kid Rock white trashes samples of Warren Zevon's "Werewolves of London" and Lynyrd Skynyrd's "Sweet Home Alabama" into his biggest hit "All Summer Long." And the re-beat goes on, for better or worse and in between.

The cover up was sweeping, extending well beyond radio to television, from the mandatory Motown of the star making microphone machinery of *American Idol* to artist's covering themselves on MTV's *Unplugged* to VH-1's short lived series *Cover Wars*, a bang a *Gong Show* update featuring David Letterman band leader Paul Shaffer as host to competition between three bands who were asked by judges to improvise popular songs. The show's conceptual blend of *American Bandstand*'s "Rate a Record" with a *Hullabaloo* and *Shindig!* atmosphere was more true to the dues paying, garage spirit of rock and roll than the shortcut to greatness avenue of the American Idolators lined up before sinister Simon Says (Cowell) and his band of has-been talent appraisers. NBC's *Hit Me Baby One More Time,* both Brit and Britney, was summer stock, 16th Minute of fame reality whose promos asked: "Where have they gone?;" then answered in *Poltergeistian*: "They'rrre baaack!" The show resurrected long gone acts such as Juice Newton, Sophie B. Hawkins, Flock of Sea Gulls, Wang Chung, the Motels and others for comatose karaoke competition requiring the has-beens to sing several of their old songs and a cover of a contemporary hit.

Shifting slightly and smartly beyond these caricatures to cartoon characters, The Power Puff Girls commemorated the 37th anniversary of the Beatles February 1964 appearance on *The Ed Sullivan Show*, with a special episode, "Meet the Beat Alls," on their Cartoon Network series. In the tale, The Beat Alls are a supervillain conglomerate, also know as "the Bad Four," who are orchestrating a "Brutish Invasion" designed to vanquish the 5-year old crime fighting Puff trio. The episode is brimming with song lines and visual references, though no backmasking that contains hidden messages.

Even ad jingles were instantly appropriated into allegedly clever covers. The rhyming "FreeCredit Report.com" tune became a novel epidemic in rotations of unsigned bands in bars and clubs across the country.

Television (*Ally McBeal, Crossing Jordan*, etc.) and film beyond *Moulin Rouge* (*I Am Sam, Oh Brother Where Art Thou?*, *de Lovely, I Shot Andy Warhol, Standing in the Shadows of Motown, The Commitments, Me, Myself and Irene, Honeymoon in Vegas, Across the Universe*, etc.) increasingly relied on versions of traditional or pop tunes for their soundtracks for narrative, montage and marketing purposes. Before *Weeds*, other series, such as *Providence* (NBC) and *I'm With Her* (ABC), incorporated covers for their opening title theme songs (Chantel Kreviazuk, The Beatles "In My Life"; and Sugar Ray, Joe Jackson's "Is She Really Going Out With Him"). In the period piece, *American Dreams* (NBC), contemporary pop stars are cast in guest portrayals of 1960s icons of *American Bandstand*, among them Kelli Clarkson (Brenda Lee), Nick Lachey (Tom Jones), Alicia Keyes (Fontella Bass) and the Duff Sisters (the Shangri Las). Biography also made it to Broadway where the "jukebox musical" emerged. Billy Joel's pop piano pieces were adapted into a Twyla Tharp choreographed musical *Movin' Out*, while Abba's sugary Swede songs were recast into *Mamma Mia* and the Beach Boys surf sounds staged in *Good Vibrations*. Other bio-musicals included Elvis (*All Shook Up*), Johnny Cash (*Ring of Fire*), Frankie Valli (*Jersey Boys*), Ray Charles (*I Can't Stop Lovin' You*) and Tharp again with Dylan (*Times Are A-Changin'*).

The critical and consumer consensus was that cover compilations and the tribute phenomenon would peak by the mid 1990s. "Most interesting in the world of trendy tributes is the simple question, 'Who's left?'" asked *Musician Magazine's* Dave DiMartino in November 1994. Apparently plenty. Since then, the number of tribute/cover record variations has been steady if not staggering, with estimates ranging between 150 and 200 releases annually. With the cover congestion, producers have been challenged to conceive new approaches. One of the emerging patterns is the album tribute. *Sgt. Pepper Knew My Father* (1987), a commemoration of the Beatle record's 20th anniversary, was a precursor to the recent replica records. Albums by Fleetwood Mac (*Legacy: A Tribute to Rumours* (1998)), Bruce Springsteen (*Badlands: A Tribute to Nebraska* (2001)), The Beatles (*The Blues "White Album"* (2002); *This Bird Has Flown: A 40th Anniversary Tribute to "Rubber Soul"* (2005)); and Bob Dylan (*The Blues "Blonde on Blonde"* (2003)) have received various artist treatments, while Mary Lee's Corvette solos Dylan's *Blood on the Tracks* (2002), recorded during one of the Arlene Grocery's "classic album nights" in New York City. Other album encores include Petra Haden's *The Who Sell Out* (2005), the Smithereens *Meet the Beatles* (2007), and the Easy Star All-Stars' reggae reversions of Pink Floyd's moon masterpiece (*Dub Side of the Moon*, 2003) and Radiohead's *OK Computer* (*Radiodread*, 2006). The album tribute trend skewed a bit more narcissistic when it splintered into further fragments when Alanis Morissette released a ten-years-after acoustic reading of her *Jagged Little Pill* (1995). The anniversary record was initially available only at Starbucks for one month prior to its wider availability.

Record labels seized the opportunity and began specializing in cover compilations and tributes. Among those who followed in Rhino Records tracks were Imaginary/Communion, Cleopatra, Big Eye, Dwell for heavy metal, Vitamin with Electronica and String Quartet re-arrrangements, and CMH with a spacious catalog of bluegrass renditions highlighted by its "Pickin' on" series. The Chicago, Rounder, Telarc, Liquid 8, Dressed to Kill, and Hip-O labels also cultivated covers. Chess, P-Vine and Catfish Records capitalized on the trend by inverting the cover formula with issues of separate compilations of "the original recordings of songs" covered by Ry Cooder, the Rolling Stones, Eric Clapton, and

Elvis Presley. These collections of originals provide historical duets that are revealing roots of deconstruction.

Plagiaristic precision performance and reverent imitation were no longer the exclusive principality of the Elvis impersonators. Mimic outfits of dead ringers such as Lynyrd Skynyrd and Dave Matthews Cover Bands, and The Led Zeppelin and Pink Floyd Experiences were common and do not conceal their imposterous intentions. At least the Abba mimes, Bjorn Again and the A*Teens, along with the irreverent all-female outfit Lez Zeppelin, came up with original names. Predictably, the Beatles brand is the closet rival to the Elvis legion in the imitation parade. There are nearly 50 Beatles tribute bands, with derivative names such as Rain, Fab Four, Fab Faux, Get Back and Bootleg Beatles. In 2007, Rain reportedly sold 100,000 tickets between Atlantic City, Las Vegas and its other tour dates. Tribute bands must pay licensing fees for permission to play an artist's songs. Though their imitation may be sincere and flattering, they are seldom endorsed by the original artists. The rationalization from the tribute ranks points to furthering the franchise. "Let's face it, having all these tribute/experience acts, it just increases their brand," says Springsteen impersonator Matt Ryan. "They're gonna sell more records, t-shirts, etc. It's almost free advertising for them. We're spreading the brand continually, so it's good for them" (CBS *Sunday Morning,* 2007).

The comical nature of the copycat condition and confusion between authentic and imitation was cleverly captured bv Grace Adler (Debra Messing) when trying to book entertainment in an episode of the sassy sitcom *Will & Grace* (NBC): "I've narrowed it down to two bands: Either a Kool and the Gang Tribute Band or Kool and the Gang." Performance mimicry solicits artistic suspicion as well as legal leery. In her video for "I'm Glad" (2003), Jennifer Lopez morphed into Jennifer Beals in *Flashdance*. An echo of the endless Michael Jackson "Thriller" choreograpohy covers, Lopez considered her routine a tribute to the memorable movements, while Paramount cried copycat and copyright infringement.

Reverent renditions balanced the novelty acts and great pretenders. In 2004, Jamie Foxx, Kevin Spacey, and Kevin Kline provided stunning reincarnations of Ray Charles, Bobby Darin, and Cole Porter, followed in 2005 by Joaquin Phoenix and Reese Witherspoon as Johnny and June Carter Cash. The performances further enhanced an impressive tradition of music bio pics that includes Buddy Holly, Ritchie Valens, Loretta Lynn, Elvis Presley, and Jerry Lee Lewis. Late legend Cash's final recordings, particularly the "American Recordings" series produced by Rick Rubin culminating with the astounding *Unearthed* (2003) box set, is filled with traditional songs, hymns, and interpretations of songs by an array of songwriters and artists including Stephen Foster, Nick Lowe, Bob Marley, Neil Young, Neil Diamond, U2, Nick Cave, Gordon Lightfoot, Nine Inch Nails, and Danzig.

Quirky cover events outside karaoke bars surfaced, from a "Sweet Jane" cover contest in Austin, Texas to "Louie Louiepalooza," an assembly of 754 guitarists gathered in Washington state in 2003 for a collective three chord tribute. That cover congregate was topped by Louie Fest in 2004 as 1000 guitarists assembled at the Tacoma Dome to break the Guinness record for a guitar ensemble playing a single song. As one of popular music's "franchises," "Louie, Louie" has its own web site, been the subject of a Dave Marsh book and a Rhino *Best of*, two volumes of versions ranging from the Richard Berry 1955 original to the Kingsmen's 1963 hit to the Rice University Marching band rendition.

Other gatherings paid homage to careers and catalogs. Commemorative, collaborative concerts recognizing careers, birthdays and anniversaries, honored artists such as Burt Bacharach, Johnny Cash, Elvis Presley, Bob Dylan, Roy Orbison, Willie Nelson, Brian Wilson, George Harrison, and Joni Mitchell. The events were documented and distributed from cablecast concert to consumer via attractive audio and video packages.

Vintage vocalists became another cover manifestation. Whether the result of a return to roots, career reinvention, or mid life creative crisis, an increasing number of "interpretive artists" entered the Ronstadt realm of routinely revisiting and rereading the American songbook. Standards became the standard. "I've done other people's songs for so long, I felt it was time to do some of my own," commented Barry Manilow during a 2001 CBS *Morning Show* concert interview. Manilow's commitment to originals was short term. By mid-decade, he implemented the "decade" as a cover concept which resulted in a series of annual, easily marketed era collections: The *Greatest Songs of the Fifties* (2006), *Sixties* (2006), *Seventies* (2007)*,* and *Eighties* (2008) and counting. In addition to Manilow, Harry Connick Jr. drew Sinatra crooning comparisons, while Rod Stewart did an about face, along with Roxy Music's Bryan Ferry, as they developed lounge leanings as chanteurs. Stewart in particular has settled into the midlife reinvention rut with four volumes of the American songbook. Michael McDonald went from Doobie to Detroit with two editions of white soul Motown makeovers. The diva domain included Madeleine Peyroux, Celine Dion, Diana Krall, Bette Midler, Cassandra Wilson, Jacinta, Vonda Shepard, and k.d. lang. Elvis Costello, Rickie Lee Jones, James Taylor, Carly Simon, Gloria Estefan, Sinead O'Connor and Cyndi Lauper are among a secondary tier who predominantly write and record their own compositions, but have more than one cover compilation in their discographies.

The younger generation of performers has also been drawn to covers. The reinterpretive route is requisite for the *American Idolaters* since most are primarily vocalists. Non-contestant, newer artists, such as Mandy Moore with *Coverage* (2003), are particularly susceptible to criticism that such projects are uninspired and detrimental to creative development. While those concerns can be directed toward any artists covering songs, there appears to be a greater consent for established artists occasionally recording an album of covers without the interpretive approach becoming a complete career reinvention. Annie Lennox, James Taylor, Patti Smith, Joan Baez, Marianne Faithfull and Bruce Springsteen's *Seeger Sessions* are among examples. Such performance permission may be attributed to the perception that older artists have paid dues longer and earned the privilege to "borrow" songs. The generational divide seemed to be marked by the youthful entitlement "past as privilege" in contrast to the mature artist view of "privilege to be a part of the past."

"Traditional Pop" Transition: Standards "Any Old Time"

Following the numerous awards for re-recordings at the 1992 Grammy ceremony, comic actor Chevy Chase remarked, "Grammy officials are guessing that songs written in the year 1992 will win Grammys in the year 2000." The glib one liner was a prophetic Cover Age comment, though Chase's projection missed by a year. At the 43rd Grammy Awards in 2001, a new generation and genre of artists was recognized for their achievements on music's standardized test. Bryan Ferry (*As Time Goes By*), Rickie Lee Jones (*It's Like This*), George Michael (*Songs From the Last Century*) and Joni Mitchell (*Both Sides Now*) joined Barbara Streisand as nominees for "Best Traditional Pop Vocal Album." The category, established in 1991 by the National Association of Recording Arts and Sciences (NARAS), honors artists who record popular standards often associated with bygone eras. Since its inception, the category had been the domain of crooners such as Tony Bennett, a six time winner. The 2001 "Traditional Pop" nominees highlighted the proliferation of covers and tribute recordings, which, as a body of work, contributed to a revision of the meaning of "standard" in American popular music during the Cover Age. "In a certain way a new generation is claiming a relationship to an older more established tradition," says *Rolling Stone* editor Anthony DeCurtis. "I think that shifts the idea of what is standard, what is traditional" (Gardner, 2001).

The traditionally recognized standards emanate from the pre-rock era and are largely defined by the mid-century show tunes of Cole Porter, the Gershwins, Irving Berlin, Harold Arlen, Lorenz Hart and Richard Rogers and early American Songbook of Stephen Foster. Though their enduring compositions are featured in pop and rock revisionist repertoires, many, including the 2001 Grammy nominees, updated their song selections. By steering toward contemporary colleagues, they further signaled, if not solidified, a modernization movement, a traditionalist transition for standards that embraced folk, rock, pop and blues songwriters and composers such as Robert Johnson, Woody Guthrie, Pete Seeger segueing into Burt Bacharach, Bob Dylan, Joni Mitchell, Paul Simon, Brian Wilson, Lennon and McCartney, Jagger and Richards, and Townes van Zandt. "I don't see (traditional) pop as a thing purely from my parents' time," said Rickie Lee Jones. "American popular music is a tradition that is hopefully being added on to a la the Beatles and Steely Dan, as well as Gershwin and (Billy) Strayhorn" (Gardner, 2001).

In 2003, Steve Forbert, whose striking folk punk debut *Alive on Arrival* (1978), earned him "the next Dylan" deadly designation, received his first Grammy nomination. Not for his own songs, but ironically for a set of his interpretations of his fellow Meridian, Mississippian, Jimmie Rodgers' tunes. The title of Forbert's tribute—*Any Old Time*—characterizes the "traditional transition" and evolving standard for standards in popular music. At the 50th Grammy Awards in 2008, Herbie Hancock's jazz tribute *River: The Joni Letters,* won Best Contemporary Jazz Album and Album of the Year. Winning the most prestigious award was a surprise to many, but further reinforced the establishment of a new catalog of song standards in popular music.

Briefly Back Tracking: A Pre-Re Era Cover Chronicle

While covering and its variations constituted a significant segment of the music marketplace from the Re Decade into The Cover Age, the practice of one artist recording or performing another composer's song, has always been an integral, multifaceted attribute of popular music. The cover genre embodies an assortment of appropriationist musical methods that spans traditional forms such as folk, protest and work songs, patriotic anthems, religious hymns, show tunes, Muzak instrumentals, Christmas classics, children's songs, and comedy to contemporary strands in karaoke, rap and sampling, soundtracks, parodies, impersonation, advertising and tributes.

In 1949, there were twenty records which had cover versions in the Top Ten, and twenty-one in 1950. Of all the records that charted between 1946 and 1950, 70% had more than one recorded version. (Peterson and Berger 1990: 143) During the 1950s, it was beg, borrow and steal as prejudice, plagiarism and profit were underpinnings of the widespread practice of covering songs. Major labels such as Decca, Columbia, RCA Victor and Capitol insisted that black artists adopt white-oriented singing styles similar to Nat King Cole or else face isolation. As a result, many songs were recorded into an "appropriate sound" by clean and cool copycats such as Pat Boone, Bill Haley and Elvis Presley.

The "borrowing" evolved with the industry's growth and as songwriting matured. The Brill Building and its songwriting machine concept, featuring dynamic duos Carole King/Gerry Goffin, Jerry Lieber/Mike Stoller, Barry Mann/Cynthia Weil, Doc Pomus/Mort Shuman, flourished in the period between Presley and the Beatles, providing hits for The Girl Groups, Spectorian superproductions, Elvis and many others. Songs became communal in the folk rock genre which emerged during the era, in large part baptized by the Byrds in 1965 with Roger McGuinn's ringing Rickenbacker and a string of Dylan adaptations that became hits. During the mid-1960s, album-length tribute recordings by major artists such as Marvin Gaye's salute to Nat King Cole and Del Shannon's homage to Hank Williams sporadically surfaced, followed by cover collections by The Band (*Moondog Matinee*), David Bowie (*Pin-Ups*), John Lennon, the Isley Brothers, and the Byrds playing Dylan in the 1970s.

During the same period, interpretation became more common. Multi instrumentalist Ry Cooder took a musicologial approach in his excavation of obscure folk, jazz and blues songs that characterized his solo recordings. Former lead singer of Brasil '66 and wife of Herb Alpert, Lani Hall, released a series of records between 1972 and 1979 that were predominantly comprised of covers. Linda Ronstadt emerged as a prototype interpretive singer. Her string of platinum selling albums and Top 40 singles featured oldies, and folk-rock, country-pop versions of many of her California contemporaries compositions. Ronstadt's career cover catalog accumulated pop standards, Nelson Riddle Orchestra collaborations, duets, show tunes, new wave, jazz, country, Christmas and traditional Mexican and Spanish material.

Cover collections expanded during the 1980s, offering renditions from various genres, ranging from country on Elvis Costello's *Almost Blue* (1981) to jazz, swing and Big Band on Carly Simon's *Torch* (1981) to reggae on UB40's *Labour of Love I* (1983) and *II* (1989). Novel variations emerged from fringe dwellers. The avant gardian Residents added to the transformation of 1960s Top 40s hits into two side-long suites (*The Residents Present the Third Reich and Roll* (1975) with the beginnings of its American Composer Series by matching George Gershwin with James Brown (*George and James* (1984)) and juxtaposing Hank Williams with John Phillip Sousa marches (*Stars and Hank Forever* (1986)). Pussy Galore remade the Rolling Stones *Exile on Main Street* (1986) while the Bollock Brothers bizarre *Never Mind the Bollocks 1983* parodies the Sex Pistols 1977 album from cover design to contents. "Weird Al" Yankovic emerged as the High Priest of Pop Parody by mutating Michael Jackson's "Beat It" into "Eat It" and the Police's "King of Pain" into "King of Suede." Multi-artist tributes records such as *Cover Me* (1983), the first of many collections of Bruce Springsteen renditions, came of age, easing above the underground and beyond the fringe to scratch the surface of the mainstream music market. In advertising, golden oldies became "stolen oldies" as songs were increasingly converted into commercial soundscapes. Soundtracks were part of the swell as well, with *The Blues Brothers* (1980), *La Bamba* (1987) and *Great Balls of Fire* (1989) among movie music makeovers.

By the early 1990s, cover song momentum as a musical movement was well established. Whether due to an overreaction to a fad, leftover excess from the 1980s, artistic convenience, or the industry's profit motivation, covers proliferated creatively and commercially, transcending trend status into a surging, re-sounding subgenre. The 1992 Grammy Awards further magnified, if not provided overdue acknowledgment, of the postmodern condition in popular music. Among the winners were Michael Bolton for his remake of Percy Sledge's 1966 hit, "When A Man Loves A Woman," and Natalie Cole, who was awarded seven Grammys, including Song, Record and Album of the Year, for her *Unforgettable* covers that featured a posthumous duet with her father Nat, a song written by Irving Gordon in 1951. Despite Natalie Cole's seemingly naive post-Grammy ceremony cover caution to other performers who planned to record standards "not to overwhelm the market with this kind of music," signs of saturation and standardization were sweeping. Cover collections and tributes were so abundant that retailers established separate display bins, or recycle bins, to accommodate the genre glut.

The 1992 recognition for re-recordings at the industry's ritual may have marked the inauguration of The Cover Age, but its arrival and pervading presence attracted critical discussion, if not backlash. Titles suggested that imitation had its limitations: "Flattery Gets You Nowhere" (DiMartino, 1994); "Tribute LPs Filled With Quirky Covers Are Just No Fun Anymore (Fricke, 1993); "How Many

Tribute Albums Does It Take to Exhaust A Fad? (Milano, 1991) Song recycling intrinsically invited issues of authenticity, unnecessary repetition, excess, gimmickry, appropriation, imitation, entitlement, lack of homage and emphasis on commodity rather than concept. One of the most common perceptions was that originality's merit had become outmoded, diminished and often replaced by the illusion of fresh within the technospace, music making machinery and mass market. By 2004, the 50th anniversary of rock and roll, questions about originality persisted. "A cynical person could wonder if all the possible good melodies and lyric ideas have been used up, especially the three-chord guitar thing," says Pete Howard, editor of *Ice* magazine. It sounds like a juvenile question but it might be a valid point: How many good new songs are there left?" (Gunderson, 2004).

New York Times music Jon Pareles identified signs of the shift at the end of the 1980s. "Music [today], in particular, is demanding we rethink our cherished notions of originality and artistic independence. In today's music, as in the culture at large, it seems that sophisticated copying of past and present has overtaken innovation" (1). Brenda Johnson Grau echoed Pareles point. "Rather than being defined as a particular style or tempo or instrumentation or even subject, rock and roll now operates as a form of incorporation or pastiche" (35). Into the 1990s, frequency and visibility of covers represented a Warholian prophecy, if not nightmare, fulfilled. The repetition of the same image to the point of cultural exhaustion that the Pop Artist depicted in his grid compositions—Campbell's soup cans, products, mythic cultural icons such as Elvis, Marilyn Monroe, Jacqueline Kennedy, Mickey Mouse and the Mona Lisa— was revealed in aural artifacts and the music industry approach and management of the recycle trend.

Tributaries: Franchising the Familiar

> The world has always needed an album with ten different versions of 'Louie, Louie,' don't you think?
>
> —Rhino records 1991–92 Music Catalog

> What makes most tribute albums useless, of course, is that by definition most should be heard precisely once. After that, astute consumers will theoretically hightail it back to the record store to pick up the complete works of the original artists and thus enjoy the Real Thing forever after.
>
> —critic Dave DiMartino, *Musician*, November 1994: 83

The sincerity of the "tribute" concept as the primary cover vehicle became tarnished as the cover categories expanded into excess. While many artists were clearly worthy of musical praise, other selections seemed arbitrary, and the product watered down, with a grab bag, thrown together, thoughtless approach to assembly other than to capitalize on the genre's popularity. Producers appeared engaged in tribute one-upmanship, seeking new and novel categories, concepts and combinations for cover compilations beyond the artists themselves. Songs, record labels (Sun, Asylum, Merge), albums, socially conscious causes and benefits, genres, regions, composers, film scores, cult bands, classics, cartoon themes, commemorations, collaborations and duets, eras, novelties, comedy parodies and celebrity sing offs were among the "tributaries," countless classifications aimed at appealing to niche audiences as well as artist and song loyalists (see Plasketes, 1992; 1995).

There were some logical steps in the progression such as a "Best of Tributes" by the independent label Imaginary Records (1992) culled from their own catalog of tribute records, and illogical entries such as *Rutles Highway Revisited* (1991) a tribute to a band that never existed except as a Beatles parody group. Evidence of excess was easily identifiable in the single song compilations. Like Rhino's humorous hoarding "Louie, Louie" and "La Bamba" into "best of" volumes that blended hysterical with historical, Suzanne Vega's *Tom's Album* (1991) featured 12 versions of her song "Tom's Diner" from her *Solitude Standing* (1987) from four years earlier.

Despite the variations, the conceptual continued to clash with the commercial intent. Critics observed that too many cover projects relied on a grab bag approach with materials thrown together with little thought, except to capitalize on the genre's popularity. They also saw the projects as attempts by labels to keep artists commercially viable in between projects.

There is no denying that covers, whether a single song or a compilation, are as much market driven as they are music motivated. The commercial appeal is inherent. Familiarity breeds artist convenience, consumer content and corporate capital, from record labels to radio stations to listeners and record buyers. That presumption remains constant with current contestants on *American Idol.* "I'm sure the ratings [for *American Idol*] would be significantly lower if they were singing new songs," says Peter Howard, editor of *Ice* magazine. "A recognizable song draws instant attention. It gives the audience something to compare against" (Gunderson 2004). On radio, a remake is inclined to catch the attention of a programmer's ear because the familiarity enables a song to "build faster" with listeners. "With a big artist and a universally loved song, you can have a surefire combination that saves a lot of time," says Sean Ross of Edison Media research (Gunderson, 2004).

Such commercial ploys foster creative convenience. Covering provides fill material and an easy way to record a record without having to write new songs. They may buy an artist time to appease their label in between original projects. There is some debate as to whether covers should be considered filler material anymore than original songs. "I've always wondered why an emerging artist puts out a CD with 15 new songs. A couple of familiar songs would make for an easier entree," observes *Ice* editor Howard. (Gunderson, 2004).

Covers also create consumer curiosity and incentive for fans and collectors, in particular completists attracted to a cut that is unavailable elsewhere, with the exception of B-sides and EPs, which have consistently been harbors for covers, and the newest domain of downloads at artist web sites. The presence of a cover song on a record contains the intrigue of hearing a familiar song being performed by another artist, which can often sway a borderline purchase decision. The marketing savvy of covers, particularly tributes, lies in the product's multiple appeal. Fans might be attracted to a record for the contributing artist(s), the honoree or a particular song or body of work. For example, the Wilson Phillips homage to the 1970s West Coast sound (Eagles, Mamas and Papas, Ronstadt, Jackson Browne, Neil and Jesse Colin Young, Fleetwood Mac, Byrds, Beach Boys) on *California* (2004) would presumably entice older, baby boomer consumers who came of age in that era. Conversely, those same listeners would be unlikely to have Wilson Phillips originals in their music collections (unless out of allegiance to the band members pop parents—Brian Wilson and Michele and John Phillips of the Mamas and Papas).

Covers prove to be enticing even when there is little need for consumer coercion, as in the case of greatest hits collections which employ a cover version as a bonus or "previously unreleased" track. Sheryl Crow's *Best of* using "The First Cut is the Deepest" as a single is but one example. Such inclusions appear a clear commercial calculation. Only months after its initial release in 1998, Sixpence None the Richer's self-titled record was reissued with one additional track, a cover of The La's "There She Goes." For anyone interested in the record, the band or the song itself, the choice was clear. The "cover up" no doubt resulted in a wave of trade-ins from purchasers of the record's original pressing. "There She Goes" also magnified the frequency of stunting soundtracks with covers, not to mention puzzling placement. The La's original and a barely indistinguishable version by the Boo Radleys bookended the *So I Married An Axe Murderer* (1993) soundtrack and were early echoes of Sixpence's replay. Such duet-like pairings of songs on the same record became commonplace, though usually with greater contrast. On *How to Deal* (2003), Beth Orton's smooth electronica reading of "Wild World" diverges from the Cat Stevens original that closes the soundtrack. Though film soundtracks may be among the accessible outlet for covers, the remake or a roots revisitation project has become a prominent producer and artist priority and practice, and an increasing requisite for records.

Commercially, cover songs both individually and collectively, also reflect the widespread franchising of cultural products. Look, or listen, no farther than the annual kid karaoke compilation *Kidz Bop*, recycled radio rotations that are approaching double digit volumes . A song re-recorded numerous times is similar to the standardization and diversified distribution—Hard Rock Cafe, Gap and its micro niches Baby Gap and Gap Kids, and television crime series such as Dick Wolf's *Law and Order* (NBC) with *SVU* and *Criminal Intent* offspring and Jerry Bruckheimer's *C.S.I.* (CBS) expansion to include Miami and New York locales. Like most entertainment forms, these series cash flow into wider distribution via syndication and DVD. Music's most thriving cover song franchises include popular Christmas songs, notably the Josef Moore and Franz Gruber's 1818 composition, "Silent Night," the all time leader in re-recording according to archivists; George Gershwin's ballad "Summertime" with an estimated 2600 versions; and the most popular of the Lennon-McCartney catalog—a franchise unto itself—"Yesterday," which has been recorded by more than 2,000 performers. "Louie, Louie's" lineage is marked by approximately 1,200 versions, while "Amazing Grace," "Bridge Over Troubled Water," and "Over the Rainbow" are among other songs with significant cover capacity.

Imitation as Flattery or Homage? Apprenticeship, Adaptation and Authenticity

> Re-creation is the sincerest form of flattery.
> —advertisement for Duran Duran's *Thank you* (1995)

> [Covering is] the highest compliment to a songwriter. Even [William] Shatner's "Rocket Man" sounds good to me.
> —Sir Elton John, *Today Show* (NBC), 30 November 1998

> One of the pleasures of life is to sing great lyrics.
> —Lucy Kaplansky, on contributing a song to *A Nod to Bob* (2001),
> *All Things Considered* (National Public Radio, 2001)

A scene in the film *Love Actually* (2003) depicts a recording studio session with a waning star struggling to convert the Troggs' "Love is All Around" into a commercial "Christmas is All Around." "I'm afraid you did it again, Bill," says the producer to the singer, who repeatedly fails to make the desired seasonal substitution in the lyrics. "It's just that I know the old version so well, you know," apologizes the singer. Not missing a beat, the producer unsympathetically responds, "Well, we all did, that's why we're making the new version."

Though artists and audience alike comfortably cling to the original, and commonly question the necessity of a cover version, there are many legitimate reasons for "making a new version." The multi dimensionality, intertextuality and contextuality of covers songs contain positive perspectives which counter the numerous critiques. Proponents recognize redeeming qualities in recyling songs such as the historical context, apprenticeship, homage, empathy, adaptation, translation, interpretation, preservation, revitalization and the value of exposing songwriters, their songs and styles, old and new, to an audience.

As a musical tradition, covering has always provided a practical point in the apprenticeship process. By employing the "playing songs we like" or "what we grew up listening to" method, bands learn form, structure, and style. "You've got to [play covers] if you're going to learn anything [about songwriting]. It's the only way to really figure it out. I can't imagine not starting that way," explains Tom Petty (Flanagan, 1986).

Canadian songwriter Ron Sexsmith characterized his dues paying as being "a Human Jukebox" playing familiar songs. He echoes Petty's point. "Covers are about learning structure and the importance of the song." Sexsmith also recognizes a sense of redemption in covering, that is, being drawn to "a song I'd aspire to write or wish I could have written." For Sexsmith, Anne Murray's "Snowbird" is his "redemption song" (*Fresh Air*, 2001).

Bill Carney, front for the New York based faux French band Les Sans Celottes, offers a playful perspective on imitation and adaptation cutting across musical styles. "I grew up all my life as a Beatles fan and I learned the canon note for note, every album inside and out. If I were to apply that, the best I could really achieve today would maybe getting to be in a Beatles tribute band. But by applying that same approach to French music, I finally got to be the Beatle that never was" (NPR *Weekend Edition*, April 2, 2005).

The arts have always borrowed from their past. The imitation intrinsic in the act of covering in music, even with the honorable intent of homage from a disciple, is incongruent with authenticity. Critics frequently cite the absence of originality and pointless duplicity of covering. After all, as Rolling Stone Mick Jagger wondered circa 1968, "What's the point listening to us doing "I'm a King Bee" when you can listen to Slim Harpo doing it?" Yet there are points beyond the popular premise expressed by Jagger and playfully proclaimed in a Dr. Pepper ad, that "Nothing is as good as the original." The adage "never expect anything original from an echo" does not necessarily ring true with covers.

The process of covering a song is essentially an adaptation, in which much of the value lies in the artists' interpretation. A song travels a slightly different course than a piece which evolves from page to stage to screen, whether silver or small. With music, the song undergoes a recontextualization, remaining in the same medium, with the artists translating the material into a particular style. Measuring the interpreter's skill, in part, lies in how well the artist uncovers and conveys the spirit of the original, enhances the nuances of its melody, rhythm, phrasing, or structure, maybe adding a new arrangement, sense of occasion or thread of irony.

Musical mirroring may not be as simple as it seems on the surface. "In the best tributes the covering artist steals a song from the original and makes it their own, while they keep, even exaggerate, its original spirit. It's a tough trick, demanding authenticity and empathy," writes D. Dasein (1994). In the process, the interpretation might offer a fresh insight into the song, its composer or a particular period. The imitative method allows artists to explore and expose their musical roots, perhaps broaden their own oeuvre with uncharacteristic materials, and pay homage not only to songs but to influential artists, composers, styles and eras. "When you do this, it's like being in the studio with a few great collaborators," explains Bryan Ferry, whose cover compilations include *Taxi* (1993), *As Time Goes By* (2001) and *Frantic* (2002) and *Dylanesque* (2007). "Goffin and King are there, saying: 'This is the tune. This is the lyric. Have a go?'" (DeCurtis, 1993).

The possibilities of place are vast; the transformations span a broad spectrum, from literal readings or clones to loose translations to shape shifters to mutations remote from the original. The blurred line between imitation and homage, for example, is demonstrated in Tom Petty's precise cover of the Byrds "I'll Feel A Whole Lot Better" on his *Full Moon Fever* (1988). Petty's version, both musically and vocally, is indiscernible from Byrd Gene Clark's original. While "what's the point?" and "Petty theft" could apply, it is more likely that his intentions were not as counterfeit as they were commemorative as a testimonial to the group as a longtime influence, in particular Roger McGuinn. During his career, Petty has appropriated the Byrds jangling sound into much of his music and also recorded McGuinn material. The vocal similarities between the two are apparent on McGuinn's "King of the Hill," a song they co-wrote and perform in duet fashion on McGuinn's *Back From Rio* (1991). Further, McGuinn's reciprocate cover of Petty's "American Girl" is ironic as it represents McGuinn covering Petty who is basically covering McGuinn to begin with.

Looser interpretations render new meanings by transporting the original song to a different musical, vocal, stylistic, social, and/or historical setting. Examples abound. The Sex Pistols version of Sinatra's "My Way," Neil Young's grungy "On Broadway," Aztec Camera's laconic reading of Van Halen's "Jump," T-Bone Burnett's equally dry rendition of the "Diamonds Are a Girl's Best Friend," made famous by Marilyn Monroe in *Gentlemen Prefer Blondes*, and Fountains of Wayne's peculiar take on Britney Spears's (Max Martin) "...One More Time." U2's chilling synth version of "Night and Day" places Cole Porter's romanticism into a frightening AIDS-era setting. Bad Company's 1970s hard rock hit "I Feel (Like Makin') Love" becomes a sweet lesbian love song through Two Nice Girls. Likewise, Elvis Costello's "Alison," Warren Zevon's "Poor Poor Pitiful Me" and "Tenderness on the Block," the Beatles "Lovely Rita" and Bruce Springsteen's "Tougher Than the Rest" derive different views through gender transposition when performed by Linda Ronstadt, Shawn Colvin, Michelle Shocked, or Tracey Thorn of Everything but the Girl. Tori Amos recasts the gender view of twelve songs written by men on *Strange Little Girls* (2002), most strikingly Eminem's wife-killing fantasy "'87 Bonnie & Clyde." Nirvana's grunge anthem, "Smells Like Teen Spirit" is playful parody for Weird Al Yankovic ("Smells Like Nirvana") and piano pity that is more despairing than angry on Amos's *Crucify* EP. L.L. Cool J's rap ballad "I Need Love" changes colors, countries, and genres when adapted into a Celtic reading by Luka Bloom on *The Acoustic Motorbike* (1992). Billy Bragg inventively beds the Left Banke's "Walk Away Renee" melody beneath a break up narrative, just as Puff Daddy layered his own rap "I'll Be Missing You" over the Police's "Every Breath You Take." Cat Power routinely provides surreal whispers of rock classics, with "(I Can't Get no) Satisfaction" among the more striking of her lovely, haunting interpretations. On *Tom's Album* (1991), Suzanne Vega's "little song about eating breakfast" is rearranged into songs about accidental pregnancy ("Daddy's Little Girl"), pop culture ("Jeanie's Diner") and the Gulf War ("Waiting at the Border").

Genre bends are among the most common alterations. The sessionists at CMH records have countrified an endless roster of popular artists' catalogs into Bluegrass just as the Bob Belden Ensemble and other Philharmonic assemblies have jazzed up popular tunes, even heavy metal, into the Muzakian mode. Jimi Hendrix's "Up from the Skies" receives a lovely treatment from Rickie Lee Jones on *Pop Pop*

(1992), her interpretations of jazz standards, obscure Broadway show tunes, and a Marty Balin Jefferson Airplane pop ballad. More rare are geographic blends. Examples include Seu Jorge's Brazilian Bowie—live acoustic *Ziggy Stardust*-era troubadorian takes in Portugese—in the film and soundtrack, *The Life Aquatic with Steve Zissou* (2004), and the David Lindley and Henry Kaiser exotic makeovers of country hits by Ray Price ("You Done Me Wrong, 1956) and Merle Haggard ("I'm a Lonesome Fugitive," 1966) and the Sonny Curtis composed Bobby Fuller Four hit "I Fought the Law," via cross cultural collaborations with musicians in Madgascar.

Re-possession: "Make them your own"

> Covers—I hate that term. To me a cover is just changing the vocal performance. I like to redesign a song. That's really a modern idea, after Dylan—that you have to write your own stuff. The idea that you can write your whole repertoire yourself seems rather conceited.
> —singer/songwriter Bryan Ferry (DeCurtis, 1993)

> In singing these songs, I believe that Joni has achieved something quite extraordinary in that she has truly sung them as if...she had written them in her own blood.
> —producer Larry Klein, liner notes, Joni Mitchell, *Both Sides Now* (2001)

> Once you embrace this idea of plagiarism as a positive thing, it's this immensely liberating experience. We all started to blossom as songwriters.
> —musician Bill Carney, Les Sans Celottes (NPR *Weekend Edition*, April 2, 2005)

The notions of ownership, repossession, borrowing, entitlement and authenticity have always converged as part of the cover song heritage, particularly with rock and roll's arrival and its blues linkages. By the mid to late 1970s, the postmodern condition and character ruptured rock culture's aesthetic, shifting emphasis away from authenticity (see Bailey, 2003). Several year ago, Levi's jeans ran a commercial depicting a young male with microphone and monitor on stage in a solo crash and burn of Petula Clark's "Downtown." "Make them your own," punctuates the voice over announcer. The phrase is fitting for the commercial's karaoke scene. The expression is also frequently conveyed by artists when discussing their approach to interpreting songs. Perspectives are plentiful, ranging from "possession of" to "possessed by." Many seem to view "making a song their own" a creative objective, challenge or exercise. "I decided to cover songs that weren't particularly my favorites but ones I could interpret, songs I could play around with and make my own," says Paul Weller regarding his cover records *Studio 150* (2003) and *Under the Influence* (2004) ("Ice Cubes", 2004). "I learned the song mainly because I felt like I could make it my own. This is more challenging than any song I've ever written," said Irish folksinger Luka Bloom about his experience re-recording L.L. Cool J's rap ballad "I Need Love" (Azerrard, 1992).

To other artists, the adaptation process is more natural, accidental or an innocent inhabitation that is sometimes the song choosing its translator. "Traditional music is a blank page. You can never imagine what the person who sang an old song originally sounded like," says British folksinger Eliza Carthy. "Interpreting [songs] is not that academic a process. Once the song is in your mouth it's just going to come out the way you are" (Lord, 2002). "[Covering] is not so much choosing a song," says jazz/blues vocalist Cassandra Wilson. "Some songs come into your consciousness and they won't go away" (*Breakfast With the Arts*, 2003). Linda Ronstadt appears to cover Wilson's quote. "I don't choose the songs, they choose me, consistently," she says. And if I don't sing them they won't leave me alone" (*CBS Sunday Morning*). And Cyndi Lauper reinforces Wilson's experiences when discussing her record of pop standards *At Last* (2003). "The songs spoke so loudly to me I lost myself in them." To Lauper, voice was also a variable in song selection. "I felt that my voice was suited to that time period and the songs of the Fifties and Sixties" (*Breakfast With the Arts*, 2004).

Before performing *Blood on the Tracks* during "classic album night" at Arlene Grocery, Mary Kortes says a series of common questions immediately presented themselves: "How do you sing a Bob Dylan song in a way that anyone should even bother listening to? How do you sing it right without imitating him? How do you make it your own? And of course, why should you?" (Kortes, 2002). John Wesley Harding, a vocal dead ringer for Elvis Costello, admits that he began covering Madonna's "Like A Prayer" during live shows as a joke, but then got so comfortable with the song and liked it so much that he re-recorded it for his EP *God Made Me Do It* (1989).

Patti Smith's decades of scrawling "countless lists for a possible covers album" finally came to fruition with *twelve* (2007)*, a set of reverent interpretations of songs by Hendrix, Dylan, the Stones, Beatles, Doors, Nirvana, Allman Brothers, Paul Simon, Jefferson Airplane, Neil Young, and Stevie Wonder. Smith's reflective perspective in the record's liner notes suggests an elusive, unpredictable and collaborative nature within the cover process:

> [The list] compiled in 1978, it was never realized, nor was the list I made in preparation for what is offered here. Many of the songs I thought to record somehow slipped away, and unexpected ones filled their slots. *Twelve* truly had a mind of its own, as if formed by an unanticipated inner narrative; like the moves on Alice's chessboard, it became a combination of what is written and what we write ourselves. (2007)

Cover versions are capable of providing preview rather than postscript. Jackson Browne found it beneficial to have Bonnie Raiit record several of his early compositions before he did. According to Browne, Raiit's renditions of

"My Opening Farewell," "Under the Falling Sky," "I Thought I Was A Child" became to some extent auditions that were instructional, revealing nuances, emotional qualities, and insights that shaped Browne's subsequent recordings of his own songs. (Marrone, 2008)

Musical appropriation can also result in a song's signature being misplaced or inherited. A familiar tune is easily and often more closely connected with the cover artist than the original songwriter. Popularity equals ownership. The uncovering of the original is marked by a moment of curious enlightenment, a revelation within the recognition of the song's familiarity, followed by the response, "I didn't know s/he sang/wrote that song?" It is as if the songwriter had to repossess his/her own song. Cases of mistaken identity or incidental inheritance in songwriting are plentiful. Dylan's "All Along the Watchtower" and "The Mighty Quinn" are Hendrix and Manfred Mann trademarks. The Byrds jingle jangled and harmonized so many of Dylan's songs into hits that David Crosby proclaimed, "We play Dylan better than Dylan." Kris Kristofferson's "Me and Bobby McGee" was a number one hit and signature song for Janis Joplin. Dolly Parton's "I Will Always Love You" is Whitney Houston's just as Jimmy Webb's "Wichita Lineman" is Glenn Campbell's, and John Hiatt's "Thing Called Love" is more closely associated with Bonnie Raitt. Jules Shear lingers in anonymity despite the success of his tunes popularized in the Big '80s by The Bangles ("If She Knew What She Wants") and Cyndi Lauper ("All Through the Night"). Shear, Webb and Hiatt are examples of singer/songwriters who have never quite broken through to the major artist level, yet their contemporaries have routinely borrowed from their songbooks for years. In 2000, Eric Clapton and B.B. King covered Hiatt's "Riding with the King," and used the song for the album's title. Three Hiatt tribute records confirm his revered status in the songwriter's circle. At the same time, they demonstrate the value of cover versions as an exposure vehicle not only for songs, but for their composers as well. Linda Ronstadt's popular interpretations helped uncover the songwriting skills of her 1970s California cronies such as Warren Zevon, J.D. Souther, Karla Bonoff, and Anna McGarrigle, just as Judy Collins folk renderings drew attention to East Coast writers and performers in the 1960s. In songwriting circles, there appears to be a mutual acceptance of the possibility of such cases of "mistaken identity." In 1976, when a radio host requested that in-studio guest performer Warren Zevon to play his song "Hasten Down the Wind," Zevon drolly corrected, "That's Linda Ronstadt."

Song "ownership" does not have to be a perception provoked by popularity. Some songs are a natural, if not better, fit for the interpreter than the composer. The greatest interpreters—from Sinatra and Ella Fitzgerald to Elvis, Willie Nelson and Patsy Cline—covered a lot of ground. They possess a vocal knack and presence to make every song they sing sound as if it was theirs from the first note, the first lyric. Tom Petty's "I Won't Back Down" is customized Johnny Cash, the lyrics and tone dressed in black, standing his ground at the gates of hell. By eliminating the rock chronicle verses in Don McLean's classic "American Pie," Madonna magnifies her own odyssey: "I knew if I had the chance that I could make those people dance."

Cover Me: Both Sides Now

"Re-possession" as a cover component is also as evident when artists rethink, rework and rerecord their own compositions. As the seemingly boundless borders of the tribute/cover genre expanded, songwriters "covering themselves" became a conspicuous offshoot that included live performances, demos, rarities, alternate mixes and B-sides. MTV's *Unplugged* franchise provided significant impetus for the self-cover subgenre, and signaled a subtle shift in rethinking "live" performances as a viable variation in The Cover Age. The series' intimate, acoustic setting provided another "place" for familiar songs. For some, such as Nirvana, the contrast was stark. For others—R.E.M., 10,000 Maniacs, John Mellencamp, Dylan—the venue slightly muted. And then there was Tony Bennett, who was never plugged in to begin with. The format induced the VH-1 variants *Storytellers* and the short-lived *Duets*, which paired performers swapping songs in similar style to CMT's (Country Music Television) *Crossroads*. In 2008, the Sundance Channel series *Spectacle: Elvis Costello With ...* integrated talk show conventions into the music mutuality and experimentation. The engaging collaborative concept was rooted in the syndicated gem *Sunday Night/Night Music*, which featured Jools Holland and David Sanborn conducting experimental musical matchmaking. Other performances originating from the House of Blues, Hard Rock Cafe and Nashville's Bluebird Café became part of the live trend as they were programmed into syndication and cable. Public Television hosted *Sound Stage* and *Sessions at West 54th,* and boasted the archetypal *Austin City Limits*, the blue print for the intimate live music performance on television.

Beyond narcissism and commercial and collector appeal, an artist covering their own songs appears to be a superfluous and uninspired approach to interpretation, a sure sign of a songwriting slump. Yet, the possibilities of a new place for a song to be heard are present even if its own composer is the one revisiting it. Eric Clapton's strumming acoustic "Layla" is a prime example. Similarly and singularly, the 1980s Men at Work hits return as *Man at Work* (2003), pared down by the band's former frontman Colin Hay. John Prine's motivation for re-recording his own songs was more legal than creative. Prine dusted off materials from his first three records for *Souvenirs* (2003) so he could own the master recordings to the songs. Amid whispers that she was no longer relevant, Joni Mitchell followed her Grammy-nominated *Both Sides Now* (2000), a conceptual cover collection tracing the arc of a modern romantic relationship, with *Travelogue* (2002), a double-disc retrospective of reinterpretations of her catalog with the London Symphony Orchestra. The choral collaboration transforms her classics into classical as tunes of pop simplicity undergo arrangements of lush grandeur. Similarly, Ray Davies rearranged Kink classics with the Crouch End Festival Chorus into *The Kinks*

Choral Collection (2009), 40 years after the Davies brothers songs were a defining sound of the British Invasion.

As precursor to Beatles pre-Spector paraphrase *Let It Be ... Naked* (2003), heartland rocker John Mellencamp reverses the self-cover process on *Rough Harvest* (1999), a document that sprinkles four covers in between nine versions of Mellencamp's own songs. Rather than re-recorded translations of his songs, Mellencamp provides the pre-recorded—the stripped down, unmixed, unplugged versions from rehearsals, sound checks, and impromptu get togethers to "make music to please themselves" (White, 1999). Before his 1986 Scarecrow Tour, Mellencamp required that his band learn nearly 100 hits from previous eras. In *Rough Harvest*'s liner notes, the late Timothy White revealed that part of Mellencamp's intent was to generate material for B-sides and surprise concert encores (1999). The covers became routine selections in the band's live playlist. Many, such as "Pretty Ballerina" and "Shama Lama Ding Dong," appeared as B-sides of Mellencamp singles. This rarities and rough cut approach, common with box set bonus material, grants a glimpse of the work in progress, from songwriting to studio sessions. White suggested the covers served another purpose beyond practical, performance and making a point; observing that Mellencamp and company used the songs to "re-center themselves" and "quietly reaffirm the rightness they feel in the path they've chosen and the playing that results from it" (White, 1999). In what was becoming a recording ritual among older artists, Mellencamp further revisited his roots on *Trouble No More* (2003), a striking set of folk blues standards. The unplugged pattern and the demo domain of stripped down songs receives regular impetus, among the notable reversions being the posthumous *John Lennon Acoustic* (2004), Cyndi Lauper's duet oriented *The Body Acoustic* (2005) and Alanis Morissette's acoustic anniversary of *Jagged Little Pill* (2006).

Something/Anything?: Twists and Re-turns, Revivals and Reincarnations

> There was no question in my mind about the appropriateness of this style to the challenge of reproducing 'sacred' favorites. How else to revive the material for myself as much as for others?
> > —Todd Rundgren, back jacket sleeve note, *With A Twist ...* (1997)

> I thought it would be good to record songs that didn't have a life but should've had a life. This is my attempt at giving them a life.
> > —Jules Shear, on his cover collection *Sayin' Hello to the Folks* (Wilder)

Todd Rundgren's *With A Twist* (1997) offers another curious case of cover contrast. The twist is Todd as the Boy from Ipanema delivering 11 of his classics, including —"I Saw the Light," "Hello It's Me," "Can We Still Be Friends," "Love is the Answer, "A Dream Goes On Forever," "It Wouldn't Have Made Any Difference," in Bossa Nova style. "Am I serious?" begins Rundgren's brief note of justification on the back cover. The line vies with "Laugh at him. Go ahead, laugh" from *Bonograph: Sonny (Bono) Gets His Share* (1992) as the best liner note lead on a cover/tribute record.

Rundgren's revivalist regard resonates as it complements Emmylou Harris's view of the necessity of songs to be sung in new places in order to stay alive. *With A Twist*, like many cover projects, may be easy to file away until a pool party, or to dismiss as a one-listen novelty fit for the Rhino Records reserve. But Rundgren deserves credit for not taking a safe route with his own material. The trendy live and unplugged approach to self covers may be more marketable and better suited to repeated listens, but artistically the songs are stranded. They essentially remain in the same place. Granted, a "new place" may not be the *best* place, or even a *better* place for the musical material to stay alive; it is merely *a* place with a different view.

Rundgren charts a curious and courageous course along the cover cartography, a vast frontier which is perhaps appropriately characterized by his early album title *Something/Anything?* Yet, among the random revisionists and reforms of the Cover Age, is classic Rundgren doing the Bossa Nova any more unusual than other tuneful twists and re-turns that have permeated the market since the 1990s: Dwight Yoakam's twangy Big Band orchestration of the Kinks' "Tired of Waiting for You?" CMH sessionists bluegrass pickings of rock classics "Purple Haze" and "Born to Run"? Reggae, country, gospel and global Dylan? String Quartets playing heavy metal or Warren Zevon's "Werewolves of London" or "Excitable Boy?" Natalie Imbruglia's sugary pop take on Ednaswap's grinding "Torn?" Alternative rock bands paying homage to composers Henri Mancini and Burt Bacharach? Lo-fi, Spectorian gymnasium recordings of The Langley Elementary School choir covering 1960s and 1970s pop hits? Old timers Willie Nelson covering Kermit the Frog's "Rainbow Connection," Dylan delivering "This Old Man," and Little Richard "Itsy Bitsy Spider"? Motown, reggae and a cappella Beatles? Dread Zeppelin's Elvis Impersonator "Tortelvis" crooning "Stairway to Heaven" over reggae and dub production accents? Trekkie covers by William Shatner ("Lucy in the Sky with Diamonds") and Leonard Nimoy ("Proud Mary")? Ozzy Osbourne's unlikely tendertake of the Beatles "In My Life?" Meat Loaf singing Gershwin's "Somebody Loves Me?" The campy, middle aged Del Rubio Triplets "Light My Fire?" Or any song sung by *American Idol*'s international lampoon William Hung?

Like Rundgren's renditions, these interpretations simultaneously attract and distract; the incompatibility of the version or vocal confounds; maybe solicits a smirk. Of course the listener asks, "Is s/he serious?" Or hums, "Look what they've done to my song." The "new place" can be so different that it is difficult to take the work seriously, despite impressive production qualities, the creator's track record, and artistic intentions. Yes, Rundgren's cheesy lounge transformations distort the familiar into something nearly unrecognizable. It's not the same old song. Yet, when considered within the broader context of history, genre, style, music market trends and "singing songs in places they've never been," Rundgrens' revivalist renditions may not be as twisted a they sound.

Other restoration projects employ a "lost and found" approach. *Lost Songs: Songs the Beatles Wrote But Never Recorded* (1999) features one band re-covering Beatles compositions recorded by Billy J. Kramer, Peter and Gordon, the Dakotas, P.J. Proby and others. The collection, recorded at the Abbey Road Studios in London, faithfully recreates the 1960s sound and the George Martin production vibe. Similarly, on *Lost Songs of Lennon & McCartney: From a Window* (2003), B-52 Kate Pierson, Graham Parker and Bill Janowitz of Buffalo Tom reinvent 17 songs that were never released by the Beatles. There may be no better illustration of "reviving material" than the Billy Bragg and Wilco *Mermaid Avenue* volumes (1998, 2000). When Woody Guthrie died in 1967, he left behind hundreds of songs that he had carried in his head and written, but they were never recorded. Guthrie's daughter, Nora, fearing the tunes were gone forever, approached Bragg about writing some new music to accompany her father's lost lyrics. The resulting recordings resurrected Guthrie's tunes with remarkable reverence. Bragg describes the approach to the ambitious project: "... Nora talked to me about breaking the mould, of working with her father to give his words a new sound and a new context. The result is not a tribute album but a collaboration between Woody Guthrie and a new generation of songwriters who until now had only glimpsed him fleetingly, over the shoulder of Bob Dylan or somewhere in the distance of a Bruce Springsteen song" (Bragg, 1998).

Lost and Found in Translation: Listening to Old Voices in New Places with New Ears

> There is nothing that says a great song cannot be interpreted at any time in any way.
>
> — producer Phil Ramone (Gardner, 2001)

> Songs need new voices to sing them in places they've never been sung in order to stay alive.
>
> —Emmylou Harris (Griffith, 1993)

The essence of the cover song may be located in the sense of heritage that the form harbors, preserves, references and reveals. Like any adaptation, the cover song points to the past and profiles its predecessor. As one of music's major forms of intertextuality, covers are not only immersed in history, they recognize, recite and reshape the past (Weinstein, 1998).

The best tribute records or cover compilations document such heritage and context in packaging that contains contributors comments, biographical, historical, cultural and musical background. The booklets and liner notes stand as affirmative works of criticism and provide context that complement the song cycle. There are a variety of archival sources of synergy. "Book covers" such as Nanci Griffith's and Joe Jackson's, *Other Voices: A Personal History of Folk Music* (1998), provide a magnificent musicological song-by-song companion piece to Griffith's reverent contemporary folk cover collaborations, *Other Voices, Other Rooms* (1993) and *Other Voices, Too: A Trip to Bountiful* (1997). Dave Marsh's *Louie Louie* (1993) lineage and Bill Moyers's documentary *Amazing Grace* (1992) demonstrate the rich cultural heritage contained in a song, whether pop or traditional. Internet access, such as the detailed "Dylan cover albums" web site designed to accommodate the voluminous Dylan cover catalog, provides convenient click outlets for avid fans and musicologists to trace a song's lineage.

A cover song invites, if not insists upon, a comparison to the original, striking a familiar chord, rousing residue of musical memory, engaging the listener in a historical duet with lyric and lineage. A distant dialogue. A delicate and dichotomous dance between past and present, place and possibility. Between the song, its composer, its interpeter(s) and listeners, connecting, disconnecting, reconnecting. Old verses, new voices, new places and possibilities, new ears.

As the versions of a song accumulate, the listener is drawn deeper into the dialogue and the dynamic of the duets. With the original framed in forefront or back of our mind, we consider the conversions and their contrasts, weighing the repetition and relocation, recognizing the potential for delight and disappointment, different or diminished meaning, noticing minor makeovers and incongruities. The We Five and Crispian St. Peter's mid 1960s hit versions of Ian and Sylvia's "You Were On My Mind" changing the lyrical reference to drinking ("I got drunk/And I got sick/And I came home again"); but The Cowsills leaving it in. Ronstadt's obvious gender transposition and softening of Warren Zevon's *Rainbow Bar* and Hyatt House rendezvous in the low self esteem "Poor Poor Pitiful Me," by changing the location to Yokohama and dropping the snarling line "I don't want to talk about it."

Greil Marcus suggests, "If musicians cover songs by recutting them, then listeners cover songs by mishearing them" (1994: 15). The B-side to Mary Chapin Carpenter's "Almost Home" is one of those hear-here cases. "This is a bummer song by somebody else," prefaces Carpenter to a cover she is about to play during a live show. The "somebody else" turns out to be Bruce Springsteen. Counter to expectations of a selection from *Nebraska, Tunnel of Love* or perhaps *Ghost of Tom Joad,* Carpenter delivers a subdued version of his spirited *Born in the USA* hit "Dancing in the Dark." The rendition is a revelation that reaches beyond the acoustic and electric disparity. The austere lament illuminates the loneliness in the lyrics. Assuredly, no fan joined Carpenter on stage to reprise Courtney Cox's dancing concert cameo in the song's 1980s video. In exuberant contrast to Carpenter's cover, any hint of despair and yearning in the original is immersed in the signature Springsteen sound and inexhaustible energy.

Just when a familiar song's cycle seems saturated, too familiar and tired, perhaps teetering on encore exhaustion, it travels to a surprising place, somewhere it had not been to or where we could not have imagined it being. Along comes the late Israel Kamakawiwo`ole's blissful, humming, ukelele strumming "Over the Rainbow" that melts into a medley with "What a Wonderful World." Out of the accumulation of the rock touchstone "Sweet Jane"—from Lou Reed to Mott the Hoople and endless alternative rock takes—emerge the Cowboy Junkies' atmospheric dirge and Two Nice Girls' gorgeous mediation that weaves Joan Armatrading's "Love and Affection" into the original.

Sometimes it is the voice itself that provides the new place, from Johnny Cash's world weary restatements of "In My Life," "Bridge Over Troubled Water," "Danny Boy" or "The First Time Ever I Saw Your Face" to Victoria Williams rustic, innocent, wounded wing warbling "Over the Rainbow," "My Funny Valentine," "Someone to Watch Over Me" and other classic compositions on her *Sings Some Ol' Songs* (2002). Sometimes the location and language are far away. On the intriguing *Masked and Anonymous* (2003) soundtrack, the voices are those of obscure international artists translating Dylan: "My Back Pages" in urgent Japanese; "If You See Her, Say Hello" in Italian folk-pop; a Swedish spoken-word version of "Most of the Time;" "One More Cup of Coffee" in Turkish pop; and an Italian hip-hop take on "Like A Rolling Stone." Dylan's down home demo-like delivery of "Dixie" enhances the exotic. According to Alan Light (2003), the film's producer/director Larry Charles wanted to find a different approach to the music. He sampled thousands of existing global covers of Dylan songs, a process which Charles described as "like falling into a big cave and stumbling onto this huge treasure trove."

While we seek treasures, listening to a song's lineage in the comforting confines of our own cover caves, sifting and sampling various versions and voices, originals and offspring, the distant dialogue becomes discerning. Preferences inevitably emerge. Maybe R.E.M.'s "Wall of Death" to Richard and Linda Thompson's original, Nanci Griffith's or Pete and Maura Kennedy's. Or still finding John Hiatt's raspy "Have A Little Faith in Me" the most majestic and meaningful amidst a pleasant progression of borrowers —Jewel, Patty Larkin, Mandy Moore, guitarist Bill Frisell. And how does one choose between the Leonard Cohen original or Bono's, John Cale's, or Jeff Buckley's "Hallelujah" or the set of versions of the Band's "The Weight?"

When a song is re-recorded, a genealogy begins to unfold into a time line, a lineage marked by artists, styles, genres, periods and generations. In his typically illuminating essay "Old Songs in New Skins," critic extraordinaire Greil Marcus (1999) suggests how a song persists, echoing the "revival" and "survival" cover convictions expressed by both Todd Rundgren and Emmylou Harris:

> One of the ways songs survive is that they mutate. Sometimes this happens subtly, around the margins, in soundtracks or commercials. The song is moved just slightly off the map we normally use to orient ourselves—but in a way that, in a year or ten, may completely change—how we hear it, what associations we bring to it. Pop songs are always talked about as the "soundtrack to our lives," when all that means is that pop songs are no more containers for nostalgia, but

lives change and so do soundtracks, even if they're made of the same songs.(374)
"... [a] song itself may be over—or, rather definitively appropriated, never to be given back ... you can think it has just begun to travel, a mutant now, limbs fallen off, strange sores appearing, the sores growing into whole new bodies. (376)

Though the covering process may preserve, sustain and revitalize music, melody and lyrics, covering is not a condition of continuity. Outstanding songs are self-sustaining. "Yesterday" was great 2000 versions ago. "Blowin' in the Wind," "(I Can't Get No) Satisfaction," "The Weight" and "Moon River" do not require restatement. Yet, when contemporary artists such as John Prine, Alison Krauss, Yo Yo Ma, Mavis Staples, Roger McGuinn and others assemble to celebrate the works of "America's first songwriter" Stephen Foster on *Beautiful Dreamer* (2004), the sound and spirit of the century-old songs awaken from where they last settled along their lineage, transported in time and place with other voices as vessels of vitality. Enduring anthems become works in progress.

Whether necessary or not, the respectful recognition inherent in a rendition contributes to the chronology and a song's survival. Of all the "re" characteristics of cover songs, the most essential may be as a reminder. A trigger of memory residue. Covers are souvenirs of songs that are great or good, favorite or familiar, songs that strike a chord or capture a moment, recall a person, place, event ritual or style. A reminder of why we learned to play the song. Why it made us laugh or cry; sing along or dance. They cue chronicle and context—the who, what, where, and when, and the reasons why we liked the song in the first place. And remind us why the song is worth repeating, reciting, replaying, revisiting, rediscovering. As Don McLean suggests when responding to Madonna's millennium revival of his epic "American Pie," "Good songs always come back when you need them the most."

Traveling the Cover Cartography: Only the Song Survives

> ... it's just the song, the image, and the clarity of paving a highway to your own sound track in your own "Bountiful" in your own time and sense of place.
>
> —Nanci Griffith (1998: 49)

> ... originals are a zillion times better, but that's not the point. The point [of covers] is outstanding songs.
>
> —critic Christian Wright (1992)

Cover songs span the songwriting spectrum as soundtracks of our lives, musical quotations, touchstones, franchises, aural artifacts that have withstood the test of time. They embody and disembody, and are cast in various contexts and complexions—as derivatives or deviants, morphs or mutants, interpretations or inhabitants, clones or copycats, shape shifters or genre benders, encores or echoes, favorites reformed or refashioned, fine tunes being fine tuned, classics being re-classified.

Perhaps as much as any categorization, in their purest sense, cover songs are simply time travelers. They traverse as reverent ricochets and resonant reminders; chronicles and containers; converted companions—rock renditions, borrowed blues, and pop portraits of the past. They are intertextual tourists, lost and found in translation; notes of nostalgia on sentimental journeys, trekking the cultural and historical songscape, twisting and turning, tracing and leaving tracks, tripping the light fantastic, transformations in transportation, covering ground along the frontier of familiar on the Musical Matrix that is the contemporary Cover Cartography, a timeless tuneful terrain.

UNDER THE COVERS:
HISTORY, IDEOLOGY, IDENTITY

Chapter 2

Charting Cultural Change, 1953–57:
Song Assimilation Through Cover Recording

B. Lee Cooper

Songs are commodities. They are products of composers/lyricists. They gain life through performance. They attain status through retail chart listing. They achieve broader acclaim through cover recording. Undeniably, repetition of a particular song is a sign of artist interest and audience appreciation. Multiple recordings of the same hit song were a common practice during the first half of the twentieth century. This practice continued at mid-century, but featured a far more diverse group of composers and performers. More importantly, songs of the '50s were drawn from previously segregated musical genres. Rhythm 'n' blues performers joined country singers in invading "Pop" charts. The cover recording battle that raged throughout the mid-1950s promoted greater national exposure, acculturation, diversity, and legitimacy in American popular music. *Billboard* and *Cash Box*, the major music trade journals of the period, provide weekly documentation of song acceptance within the public forum. These two journals also trace the rise and fall of particular recording artists. By the end of the 1950s, a new popular music galaxy was established. Some old stars remained (Dean Martin, Frank Sinatra, Tony Bennett, Bing Crosby, Dinah Shore, and Peggy Lee); many new stars were born (Elvis Presley, Pat Boone, Jackie Wilson, Hank Ballard, The Platters, James Brown, The Drifters, and Bill Haley and His Comets); several old stars disappeared (Georgia Gibbs, Fontane Sisters, Hilltoppers, Guy Mitchell and Teresa Brewer); and numerous new performers flashed brightly and burned out (Boyd Bennett, Otis Williams and His Charms, Maurice Williams, Nervous Norvis, Billy Lee Riley, Larry Williams, and The Five Satins).

This study examines public song assimilation through cover recording. It utilizes two weekly popular music charts—*Billboard* and *Cash Box*—to track expanding commercial interest in new music, whether it was performed by traditional stylists or by new artists. The conclusion is that the American musical culture shifted dramatically at mid-century (1953–57) because of the cross-pollination of singing and instrumental styles exhibited in multiple performances of new hit songs.

The Tradition of Cover Recording, 1933–52

For composers, duplication is the sincerest form of flattery. Repetition of their songs, with royalty benefits streaming from multiple record sales, is an unspoken goal among songwriters. The tradition of cover recording emerged early in the twentieth century. Good songs attracted several artists. Why should the first performer be the only one to benefit from a popular lyric or a catchy melody? Immediate covers were designed to capture the initial moment of audience awareness. Obviously, the financial pie of total public purchases was divided into smaller pieces when two or more renditions of a single tune reached the market during the same year. The original artist understandably griped. So did the record company producing the first release. But the composer couldn't conceal glee at the prospect of increased visibility and broadened sales. With numerous versions of the same song being played on pianos, victrolas, juke boxes, and in live performances by multiple artists, the songwriter's ultimate dream of producing a life-time "standard" was within reach.

The test of particular songs attaining long-range impact is not the immediate cover, but the future cover. From 1933 to 1952 only a handful of the thousands of songs recorded during those two decades received both immediate and future covers. Clearly, novelty songs like "Mairzy Doats" (1944) and "Open the Door, Richard" (1947) spawned many renditions in their single year of popularity. But never again. Similarly, classic World War II tunes like "Miss You" (1942) and "(There'll Be Bluebirds Over) the White Cliffs of Dover" (1942) charted in multiple versions, but not beyond their initial year of appearance. On the other hand, some recordings demonstrated renewable popularity. The most dominant song in this category is "White Christmas." This American standard was initially charted by four different performers in 1942 (Bing Crosby, Charlie Spivak, Gordon Jenkins, and Freddy Martin). The Crosby version returned to popular acclaim from 1944–45, 1947–50, 1952, and beyond. Other versions of "White Christmas" were released by Frank Sinatra (1944), Jo Stafford (1946), Eddy Howard (1947), Perry Como (1947), and Mantovani (1952). Irving Berlin's holiday classic is the poster boy illustration for both immediate and future cover recording. Table 2.1 features an alphabetical listing of songs that were hits with more than one version being released initially and then were popularized again through the rebirth of at least one new charted rendition. Data for this chart was drawn from the following sources: (Jacobs and Jacobs, 1994; Lax and Smith, 1989; Whitburn, 2002, 1986).

The practice of cover recording can be viewed as aesthetic robbery. An original artist may lose sales revenue because a second or a third performer elects to release the same song during the same period. As noted earlier, composers reap financial benefits regardless of who records their songs. For this reason, songwriters often shop their tunes to record companies even after an initial recording has been released. Why not? What is seldom recognized and rarely discussed are the unintended consequences of cover recording. Finances aside, an ever-increasing portion of the American listening public can be exposed to a single tune through multiple releases. While arrangements and singing styles may vary, the song itself gains greater currency in the popular hit treasury. The two decades prior to the emergence of doo-wop, rockabilly, and rock 'n' roll illustrate the rich realm of cover recording. From 1933 to 1952 hundreds of songs were covered. Some tunes were borrowed from country music ("Cold, Cold Heart" and "Jambalaya"); some poked fun at other pop hits ("Baby, It's Cold Outside" by Homer and Jethro and "Temptation (Tim-Tayshun)" by Red Ingle and the Natural Seven); and some sought to introduce special jazz rhythms or rich orchestral arrangements to relatively simple pop tunes. The result of hybrid or highbrow covers was a growing diversity within American popular music. Slowly but surely, the record listening public moved from traditional pop toward a much richer musical stream of more diverse sounds. There was greater acceptance of ethnic diversity, more adaptation of country and R & B rhythms, enhanced accommodation for varied vocal styles, and broadened acculturation in regard to both humor and topical lyrics. The chronological list of songs provided in Table 2.2 were covered immediately during the 1933–52 period and established the base of behavior for the transition years of 1953–57. Data for this chart was drawn from the following sources: (Lax and Smith, 1989; Whitburn, 1986).

Cover Recording as Acculturation, 1953–57

Vitality and diversity in recorded music following the Second World War was sparked by artists like Mahalia Jackson, Roy Brown, Bing Crosby, Johnny Ray, Louis Jordan, Patti Page, Duke Ellington, Hank Williams, and Billie Holiday. Celebrity recognition, however, did not always translate into pop chart success for many country, gospel, jazz and R & B artists. While inroads occurred during 1933–52, the top of the musical integration mountain wasn't reached until mid-century. What changed? Briefly, numerous independent record companies emerged; new songs and new singers moved from regional to nationwide promotion; key markets were penetrated by enhanced radio airplay and increased television exposure; and performing venues broadened dramatically.

Cover recordings of 1953 through 1957 demonstrated continuity of practice, but change in public acceptance. As always, listeners were exposed to new songs by original performers and traditional cover artists. Yet during these crucial five years, emerging stars of doo-wop, rockabilly, rhythm and blues, and rock and roll frequently achieved pop chart recognition either parallel to or superior to established performers. This transition is often described as a musical revolution. It wasn't. Youthful record buyers were attracted to Elvis Presley, Gene Vincent, Little Richard, Frankie Lymon, Eddie Cochran, and Carl Perkins. Adults purchased releases by Pat Boone, The Diamonds, Connie Francis, The Crew-Cuts, and The Hilltoppers. Songs changed, too. But once again, it was the composers who rejoiced as rampant cover recording continued.

Billboard and *Cash Box* tell the tale. Between 1953 and 1957 the chart presence of country-rooted performers (Patsy Cline, Johnny Cash, Marty Robbins, Wanda Jackson, Brenda Lee, Carl Perkins, and Elvis Presley) and R & B artists (Hank Ballard, James Brown, Ruth Brown, Ivory Joe Hunter, Joe Turner, LaVern Baker, and Etta James) increased dramatically. Greater song exposure promoted adaptation, accommodation, and (ultimately) assimilation. Ignore the motives behind cover recording. Assess the results. *Billboard* and *Cash Box* illustrate the monumental pronoun shift from deriding *their* songs to celebrating *our* songs. Cover recordings functioned as a catalyst for a massive transition in popular musical taste. Lesser-known artists like Ronnie Hawkins functioned below the chart-keeping radar to spread the acceptance of new tunes written by Chuck Berry, Larry Williams, Bo Diddley, and Jerry Leiber/Mike Stoller. Meanwhile new celebrities such as Rick Nelson (television) and The Everly Brothers (radio) launched recording careers from high profile backgrounds.

Evidence demonstrating how crossover song acceptance was achieved through audience acceptance of multiple renditions is provided in Table 2.3. Data for this chart was drawn from the following sources: (Downey, Albert, Hoffman, 1994); Lax and Smith, 1989; Lonergan, 2005; Pavlow, 2001; Whitburn, 1992; 2002; 2003).

Continuing Cover Recording, 1958 to The Beatles

After 1957 the American recording industry faced a popular music audience that had accepted new songs and new artists as the norm rather than the exception. "Blue Suede Shoes" fit both Carl Perkins and Elvis Presley. "Rip It Up" was acceptable by either Little Richard or Bill Haley and His Comets. "Two Hearts" could be sung by The Charms or Pat Boone. And "Tweedle Dee" was a reasonable tune by either LaVern Baker or Georgia Gibbs. Cover recording remained a staple – especially for the breakthrough artists of 1953–57. Fats Domino revived "Coquette," "When the Saints Go Marching In," "Margie," "Put Your Arms Around Me Honey," "Ain't That Just Like a Woman," "Jambalaya (On the Bayou)," "You Win Again," "Did You Ever See a Dream Walking," and "Red Sails in the Sunset" between 1958 and 1963. During the same six-year period Pat Boone re-issued "It's Too Soon to Know," "Cherie, I Love You," "That's How Much I Love You," "With the Wind and the Rain in Your Hair," "Good Rockin' Tonight," "Beyond the Sunset," "Walking the Floor Over You," Dear John," and "I'll See You in My Dreams." Not to be outdone in the realm of cover recording that he had dominated from 1954 through 1957, Elvis Presley provided new renditions of the following songs between 1958 and 1963: "One Night," "(Now and Then There's) A Fool Such as I," "Are You Lonesome To-Night?," "I Feel So Bad," and "Witchcraft."

Beyond Chuck Berry, the initial and best singer-songwriter of the early rock era, vocalists continued to rely upon previously charted songs to meld with new numbers over lengthy (5–8 years) record charting careers. Obviously, touring and performing in club venues often continued well beyond *Billboard* and *Cash Box* chart recognition days. (This situation may be difficult to imagine in light of the post-1960 success of self-contained composers and vocalists like Bob Dylan, Smokey Robinson, Billy Joel, Lennon and McCartney, Elton John, Jagger and Richards, Carole King, Paul Simon, and hundreds of others.) It is especially interesting to note the large number of new hit songs from the 1953–57 transition period that were revived within the following six years. Among these new standards are "Ain't That a Shame" (Four Seasons, 1963), "At My Front Door" (Dee Clark, 1960), "Earth Angel" (Johnny Tillotson, 1960), "Gee" (Pixies Three, 1964), "Hearts of Stone" (Bill Black's Combo, 1961), "I Hear You Knocking" (Fats Domino, 1961), "I'll Be Home" (Platters, 1966), "Ko Ko Mo (I Love You So)" (Flamingos, 1961), "Ling, Ting, Tong" (Buddy Knox, 1961), "Lovey Dovey" (Buddy Knox, 1960), "Only You" (Franck Pourcel's French Fiddles, 1959), "Only You" (Mr. Acker Bilk, 1963), "Pledging My Love" (Roy Hamilton, 1958), "Pledging My Love" (Johnny Tillotson, 1960), "Seventeen" (Frankie Ford, 1961), "Skokiaan" (Bill Haley and His Comets, 1960), and "Teach Me Tonight" (George Maharis, 1962).

It is even more fascinating to recognize that many, many pre-1953 hit songs became chart material for new pop performers during the 1958–63 period. Once again, cover recording provided established tunes that could be stylistically adapted by contemporary artists. As noted earlier, Fats Domino, Pat Boone, and Elvis Presley frequently borrowed old tunes from the '20s, '30s, and '40s. Other new performers revived standard songs as well: "Baby Face" (Little Richard, 1958), "Baby Face" (Bobby Darin, 1962), "Baby It's Cold Outside" (Ray Charles and Betty Carter, 1962), "Besame Mucho" (Coasters, 1960), "Beyond the Sea" (Bobby Darin, 1960), "Blue Moon" (Marcels, 1961), "Come Rain or Come Shine" (Ray Charles, 1960), "Georgia On My Mind" (Ray Charles, 1960), "Harbor Lights" (Platters, 1960), "Heartaches" (Marcels, 1961), "I Only Have Eyes For You" (Flamingos, 1959), "I'll Be Seeing You" (Five Satins, 1960), "If I Didn't Care" (Platters, 1961), "In the Still of the Night" (Dion and The Belmonts, 1960), "Lazy River" (Bobby Darin, 1961), "Moonlight Bay" (Drifters, 1958), "My Melancholy Baby" (Marcels, 1962), "Once in a While" (Chimes, 1961), "Red Sails in the Sunset" (Platters, 1960), "Shimmy Like Kate" (Olympics, 1960), "Signed, Sealed, and Delivered" (Rusty Draper, 1961), "Smoke Gets in Your Eyes" (Platters, 1958), "Summertime" (Marcels, 1961), "That Lucky Old Sun" (Ray Charles, 1963), "Time After Time" (Frankie Ford, 1960), "It's Too Soon to Know" (Etta James, 1961), "To Each His Own" (Platters, 1960), "Twilight Time" (Platters, 1958), "You Are My Sunshine" (Ray Charles, 1962), "You Must Have Been a Beautiful Baby" (Bobby Darin, 1961), "When You Wish Upon a Star" (Dion and The Belmonts, 1960), and "Where or When" (Dion and The Belmonts, 1959).

Conclusion

Popular music rankings reported in *Billboard* and *Cash Box* illustrate week-to-week song popularity. During the 1950s these trade journal charts documented a cultural transition. American pop music tastes broadened, a multitude of new artists emerged, and the age of rock was born. A network of technological innovations, radio broadcasting personalities, record company marketing techniques, and the financial strength of youthful record buyers fed this so-called "revolution". But the heart of the matter was the new songs composed by new songwriters and performed by both new and traditional artists.

During any period of cultural shift, old habits are sustained. Similarly, persons with vested interests in established patterns of behavior are reluctant to acknowledge or to accept innovation. Post-World War II song production and record distribution had been slowly moving away from a monolithic music model. Country songs and rhythm 'n' blues tunes were beginning to gain the attention of an increasingly broad audience. Pop singers borrowed freely and widely from an array of non-Tin Pan Alley and non-Broadway tunesmiths. Hank Williams and Louis Jordan alone provided significant song material for Dinah Shore, Patti Page, Dean Martin, Frankie Laine, Perry Como, and many others. This acculturation, integration, and adaptation via cover recording created the receptivity for dramatic change that culminated between 1953 and 1957. Songs reigned while music stylists battled. What emerged was more than just rock 'n' roll. It was a new vibrance in American popular music that would echo the US and Europe over the next three decades. The expanding American musical taste was achieved through magnified exposure to new songs. This tale of the crucial 1953–57 period is clearly documented in the pop charts of *Billboard* and *Cash Box*.

Table 2.1   Selected popular recordings initially covered by several artists and revived in future years, 1900–52

Song title (Composer)	Years charted	Number of versions released
1. "Baby Face" (Benny David/Harry Akst)	1926 1948	8
2. "Body and Soul" (Edward Heyman/ Robert Sour/Frank Eyton/John Green)	1930 1931 1932 1935 1937 1940 1947 1949	14
3. "Darktown Strutters' Ball" (Shelton Brooks)	1917 1918 1927 1948	6
4. "Dinah" (Sam Lewis/Joe Young/Harry Askt)	1926 1930 1932 1935 1936 1946	10
5. "Harbor Lights" (Jimmy Kennedy/ Will Grosz)	1937 1950	9
6. "I Can't Give You Anything But Love" (Dorothy Fields/Jimmy McHugh)	1928 1929 1936 1948	8
7. "(I Love You) For Sentimental Reasons" (Deek Watson/William Best)	1946 1947	6
8. "I'll Walk Alone" (Sammy Cahn/Jule Styne)	1944 1952	7
9. "I'm Always Chasing Rainbows" (Joseph McCarthy/Harry Carroll)	1927 1948	7
10. "I'm Looking Over a Four-Leaf Clover" (Moat Dixon/Harry MacGregor Woods)	1927 1948	9
11. "I've Got My Love to Keep Me Warm" (Irving Berlin)	1937 1949	8

Song title (Composer)	Years charted	Number of versions released
12. "It Had to Be You" (Gus Kahn/ Isham Jones)	1924 1930 1941 1944	12
13. "Margie" (Benny Davis/Con Conrad/ J. Russell Robinson)	1920 1921 1934 1939	7
14. "Marie" (Irving Berlin)	1929 1937 1938	5
15. "My Mommy" (Sam Lewis/Joe Young/ Walter Donaldson)	1921 1928 1947	7
16. "My Man" (Channing Pollock/ Maurice Yvain)	1922 1928 1929 1938 1939 1947	8
17. "Peg O' My Heart" (Alfred Bryan/ Fred Fisher)	1913 1914 1947	9
18. "Pennies From Heaven" (Johnny Burke/ Arthur Johnston)	1936 1937	6
19. "Red Sails in the Sunset" (Jimmy Kennedy/ Hugh Williams)	1935 1936 1951	6
20. "Shine On, Harvest Moon" (Jack Norworth/Nora Bayes)	1909 1910 1931 1943	7
21. "Tea For Two" (Irving Caesar/ Vincent Youmans)	1925 1930 1937 1939	6

Song title (Composer)	Years charted	Number of versions released
22. "Temptation" (Arthur Freed/ Nacio Herb Brown)	1934 1944 1945 1946 1947	7
23. "That Old Gang of Mine" (Billy Rose/ Mort Dixon/Ray Henderson)	1923 1924 1938	6
24. "Thinking of You" (Bert Kalmar/ Harry Ruby)	1928 1936 1950	7
25. "Together" (B.G. Sylva/Lew Brown/ Ray Henderson)	1928 1944	6
26. "Toot Toot Tootsie (Goodbye)" (Gus Kahn/ Ernie Erdman/Ted Fiorita/Robert A. King)	1923 1949	6
27. "What is This Thing Called Love?" (Cole Porter)	1930 1939 1942 1948	6
28. "What'll I Do?" (Irving Berlin)	1924 1948	8
29. "When You Were Sweet Sixteen" (James Thornton)	1900 1901 1947	7
30. "Whispering" (John Schonberger/ Richard Coburn/Vincent Rose	1920 1921 1951	5
31. "White Christmas" (Irving Berlin)	1942 1944 1945 1946 1947 1948 1949 1950 1952	21
32. "Who's Sorry Now?" (Bert Kalmar/ Harry Ruby/Ted Snyder)	1923 1946	6

Table 2.2   Selected illustrations of immediate cover recording practices in American popular music, 1933–52

1933

"Last Round-Up" (William Hill)
Guy Lombardo (Brunswick)
George Olsen (Columbia)
Don Bestor (Victor)
Bing Crosby (Brunswick)
Victor Young (Brunswick)
Gene Autry (Melotone)
Conrad Thibault (Victor)

"Stormy Weather" (Ted Koehler/Harold Arlen)
Leo Reisman, with Harold Arlen (Victor)
Ethel Waters (Brunswick)
Guy Lombardo (Brunswick)
Duke Ellington (Brunswick)
Ted Lewis (Columbia)

1934

"Smoke Gets In Your Eyes" (Otto Harbach/Jerome Kern)
Paul Whiteman (Victor)
Leo Reisman (Brunswick)
Emil Coleman (Columbia)
Ruth Etting (Brunswick)

"Two Cigarettes in the Dark" (Paul Francis Webster/Lew Pollack)
Johnny Green (Columbia)
Bing Crosby (Decca)
Jerry Johnson (Victor)
Frank Parker (Columbia)
Glen Gray (Brunswick)

1935

"Lullaby of Broadway" (Al Dubin/Harry Warren)
Dorsey Brothers Orchestra (Decca)
Little Jack Little (Columbia)
Reginald Foresythe (Columbia)
Hal Kemp (Brunswick)
Chick Bullock (Melotone)

"You Are My Lucky Star" (Arthur Freed/Nacio Herb Brown)
Eddy Duchin (Victor)
Dorsey Brothers Orchestra (Decca)
Louis Armstrong (Decca)
Tommy Dorsey, with Eleanor Powell (Victor)

1936

"These Foolish Things" (Holt Marvell/Jack Strachey/Harry Link)
Benny Goodman (Victor)
Teddy Wilson, with Billie Holiday (Brunswick)
Nat Brandywynne (Brunswick)
Carroll Gibbons (Columbia)
Joe Sanders

"Until the Real Thing Comes Along" (Sammy Cahn/Saul Chaplin/L.E. Freeman/
    Mann Holiner/Alberta Nichols)
Andy Kirk (Decca)
Fats Waller (Victor)
Jan Garber (Decca)
Erskine Hawkins (Vocalion)

1937

"They Can't Take That Away From Me" (Ira Gershwin/George Gershwin)
Fred Astaire (Brunswick)
Ozzie Nelson (Bluebird)
Tommy Dorsey (Victor)
Billie Holiday (Vocalion)

"When My Dream Boat Comes Home" (Cliff Friend/Dave Franklin)
Guy Lombardo (Victor)
Henry Allen (Vocalion)
Shep Fields (Bluebird)

1938

"Bei Mir Bist D Schoen" (Jacob Jacobs/Sammy Cahn/Saul Chaplin/Sholom Secunda)
Andrews Sisters (Decca)
Guy Lombardo (Victor)
Russ Morgan (Brunswick)
Benny Goodman (Victor)
Jerry Blaine (Bluebird)
Kate Smith (Victor)

"You Must Have Been a Beautiful Baby" (Johnny Mercer/Harry Warren)
Bing Crosby (Decca)
Tommy Dorsey (Victor)

1939

"South of the Border" (Jimmy Kennedy/Michael Carr)
Shep Fields (Bluebird)
Guy Lombardo (Decca)
Gene Autry (Vocalion)
Tony Martin (Decca)

"What's New?" (Johnny Burke/Robert Haggart)
Bing Crosby (Decca)
Benny Goodman (Columbia)
Bob Crosby (Decca)
Hal Kemp (Victor)

1940

"When You Wish Upon a Star" (Ned Washington/Leigh Harline)
Glen Miller (Bluebird)
Guy Lombardo (Decca)
Cliff Edwards (Victor)
Hoarce Hiedt (Columbia)

"With the Wind and the Rain in Your Hair" (Jack Lawrence/Clara Edwards)
Bob Crosby (Decca)
Kay Kyser (Columbia)
Bob Chester (Bluebird)

1941

"I Don't Want to Set the World on Fire" (Eddie Seiler/Sol Marcus/
    Bennie Benjamin/Eddie Durham)
Horarce Heidt (Columbia)
Ink Spots (Decca)
Tommy Tucker (OKEH)
Mitchell Ayres (Bluebird)

"You Are My Sunshine" (Jimmie Davis/Charles Mitchell)
Bing Crosby (Decca)
Wayne King (Victor)
Gene Autry (OKEH)

1942

"Miss You" (Charles Tobias/Harry Tobias/Henry Tobias)
Dinah Shore (Bluebird)
Bing Crosby (Decca)
Eddy Howard (Columbia)
Freddy Martin (Bluebird)

"(There'll Be Bluebirds Over) The White Cliffs of Dover" (Nat Burton/
   Walter Kent)
Kay Kyser (Columbia)
Glenn Miller (Bluebird)
Kate Smith (Columbia)
Sammy Kaye (Victor)
Jimmy Dorsey (Decca)

1943

"You'd Be So Nice to Come Home To" (Cole Porter)
Dinah Shore (Victor)
Six Hits and A Miss (Capitol)

"You'll Never Know" (Mack Gordon/Harry Warren)
Dick Haymes (Decca)
Frank Sinatra (Columbia)
Willie Kelly (Hit)

1944

"Long Ago (And Far Away)" (Ira Gershwin/Jerome Kern)
Helen Forrest and Dick Haymes (Decca)
Bing Crosby (Decca)
Jo Stafford (Capitol)
Perry Como (Victor)
Guy Lombardo (Decca)
Three Suns (Hit)

"Mairzy Doats" (Milton Drake/Al Hoffman/Jerry Livingston)
Merry Macs (Decca)
Al Trace (Hit)
Pied Pipers (Capitol)
Lawrence Welk (Decca)
King Sisters (Bluebird)

1945

"Bell-Bottom Trousers" (Traditional Sea Chantey)
Guy Lombardo (Decca)
Tony Pastor (Victor)
Kay Kyser (Columbia)
Louis Prima (Majestic)
Jerry Colonna (Capitol)
Jesters (Decca)

"Saturday Night (Is the Loneliest Night of the Week)" (Sammy Cahn/Jule Styne)
Frank Sinatra (Columbia)
Sammy Kaye (Victor)
Frankie Carle (Columbia)
Woody Herman (Decca)
King Sisters (Victor)

1946

"The Gypsy" (Billy Reid)
Ink Spots (Decca)
Dinah Shore (Columbia)
Sammy Kaye (RCA Victor)
Hildegarde, with Guy Lombardo (Decca)
Hal McIntyre (Cosmo)
Jan Garber (Black and White)

"To Each His Own" (Jay Livingston/Ray Evans)
Eddy Howard (Majestic)
Ink Spots (Decca)
Freddy Martin (RCA Victor)
Modernaires, with Paula Kelly (Columbia)
Tony Martin (Mercury)

1947

"Near You" (Kermit Goell/Francis Craig)
Francis Craig (Bullet)
Andrews Sisters (Decca)
Larry Green (RCA Victor)
Alvino Rey (Capitol)
Elliot Lawrence (Columbia)
Two-Ton Baker (Mercury)

"Open the Door, Richard" ("Dusty" Fletcher/John Mason/Jack McVea/
    Dan Howell)
Count Basie (Victor)
Three Flames (Columbia)
"Dusty" Fletcher (National)
Jack McVea (Black and White)
Charioteers (Columbia)
Louis Jordan (Decca)
Pied Pipers (Capitol)

1948

"Baby Face" (Benny Davis/Harry Akst)
Art Mooney (MGM)
Sammy Kaye (RCA Victor)
Jack Smith (Capitol)
Henry King (Decca)

"You Call Everybody Darling" (Sam Martin/Ben L. Trace/Clem Watts/
    Albert J. Trace)
Al Trce (Regent)
Ann Vincent (Mercury)
Andrews Sisters (Decca)
Jack Smith (Capitol)
Jerry Wayne (Columbia)
Bruce Hayes (DeLuxe)
Art Lund (MGM)
Jack Lathrop (RCA Victor)

1949

"Cruising Down the River" (Eily Beadell/Nell Tollerton)
Blue Barron (MGM)
Russ Morgan (Decca)
Jack Smith (Capitol)
Frankie Carle (Columbia)
Three Suns (RCA Victor)
Primo Scala (London)
Ames Brothers (Coral)
Helen Carroll (Mercury)

"Riders In The Sky" (Stan Jones)
Vaughn Monroe (RCA Victor)
Peggy Lee (Capitol)

Bing Crosby (Decca)
Burl Ives (Columbia)

"Some Enchanted Evening" (Oscar Hammerstein II/Richard Rodgers)
Perry Como (RCA Victor)
Bing Crosby (Decca)
Jo Stafford (Capitol)
Frank Sinatra (Columbia)
Ezio Pinza (Columbia)
Paul Weston (Capitol
John Laurenz (Mercury)

"That Luck Old Sun" (Haven Gillespie/Beasley Smith)
Frankie Laine (Mercury)
Vaughn Monroe (RCA Victor)
Sarah Vaughan (Columbia)
Frank Sinatra (Columbia)
Louis Armstrong (Decca)
Bob Houston (MGM)

1950

"I Wanna Be Loved" (Billy Rose/Edward Heyman/Johnny Green)
Andrews Sisters (Decca)
Billy Eckstine (MGM)
Hugo Winterhalter (RCA Victor)
Dinah Washington (Mercury)
Dottie O'Brien (Capitol)
Jan Garber (Capitol)

"If I Knew You Were Comin' (I'd've Baked a Cake)" (Al Hoffmann,
    Bob Merrill, Clem Watts)
Eileen Barton (National)
Georgia Gibbs (Coral)
Benny Strong (Capitol)
Ethel Merman and Ray Bolger (Decca)
Art Mooney (MGM)

"Play a Simple Melody" (Irving Berlin)
Gary Crosby and Bing Crosby (Decca)
Jo Stafford (Capitol)
Georgia Gibbs and Bob Crosby (Coral)
Phil Harris (RCA Victor)

"Rag Mop" (Deacon Anderson, Johnnie Lee Wills)
Ames Brothers (Coral)
Ralph Flanagan (RCA Victor)
Lionel Hampton (Decca)
Johnnie Lee Wills (Bullet)
Starlighters (Capitol)

1951

"Cold, Cold Heart" (Hank Williams)
Tony Bennett (Columbia)
Fontane Sisters (RCA Victor)
Eileen Wilson (Decca)
Hank Williams (MGM)
Tony Fontane (Mercury)

"Come On-A My House" (Ross Bagdasarian/William Saroyan)
Rosemary Clooney (Columbia)
Kay Starr (Capitol)
Richard Hayes (Mercury)
Mickey Katz (Capitol)

"Cry" (Churchill Kohlman)
Johnny Ray (OKEH)
Georgia Gibbs (Mercury)
Eileen Barton (Coral)
Four Knights (Capitol)

"Good Morning, Mister Echo" (Jane Turzy)
Jane Turzy Trio (Decca)
Margaret Whiting (Capitol)
Georgia Gibbs (Mercury)

"My Heart Cries For You" (Percy Faith/Carl Sigman)
Guy Mitchell (Columbia)
Dinah Shore (RCA Victor)
Vic Damone (Mercury)
Jimmy Wakely (Capitol)
Bill Farrell (MGM)

"Tennessee Waltz" (Redd Steward/Pee Wee King)
Patti Page (Mercury)
Guy Lombardo (Decca)
Les Paul and Mary Ford (Capitol)
Spike Jones (RCA Victor)

1952

"I'm Yours" (Robert Mellin)
Don Cornell (Coral)
Eddie Fisher (RCA Victor)
Four Aces (Decca)
Toni Ardan (Columbia)

"Jambalaya" (Hank Williams)
Jo Stafford (Columbia)
Hank Williams (MGM)

"Kiss of Fire" (Lester Allen/Robert B. Hill)
Georgia Gibbs (Mercury)
Tony Martin (RCA Victor)
Toni Arden (Columbia)
Billy Eckstine (MGM)
Louis Armstrong (Decca)
Guy Lombardo (Decca)

"Wheel of Fortune" (Bennie Benjamin/George Weiss)
Kay Starr (Capitol)
Bobby Wayne (London)
Bell Sisters (RCA Victor)
Eddie Wilcox, with Sunny Gale (Derby)

"You Belong to Me" (Pee Wee King/Redd Steward/Chilton Price)
Patti Page (Mercury)
Dean Martin (Capitol)
Jo Stafford (Columbia)

Table 2.3   A chronological profile of selected *Billboard* and *Cash Box* charted songs that illustrate how cover recording practices and crossover audience acceptance launched rock era music, 1953–57

	Weeks charted	
	Billboard	*Cash Box*
1953		
"April in Portugal" (José Galhardo/Jimmy Kennedy/ Raul Ferrao)		
Les Baxter (Capitol)	22	17
Vic Damone (Mercury)	7	0
Richard Hayman (Mercury)	11	0
Freddy Martin (RCA Victor)	3	0
Tony Martin (RCA Victor)	1	0
"Crazy, Man, Crazy" (Bill Haley)		
Bill Haley (Essex)	10	4
Ralph Marterie (Mercury)	4	0
"Crying in the Chapel" (Artie Glenn)		
June Vallie (RCA Victor)	17	12
Orioles (Jubilee)	10	8
Rex Allen (Decca)	15	10
Darrell Glenn (Valley)	13	12
Ella Fitzgerald (Decca)	2	0
"Don't Let the Stars Get in Your Eyes" (Slim Willet)		
Perry Como (RCA Victor)	21	16
Gisele MacKenzie (Capitol)	2	0
"I Saw Mommy Kissing Santa Claus" (Tommie Connor)		
Jimmy Boyd (Columbia)	5	4
Spike Jones (RCA Victor)	3	0
Molly Bee (Capitol)	1	0
"Oh Happy Day" (Nancy Binns Reed/Don Howard Koplow)		
Don Howard (Essex)	15	5
Lawrence Welk (Coral)	10	0
Four Knights (Capitol)	6	0
"Oh! My Pa-Pa (O Mein Papa)" (John Turner/ Geoffrey Parsons/Paul Burkhard)		
Eddie Fisher (RCA Victor)	19	17

| | Weeks charted | |
	Billboard	*Cash Box*
Eddie Calvert (Essex)	14	8
Ray Anthony (Capitol)	4	0
"Ruby" (Mitchell Parish/Heinz Roemheld)		
Richard Hayman (Mercury)	19	13
Les Baxter (Capitol)	12	0
Harry James (Columbia	1	0
Victor Young (Decca)	1	0
"Till I Waltz Again With You" (Sidney Prosen)		
Teresa Brewer (Coral)	24	20
Dick Todd (Decca)	1	0
Russ Morgan (Decca)	0	0
Harmonicats (Mercury)	0	0
"Why Don't You Believe Me" (Lewis Douglas/King Laney/ Roy Rodde)		
Joni James (MGM)	23	17
Patti Page (Mercury)	13	0
Margaret Whiting (Capital)	0	0
"Your Cheatin' Heart" (Hank Williams)		
Hank Williams (MGM)	0	0
Joni James (MGM)	17	14
Frankie Laine	2	0

1954

"Changing Partners" (Joe Darion/Larry Coleman)		
Patti Page (Mercury)	19	14
Kay Starr (Capitol)	13	0
Dinah Shore (RCA Victor)	3	0
Bing Crosby (Decca)	2	0
"Goodnight, Sweetheart, Goodnight" (Calvin Carter, James Hudson)		
Spaniels (Vee-Jay)	0	0
Gloria Mann (Sound)	0	0
McGuire Sisters (Coral)	15	10
Sunny Gale (RCA Victor)	2	7

	Weeks charted	
	Billboard	*Cash Box*
"Hernando's Hideaway" (Richard Adler/Jerry Ross)		
Archie Bleyer (Cadence)	17	13
Guy Lombardo (Decca)	4	0
Johnny Ray (Columbia)	7	0
"If I Give My Heart to You" (Jimmie Crane/Al Jacobs/ Jimmy Brewster)		
Doris Day (Columbia)	17	14
Denise Lor (Majar)	14	14
Connee Boswell (Decca)	11	0
"Let Me Go, Lover!" (Jenny Lou Carson, Al Hill)		
Joan Weber (Columbia)	16	9
Patti Page (Mercury)	7	0
Teresa Brewer (Coral)	12	0
"Mr. Sandman" (Pat Ballard)		
Chordettes (Cadence)	20	16
Buddy Morrow (Mercury)	1	0
Four Aces (Decca)	14	0
"Sh-Boom" (James Edwards, Carl Feaster, Claude Feaster, James Keyes, Floyd McRae)		
Chords (Cat)	16	12
Crew-Cuts (Mercury)	20	15
Stan Freberg (Capitol)	1	0
"Shake, Rattle and Roll" (Charles Calhoun)		
Joe Turner (Atlantic)	0	0
Bill Haley (Decca)	27	10
"Skokiaan" (Tom Glazer/August Machon Musarurgwa)		
Ralph Marterie (Mercury)	15	11
Four Lads (Columbia)	12	11
Bulawayo Sweet Rhythms Band (London)	8	11
Ray Anthony (Capitol)	5	0
"Somebody Bad Stole De Wedding Bell" (Bob Hilliard/ Dave Mann)		
Eartha Kitt (RCA Victor)	4	0
Georgia Gibbs (Mercury)	4	0

	Weeks charted	
	Billboard	*Cash Box*
"Teach Me Tonight" (Sammy Cahn/Gene DePaul)		
Jo Stafford (Columbia)	6	0
DeCastro Sisters (Abbott)	20	13

1955

"Ain't That a Shame" (Dave Bartholomew, Antoine Domino)		
Fats Domino (Imperial)	13	7
Pat Boone (Dot)	20	16
"Are You Satisfied" (Homer Escamilla/Sheb Wooley)		
Rusty Draper (Mercury)	18	0
Sheb Wooley (MGM)	1	0
Toni Arden (RCA Victor)	1	0
"At My Front Door (Crazy Little Mama)" (Ewart Abner, John Moore)		
El Dorados	11	3
Pat Boone	14	3
"Autumn Leaves" (Joseph Kosma, Johnny Mercer)		
Roger Williams (KAPP)	26	15
Steve Allen, with George Cates (Coral)	12	0
Ray Charles Singers (MGM)	8	0
Jackie Gleason (Capitol)	9	0
Mitch Miller (Columbia)	14	0
Victor Young (Decca)	11	0
"Ballad of Davy Crockett" (Tom Blackburn, George Bruns)		
Bill Hayes (Cadence)	20	15
Fess Parker (Columbia)	17	0
Tennessee Ernie Ford (Capitol)	17	0
Voice of Walter Schumann (RCA Victor)	6	0
"Band of Gold" (Bob Musel, Jack Taylor)		
Hi-Fi Four (King)	1	0
Kit Carson (Capitol)	22	0
Don Cherry (Columbia)	22	9

	Weeks charted	
	Billboard	*Cash Box*
"Black Denim Trousers and Motorcycle Boots" (Jerry Leiber and Mike Stoller)		
Vaughn Monroe (RCA Victor)	4	0
Cheers (Capitol)	11	0
"Burn That Candle" (Winfield Scott)		
Cues (Capitol)	1	0
Bill Haley (Decca)	17	0
"Cherry Pink and Apple Blossom White" (Jacques/Larve/ Luis Guglielmi/David Mack)		
Perez "Prez" Prado	26	20
Alan Dale (Coral)	7	0
"Daddy-O" (Charlie Gore, Buford Abner, Louie Innis)		
Bonnie Lou (King)	15	1
Fontane Sisters (Dot)	16	1
"Don't Be Angry" (Rose Marie McCoy, Nappy Brown)		
Nappy Brown (Savoy)	4	2
Crew-Cuts (Mercury)	8	2
"Earth Angel (Will You Be Mine)" (Jesse Belvin)		
Penguins (Dootone)	15	9
Gloria Mann (Sound)	2	0
Crew-Cuts (Mercury)	13	9
"Hearts of Stone" (Randy Jackson, Eddy Ray)		
Jewels (R and B)	0	0
Charms (DeLuxe)	15	0
Fontane Sisters (Dot)	20	14
"I Hear You Knocking" (Dave Bartholomew, Pearl King)		
Smiley Lewis (Imperial)	0	0
Gale Storm (Dot)	18	10
"It's Almost Tomorrow" (Wade Buff/Eugene Adkinson)		
Dream Weavers (Decca)	23	9
Snooky Lanson (Dot)	16	0
David Carroll (Mercury)	16	0
Jo Stafford (Columbia)	20	0

	Weeks charted	
	Billboard	*Cash Box*
"Ko Ko Mo" (Eunice Levy/Jake Porter/Forest Wilson)		
Gene and Eunice (Combo)	0	0
Perry Como (RCA Victor)	14	0
Crew-Cuts (Mercury)	14	0
Flamingos (Parrot)	0	0
"Ling, Ting, Tong" (Mabel Godwin)		
Charms (DeLuxe)	3	0
Five Keys (Capitol)	2	0
"Love is a Many Splendored Thing" (Paul Francis Webster, Sammy Fain)		
Don, Dick 'n' Jimmy (Crown)	2	0
Four Aces (Decca)	21	16
Don Cornell (Coral)	9	0
Woody Herman (Capitol)	6	0
David Rose (MGM)	10	0
"Maybelline" (Chuck Berry, Russ Frato, Alan Freed)		
Chuck Berry (Chess)	11	5
Jim Lowe (Dot)	0	0
Ralph Marterie (Mercury)	0	0
"Melody of Love" (Tom Glazer, Hans Engelmann)		
Leo Diamond (RCA Victor)	1	0
Billy Vaughn (Dot)	27	19
David Caroll (Mercury)	17	19
Four Aces (Decca)	21	19
Frank Sinatra and Ray Anthony (Capitol)	4	0
"Memories are Made of This" (Richard Dehr/Terry Gilkyson/ Frank Miller)		
Dean Martin (Capitol)	24	14
Mindy Carson (Columbia)	13	0
Gale Storm (Dot)	16	0
"My Boy Flat-Top" (Boyd Bennett, John Young)		
Boyd Bennett (King)	17	0
Dorothy Collins (Coral)	15	0

	Weeks charted	
	Billboard	*Cash Box*
"No Arms Can Ever Hold You" (Art Crafter/Jimmy Nebb)		
Pat Boone (Dot)	11	0
Gaylords (Mercury)	8	0
Georgie Shaw (Decca)	12	0
"Nuttin' for Christmas" (Roy Bennett/Sid Tepper)		
Fontane Sisters (Dot)	4	0
Art Mooney and Barry Gordon (MGM)	4	0
Joe Ward (King)	4	0
Ricky Zahnd (Columbia)	4	0
Stan Freberg (Capitol)	3	0
"Only You (And You Alone)" (Buck Ram, Ande Rand)		
Platters (Mercury)	22	13
Hilltoppers (Dot)	19	0
"Pledging My Love" (Ferdinand Washington, Don Robey)		
Johnny Ace (Duke)	9	5
Teresa Brewer (Coral)	3	5
"Rollin' Stone" (Robert Riley)		
Fontane Sisters (Dot)	6	0
Marigolds (Excello)	0	0
"Seventeen" (Boyd Bennett, Chuck Gorman, John Young)		
Boyd Bennett (King)	17	0
Rusty Draper (Mercury)	4	0
Fontane Sisters (Dot)	15	10
"Shifting Whispering Sands" (V. C. Gilbert/Mary Hadler)		
Billy Vaughn (Dot)	15	8
Rusty Draper (Mercury)	16	8
"Sincerely" (Alan Freed/Harvey Fuqua)		
Moonglows (Chess)	1	0
McGuire Sisters (Coral)	21	14
"Sixteen Tons" (Merle Travis)		
Tennessee Ernie Ford	22	15
Johnny Desmond	11	0

	Weeks charted	
	Billboard	*Cash Box*
"Story Untold" (Leroy Griffin)		
Nutmegs (Glory)	0	0
Crew-Cuts (Mercury)	7	0
"Suddenly There's a Valley" (Biff Jones/Chuck Meyer)		
Gogi Grant (Era)	11	4
Julius LaRosa (Cadence)	9	4
Jo Stafford (Columbia)	12	4
Patty Andrews (Capitol)	5	0
Mills Brothers (Decca)	9	0
"Teach Me Tonight" (Sammy Cahn/Gene DePaul)		
Dinah Washington (Mercury)	0	0
Jo Stafford (Columbia)	6	0
DeCastro Sisters (Abbott)	20	13
"A Teen Age Prayer" (Bix Reichner/Bernie Lowe)		
Gloria Mann (Sound)	13	7
Gale Storm (Dot)	15	7
Kitty White (Mercury)	6	0
"Tweedle Dee" (Winfield Scott)		
Lavern Baker (Atlantic)	11	7
Georgia Gibbs (Mercury)	19	16
"Unchained Melody" (Alex North, Hy Zaret		
Al Hibbler (Epic)	19	19
Roy Hamilton (Epic)	16	19
June Valli (RCA Victor)	1	0
Les Baxter (Capitol)	21	19
"Two Hearts" (Henry Stone/Otis Williams)		
Pat Boone (Dot)	12	0
Charms (DeLuxe)	3	0
"White Christmas" (Irving Berlin)		
Drifters (Atlantic)	1	0
Bing Crosby (Decca)	3	0
"Why Don't You Write Me?" (Laura Hollins)		
Jacks (RPM)	3	0
Snooky Lanson (Dot)	2	0

	Weeks charted	
	Billboard	*Cash Box*
"Yellow Rose of Texas" (Don George)		
Mitch Miller (Columbia)	19	15
Johnny Desmond (Coral)	16	15
Stan Freberg (Capitol)	9	0
1956		
"Blue Suede Shoes" (Carl Perkins)		
Carl Perkins (Sun)	21	12
Boyd Bennett (King)	10	0
Elvis Presley (RCA Victor)	12	0
"Blueberry Hill" (Al Lewis, Larry Stock, Vincent Rose)		
Fats Domino (Imperial)	27	22
Louis Armstrong with Gordon Jenkins (Decca)	11	0
"Bo Weevil" (Fats Domino, Dave Bartholomew)		
Teresa Brewer (Coral)	15	0
Fats Domino (Imperial)	9	0
"Church Bells May Ring" (Morty Craft, Richard Davis, Joe Martin, Ralph Martin, Tony Middleton)		
Diamonds (Mercury)	17	0
Willows (Melba)	11	0
"Cindy, Oh Cindy" (Bob Barron, Burt Long)		
Vince Martin and The Tarriers (Glory)	19	19
Eddie Fisher (RCA Victor)	19	19
"Eddie My Love" (Aaron Collins, Maxwell Davis, Sam Ling)		
Chordettes (Dot)	12	0
Teen Queens (RPM	12	0
Fontane Sisters (Dot)	17	0
"The Fool" (Naomi Ford)		
Sanford Clark (Dot)	21	17
Gallahads (Jubilee)	9	10
"Friendly Persuasion (Thee I Love)" (Paul Francis Webster/ Dimitri Tiomkin)		
Pat Boone (Dot)	24	19
Four Aces (Decca)	18	6

	Weeks charted	
	Billboard	*Cash Box*
"Heartbreak Hotel" (Mae Boren Axton/Tommy Durden/ Elvis Presley)		
Elvis Presley (RCA Victor)	27	11
Stan Freberg (Capitol)	2	0
"I Could Have Danced All Night" (Alan Jay Lerner/ Frederick Loewe)		
Rosemary Clooney (Columbia)	13	1
Sylvia Syms (Decca)	14	1
Dinah Shore (RCA Victor)	5	1
"I'll Be Home" (Stan Lewis, Ferdinand Washington)		
Pat Boone (Dot)	22	9
Flamingos (Checker)	0	0
"I'm In Love Again" (Fats Domino/Dave Bartholomew)		
Fats Domino (Imperial)	23	7
Fontane Sisters (Dot)	14	0
"Ivory Tower" (Jack Fulton, Lois Steele)		
Charms (DeLuxe)	21	11
Cathy Carr (Fraternity)	24	11
Gale Storm (Dot)	18	8
"Ka-Ding Dong" (Ronnie Jordan, John McDermott)		
G-Clefs (Pilgrim)	13	11
Diamonds (Mercury)	9	11
Hilltoppers (Dot)	10	11
"Long Tall Sally" (Robert Blackwell, Enotris Johnson, Richard Penniman)		
Little Richard (Specialty)	19	4
Pat Boone (Dot)	15	0
"Love, Love, Love" (Mack David, Ted McRae, Sid Wyche)		
Clovers (Atlantic)	13	3
Diamonds (Mercury)	14	0
"Love Me Tender" (Vera Matson/Elvis Presley)		
Elvis Presley (RCA Victor)	23	21
Henri Rene (RCA Victor)	8	0

	Weeks charted	
	Billboard	*Cash Box*
"Mack the Knife" (Bertolt Brecht/Kurt Weill/Marc Blitzstein)		
Dick Hyman Trio (MGM)	20	5
Richard Hayman and Jan August (Mercury)	15	0
Billy Vaughn (Dot)		
Louis Armstrong (Columbia)	15	0
Les Paul (Capitol)	12	0
Lawrence Welk (Coral)	11	0
"Man With the Golden Arm" (Sylvia Fine/Elmer Bernstein)		
Elmer Bernstein (Decca)	15	0
Richard Maltby (Vik)	16	0
Billy May (Capitol)	14	0
Bobby Morrow (Wing)	4	0
McGuire Sisters (Coral)	11	0
Dick Jacobs (Coral)	14	0
"Memories Are Made of This" (Richard Dehr, Terry Gilkyson, Frank Miller)		
Dean Martin (Capitol)	24	14
Gale Storm (Dot)	16	0
Mindy Carson (Columbia)	13	0
"Moonglow and the Theme From Picnic" (Will Hudson)		
George Cates (Coral)	22	18
Morris Stoloff (Decca)	27	18
McGuire Sisters (Coral)	20	0
Ralph Marterie (Mercury	7	0
"Rip It Up" (Robert Blackwell, John Mnrascalco)		
Little Richard (Specialty)	18	9
Bill Haley (Decca)	14	24
"Rock Island Line" (Lonnie Donegan)		
Lonnie Donegan (London)	17	3
Don Cornell (Coral)	8	0
"See Saw" (Billy David, Charles Sutton, Harry Pratt)		
Moonglows (Chess)	14	8
Don Cornell (Coral)	6	0

	Weeks charted	
	Billboard	*Cash Box*
"Seven Days" (Willis Carroll, Carmen Taylor)		
Crew-Cuts (Mercury)	11	0
Dorothy Collins (Coral)	10	0
Clyde McPhatter (Atlantic)	5	0
"Singing the Blues" (Melvin Endsley)		
Guy Mitchell (Columbia)	26	23
Marty Robbins (Columbia)	18	1
"Slow Walk" (Sil Austin)		
Sil Austin (Mercury)	14	11
Bill Doggett (King)	12	11
"Standing on the Corner" (Frank Loesser)		
Mills Brothers (Decca)	10	0
Four Lads (Columbia)	20	12
Dean Martin (Capitol)	15	0
"Stranded in the Jungle" (James Johnson, Ernestine Smith)		
Cadets (Modern)	11	5
Jayhawks (Flash)	11	5
Gadabouts (Mercury)	8	0
"Tell Me Why" (Titus Turner)		
Gale Storm (Dot)	6	0
Crew-Cuts (Mercury)	5	0
"Tonight You Belong to Me" (Lee David, Billy Rose)		
Karen Chandler and Jimmy Wakely (Decca)	9	0
Lawrence Welk, with The Lennon Sisters (Coral)	13	11
Patience and Prudence (Liberty)	25	20
"Too Young to Go Steady" (Harold Adamson/ Jimmy McHugh)		
Nat King Cole (Capitol)	12	0
Patti Page (Mercury)	3	0
"Tra La La" (Johnny Parker)		
Lavern Baker (Atlantic)	12	0
Georgia Gibbs (Mercury)	7	5

	Weeks charted	
	Billboard	*Cash Box*
"Tutti Frutti" (Richard Penniman, Dorothy LaBostrie, Joe Lubin)		
Pat Boone (Dot)	18	0
Little Richard (Specialty)	12	0
"Wayward Wind" (Stan Lebowsky, Herb Newman)		
Tex Ritter (Capitol)	13	0
Gogi Grant (Era)	28	6
"Why Do Fools Fall in Love" (Jimmy Merchant, Herman Santiago)		
Frankie Lymon and The Teenagers (Gee)	21	12
Diamonds (Mercury)	17	0
Gale Storm (Dot)	18	0
Gloria Mann (RCA)	5	0

1957

"And That Reminds Me" (Al Stillman/Camillo Bargoni)		
Della Reese (Jubilee)	18	17
Kay Starr (RCA Victor)	12	0
"Around the World in 80 Days" (Harold Adamson/ Victor Young)		
Victor Young (Decca)	34	26
Mantovani (London)	32	23
Bing Crosby (Decca)	31	0
McGuire Sisters (Coral)	6	0
"At the Hop" (John Madara/Arthur Singer/David White)		
Danny and The Juniors (ABC-Paramount)	21	18
Nick Todd (Dot)	6	0
"Banana Boat Song" (Alan Arkin/Bob Carey/Erik Darling)		
Tarriers (Glory)	19	18
Fontane Sisters (Dot)	18	1
Sarah Vaughan (Mercury)	14	1
Steve Lawrence (Coral)	14	2
Harry Belafonte (RCA Victor)	20	17
Stan Freberg (Capitol)	7	4

	Weeks charted	
	Billboard	*Cash Box*
"Butterfly" (Bernie Lowe, Kal Mann)		
Charlie Gracie (Cameo)	17	17
Andy Williams (Cadence)	20	17
Bob Carroll (Bally)	7	0
"Bye Bye Love" (Felice Bryant, Boudleaux Bryant)		
Webb Pierce (Decca)	9	0
Everly Brothers (Cadence)	27	20
"Cinco Robles (Five Oaks)" (Larry Sullivan/Dorothy Wright)		
Russell Arms (Era)	15	14
Les Paul and Mary Ford (Capitol)	14	5
Lawrence Welk (Coral)	0	1
"Dark Moon" (Bonnie Guitar)		
Bonnie Guitar (Dot)	22	19
Gale Storm (Dot)	23	18
"Empty Arms" (Ivory Joe Hunter)		
Ivory Joe Hunter (Atlantic)	16	12
Teresa Brewer (Coral)	17	12
"Fabulous" (Harry Land, Jon Sheldon)		
Charlie Gracie (Cameo)	15	9
Steve Lawrence (Coral)	7	0
"Four Walls" (Marvin Moore, George Campbell)		
Jim Reeves (RCA Victor)	22	14
Jim Lowe (Dot)	18	10
"Gonna Find Me a Bluebird" (Marvin Rainwater)		
Joyce Hahn (Cadence)	4	0
Eddy Arnold (RCA Victor)	6	0
Marvin Rainwater (MGM)	22	14
"I'm Stickin' With You" (Jimmy Bowen, Buddy Knox)		
Fontane Sisters (Dot)	2	0
Jimmy Bowen (Roulette)	17	15
"I'm Walkin'" (Dave Bartholomew/Fats Domino)		
Fats Domino (Imperial)	25	15
Ricky Nelson (Verve)	17	7

	Weeks charted	
	Billboard	*Cash Box*
"Joker (That's What They Call Me)" (Billy Myles)		
Hilltoppers (Dot)	13	10
Billy Myles (Ember)	14	10
"Little Bitty Pretty One" (Robert Byrd)		
Thurston Harris (Aladdin)	17	14
Bobby Day (Class)	8	14
"Little By Little" (Rosemary McCoy/Kelly Owens)		
Micki Marlow (ABC-Paramount)	4	0
Nappy Brown (Savoy)	9	8
"Little Darlin'" (Maurice Williams)		
Gladiolas (Excello)	11	0
Diamonds (Mercury)	26	19
"Long Lonely Nights" (Mimi Uniman, Bernice Davis, Lee Andrews, Doug Henderson)		
Lee Andrews and The Hearts (Chess)	10	9
Clyde McPhatter (Atlantic)	13	9
"Lucky Lips" (Jerry Leiber, Mike Stoller)		
Gale Storm (Dot)	5	0
Ruth Brown (Atlantic)	9	9
"Marianne" (Richard Dehr, Terry Gilkyson, Frank Miller)		
Hilltoppers (Dot)	16	14
Terry Gilkyson and The Easy Riders (Columbia)	19	15
Lane Brothers (RCA Victor)	4	0
Burl Ives (Decca)	5	0
"Ninety-Nine Ways" (Charlie Gracie)		
Charlie Gracie (Cameo)	0	0
Tab Hunter (Dot)	11	10
"Party Doll" (Jimmy Bowen, Buddy Knox)		
Steve Lawrence (Coral)	20	18
Buddy Knox (Roulette)	23	18
Roy Brown (Imperial)	2	0
Wingy Manone (Decca)	7	0

| | Weeks charted | |
	Billboard	*Cash Box*
"Raunchy" (Bill Justis, Sid Manker)		
Ernie Freeman (Imperial)	18	16
Bill Justis (Phillips)	20	17
Billy Vaughn (Dot)	22	1
"Silhouettes" (Bob Crewe, Frank Slay)		
Rays (Cameo)	20	17
Diamonds (Mercury)	11	0
Steve Gibson (ABC-Paramount)	5	0
"Since I Met You Baby" (Ivory Joe Hunter)		
Ivory Joe Hunter (Atlantic)	22	17
Mindy Carson (Columbia)	12	0
"Sittin' in the Balcony" (John D. Loudermilk)		
Johnny Dee (Colonial)	11	11
Eddie Cochran (Liberty)	13	11
"Stardust" (Hoagy Carmichael, Mitchell Parish)		
Nat King Cole (Capitol)	4	0
Billy Ward ad His Dominoes (Liberty)	24	0
"White Sport Coat (And a Pink Carnation)" (Marty Robbins)		
Marty Robbins (Columbia)	26	18
Johnny Desmond (Coral)	2	0
"You Send Me" (Charles Cooke)		
Teresa Brewer (Coral)	12	2
Sam Cooke (Keen)	26	17
"Young Love" (Ric Cartey, Carole Joyner)		
Tab Hunter (Dot)	21	18
Sonny James (Capitol)	21	19
Crew-Cuts (Mercury)	12	0

Chapter 3

The Cover Song as Historiography, Marker of Ideological Transformation

Sheldon Schiffer

The cover song is one of the more revealing cultural artifacts derived from the production of popular music because its meaning is so dependent on context and reception, as much as on musical signification. The selection of songs to re-perform and re-record, and the elective process of what musical and extra-musical elements to preserve, alter, augment or delete, all are signifying elements in the construction of meaning around and in a re-performed and re-recorded song. Michael Coyle describes the delimiting signifying practices of the major record labels of the 1930s to 1950s that "hijacked" black hits for a youthful white audience. Coyle contends that before Elvis Presley, many performers "faked" their relationship to "blackness" through selective editing of appearances; cultural "whiteness" supplanted cultural "blackness" in style and fashion, though often not in musicality, yielding profit to labels that exploited this selective difference. With the arrival of Presley and his forthright admission of his appropriation of, and identification with black music (Coyle, 2002: 146), and his performance of its dance culture and more overt sexuality, Coyle observes an ideological shift: America through Presley's covers progressed (however slightly) in accepting its blackness, and made it possible for cross-over musicians, like Otis Redding and other black musicians, to perform before white audiences, and hear their songs played on white radio stations (2002: 139–45). I will offer an extension of Coyle's argument on the use of the cover song as a marker and force that reshapes ideology beyond the boundaries of race. I will also argue that a cover song is not only understood by its musical content, but also by the context of other forms of cultural expression that indicate even more clearly a song's association with specific societal strains, namely politics and its representation, as well as fashion and style, as they indicate affiliation with subculture, generation and class.

A recording artist, producer or label may select cover songs in response to ideological assertions from one community to affiliate itself with aspects of another, as well as to mock or critique that "other" community and its beliefs, or even apply the same criticism to its own beliefs. The process of "covering" is rarely as simple as attempting to mimetically reproduce an original version, though history indicates that cover songs began with that intention (Inglis, 2005: 163–70). But the act of selecting a song to cover can itself be an assertion of ideology, that when a cover song gets traction from a fan base, the social groups that make up that base find that the new meanings implied in the cover song suggest that their ideas are transforming in a historical process.

The Singer, the Songwriter, and the Rise of the Recording Star

The premise of "covering" music requires some historical notation to shed light on the differences in what a cover song was, when the term was coined (Coyle, 2002: 154),[1] and what the term is, at *this* moment of hyper-polymorphic expressiveness. Popular music in the very early years of the twentieth century was largely performed live and distributed with sheet music (Coyle: 137). The original songwriter and/or performer often traveled more slowly than the sheet music he or she authored. And, the musicians who frequented urban centers brought back to their provincial music halls, songs that would keep them employed as live musicians. With the dissemination of record players, and provincial recording industries, often these musicians who made their livelihood performing songs gaining in popularity in London or New York (for the English-speaking world), would contract with phonograph makers to record those same songs rising in popularity (Frith, 1992: 54). The performer was often a local musician whose role it was to quickly provide a recording to vinyl for local music markets. In a brief history of Embassy Records, Ian Inglis describes how the phonograph and recording companies, Decca, Crown and later Embassy, often provided competing recordings of the same song to cover the demand for a particular song across a widely dispersed market (Inglis, 2005: 163–4). The songwriter was seen as the authorial source in this model; the sheet music and any vinyl recording was the commodity.

This historical reference suggests a transformation started in the 1920s of the cultural production of performing art into recording art. Each mechanical reproduction of music competed with both the consumption of live music – that created by an "original" performer, and subsequent re-performers who accessed sheet music renderings – and with other musical recordings. Promoters had to draw a distinction of primacy between the "original" and the "copy" or "cover" if they were to maximize the profits of the songs they recorded, and spend less on recording more music. But contrary to the interests of music promoters, the music-consuming public more often bought music because they wanted to possess a particular song. Until promoters could devise a way to consolidate interest around a single performer, this affiliation between song and consumer made "covering" profitable. A song with substitute recording artists in more remote regions could cut into the profits of the recording label that first recorded the song. The producers of popular music realized that if they could manufacture a loyalty to the performer, then they could profit from both the sale of recordings and they could use live performance, appearance in popular films, and also physical and visual presentation

---

[1]   Coyle relates the making of lacquer discs as protection copies of the wax master originals (p. 154).

as a means to promote the sale of that same recording. Simon Frith connects the early strategies of employing musical performers to record popular dance and theater compositions as new "versions" that later became the model for "cover versions" of the 1950s. Frith highlights Decca and the arrival of Bing Crosby as the turning point where a recording star system that emphasized big sales of fewer recording artists was more profitable than selling many recordings by a greater variety of musicians (Frith, 1992: 57). In this new model, the subtle characteristics of style and fashion were part of what distinguished individual recording artists. Marketing music became as much a sales pitch to the eyes as it was to the ears, and that meant manufacturing recording artists and their images, rather than waiting for the public to recognize the musical talents of a wider variety of acts (Frith: 57).

Walter Benjamin, in his seminal essay *The Work of Art in the Age of Mechanical Reproduction*, described how printed reproductions of masterpieces diminished the "aura" of the original, and hence socializes the exchange value of the art, while enhancing its use value as discursive cultural production (2001: 51–2). The problematic of recorded popular music complicated his schema, as there was no obvious fetishized object considered for fiscal or social appraisal. The recorded song, unlike a reproduction of a Rembrandt painting, had no unique referent as long as the singer was a replaceable component, and the vinyl recording an even more salient commodity. Benjamin wrote his essay in 1935, and while not elaborating much on the music recording industry or popular music, he anticipated that the "spell of personality" would supplant "shriveling aura" for cinema with its resulting "unapproachability" of the star performer as commodity (2001: 65). During the 1930s and World War II, the radio and its DJs used the connection of songs to specific performers to reinforce an American identity against the constant wartime exposure to foreign cultural influence. The music industry, through the likes of Crosby and other radio-recording artists-cum-movie-stars, found a way to inject "aura" into their product when America was most vulnerable to identity confusion.

The culture critic Theodor Adorno observed that the music industries had formulated mechanistic systems of producing songs that involved songwriters, publishers, and distributors. While Adorno blamed the loss of "authentic" musical enculturation (listening to "serious music") on the barons of the recording industry, he also recognized that the "fetishized" composition was a means of consolidating a product with an historical identity. Most notably, he describes the creation of a "pseudo-individuality" that propagated the myths of composers and singers through the dissemination of their recordings (2005: 36–8). He is describing what today might relate to "branding"—the construction of ideologies and pseudo-histories associated with a product primarily to encourage a specific community to identify with a commodity. Paralleling the myth-making propaganda of Hollywood movie stars, music marketers took an interest in revealing the personal characteristics of their recording artists. The war and its ration of shellac and the American Federation of Musician's strike and recording ban from 1941–42 also encouraged a shift of investment in widely known recording artists with existing hits (Jones, 2006: 4–8). Songs promoted with movies and live radio performances could yield more predictable returns during this period of industry instability.

The evolution of the recording artist star system began in the early twentieth century with opera tenor Enrico Caruso, through to Crosby in the 30s, and was finally consolidated through film, television and print media. First Bill Haley and the Comets on television shows, then Elvis Presley in movies, and ultimately the Beatles in film and electronic media and the popular youth culture press—these were among the most efficacious at adapting the movie star-making system through all forms of visual media (Bennett, 2001, 14–15). But some characteristics were more "interesting" to the music-consuming public than others. The challenge for music marketers was to selectively choose the characteristics that best sold the music, and therefore that best catalyzed the evolving ideologies of their fans. The music marketer and his client could use the cover song as a means to shape the fans' perception of the performer. Appearances on television, at parties, press releases and all forms of publicity were each opportunities to create mythic narratives from the lives of their artist clients to which the cover song was another means to validate affiliation. Sometimes the effect was to "cleanse" the music from more "threatening" aspects of its cultural origins, as sociologist Andy Bennett qualifies with Bill Haley's early rock recordings (2001: 12), or to use an association with more "authentic" origins as a means to sexualize the youth culture. Presley's personal affiliation with "blackness", as exemplified by his cover of Wyonie Harris's "Good Rockin, Tonight," is evidence to this effect. Or, the cover song might demonstrate resistance to the mainstream with a version that "valorize[d] blackness" with its use of language that is less than official, as Coyle describes the British Invaders of the mid 1960s, and their use of covers of R & B tunes (2002: 146–7).

What is important to highlight early in this discussion is that the function of the cover song (as we might think of it now) changed as the economy of music changed, and as that economy adapted to the ideological shifts of the societies that played the covers at that time. The first covers, as noted earlier, were a means to capitalize on popular songs, not on performers, and thereby produced what philosopher Kurt Mosser calls "re-duplication" covers (2008: §II). The second use of the cover capitalized on a growing (and covert) interest in black culture by a young and restless white youth culture, where the performers' extra-musical characteristics provided the re-signification of identity, and as Coyle contends, a means to conceal the "blackness" of the previous version so that white sexuality could revise itself (2002: 139–41). These covers required acts of "interpretation," in both "minor" and "major" proportions, to use Mosser's terms (2008: §II).

But what of those songs that seem ineffably tied to a particular performer, more than anyone else? Patsy Cline's version of Willie Nelson's "Crazy", for example, indelibly portrayed her as a woman victimized by conventional roles of marriage and fidelity. (The releases of details of her personal life reinforced this portrayal.) Such songs, coupled with the photogenic promotion of their star performers, provided the signifiers that congealed the myths of artistic creation and originality that amplified the promotion and sale of all forms of commercial culture, and that was perfected earlier by the star system of Hollywood (Dyer, 2004: 4). These star-making covers, which may be either "re-duplications" or "interpretations," ultimately steal the thunder from previous "original" recordings (which often times were covers themselves). The earlier "cover" artist recording in the provincial towns of America and elsewhere were demoted to mere local substitutes. And the "original" star performers, to the likes of Crosby and Presley, who were lauded as innovators, covered songs as a part of the creation of their star persona.

As mid-twentieth-century America engaged the battles of civil rights, the use of the cover song gained a degree of overt socio-political intention. And this new use of the cover song was also exploitable. The conflictive discourses of the late twentieth century provided opportunity for music producers to use cover songs whose singer's perceived affiliation of one ideological orientation and its social groups gave impetus to appropriation by another singer. Songs "intended" to validate relations between God and its human subjects were sexualized (Sister Rosetta Tharpe's 1940s "Nobody's Fault But Mine" versus Led Zeppelin's 1970s). Songs intended to validate heterosexual romance and sexual roles could validate homosexual love or alternative sex roles (Rod Stewart's "Tonight's the Night" 1970s versus Janet Jackson's 2000s). Songs meant to personify one ethnic or national group could augment another ethno-national identity (David Bowie's "Changes" 1970s versus Seu Jorge's in 2004). With each of these "interpretive" cover songs reaching back 30 years to an earlier version, we notice markers of social and cultural transformation in ideas related to sexuality and identity. When a recording star affiliates with one social group or subculture and openly references that of another, ideology transforms as it exchanges adherents whose own beliefs were historically different. While all cultural production gleans some meaningfulness from other forms of expression at specific historic moments, ultimately it is the signification process, of ideas moving from one listener to the next, that enables the construction of meaning for a cover song. The recording star persona, utilizing the cover song to construct its own identity, by affiliation, alters the beliefs of its listeners.

The transition from a live music culture to a recorded one necessitated an evolved aesthetic to determine how to promote and market the music (however primitively at first), and how to judge one recording as more salient than another. Gradually, valuing qualities of mimetic accuracy gave way to qualities of interpretive resonance.[2] A performer's unique characteristics (voice, instrumental style, fashion, personal history) become an interpretive inter-textual element that made a cover song legible to a particular audience with which the recording artist

---

[2]   With the rise of cover and tribute bands, this trend reversed. As culture drifted into nostalgia during the 1990s, Internet access and Karaoke performers perused the catalogues of record labels. The aesthetic of mimetic reduplicative covers has strongly re-established itself.

affiliated. A performer, marketer or music producer could test the shifts in the ideological climate with a new interpretation of a cover song.

The Implicit Dialectics of Genre and Generation

These two words, *genre* and *generation*, share the Latin root, *generis*, of or pertaining to a procreative origin—a *genus* (Partridge, 1979: 249–50). In cultural production of all sorts, and with music in particular, generations of cultural consumers manifest and/or associate themselves with genres of style. These genres are embedded with ideological tendencies that often reject the genres of their immediate ancestors and appropriate the genres of more distant ones. These affections of youths are inherently contradictory because youth negotiate the ideas of their parents and grandparents, as their social situation requires. As sociologist Dan Laughey observed recently of British youth culture, youth select the resonant and sometimes oppositional ideological themes from any living elder generation in order to define itself. This inheritance provides a transient dialectic between a person's deeply embedded need to affiliate and identify, and through a need to differentiate from the controlling will and worry of parents and the dominant society (2006: 132–6, 203–13). This inter-generational model Laughey describes as "situational-interactionist," and is useful in that it accounts for how the cover song listener and performer begin to apprehend meaning over a span of time through ritualized practices, such as clubbing and the fashion it requires. A look at the fashion and style signifiers of "clubbing" as projected by the Kennedy's through the 1960s to their swinger constituents, illustrates how the song "My Way" became an inter-generational theme responsive to shifting ideologies within an extended historical timeframe.

"My Way" and The Inter-generational Inter-textuality of the Rat Pack

The generation that came of age fifteen plus years after World War II exemplifies this problematic through its celebration of the Rat Pack—that tuxedo-clad collective of Frank Sinatra, Dean Martin, Sammy Davis, Jr., Peter Lawford and Joey Bishop. This 1960s troupe of stage and film performers has been referenced many times through film characterizations (*The Blues Brothers*, *Swingers, Reservoir Dogs*) and even "covered" through a re-made film franchise (*Ocean's Eleven, Twelve,* and *Thirteen*). Their creative exploits and subsequent popularization serves as a model of "cover" modalities in that their image and sound, however fragmented into various tele-visual forms of character, voice and myth, has been referenced and duplicated repeatedly. The song "My Way" demonstrates the complexities of signification and ideological permutation through its versions (Sid Vicious, Arturo Sandoval, Celine Dion, Aretha Franklin, and many more), and through its own invention as a trans-cultural remake of its French antecedent, the song "Comme d'habitude." As we parse through a reading of this song, it is important to give attention to the historical and cultural context.

By 1960, several things aligned. The years of depression and war gave way to a period of prosperity that, while stalled and restarted twice with mild recessions (1953 and 1957), provided a milieu for a thriving entertainment economy. The popularization of theme-based entertainment establishments, both restaurants and amusement parks, were mere G-rated variations of what was built in the Nevada desert. Las Vegas and its panoply of themed casinos and vaudevillian show halls became a destination for a generation of post-war adults whose childhood was spent in the wraps of war and depression, and whose adolescence enjoyed the evolution of a youth culture and its requisite leisure time. Second, a culture of youth emerged into the political sphere with the election of John F. Kennedy. John and his Attorney General and brother Robert, were a fusion of youth and power. The Kennedys were represented through costume and rumor to appeal to two generations. They were young enough in looks, progressive enough in political attitude, and daring enough in their personal behaviors to attract a substantial youth following. Meanwhile, their war record and anti-communist rhetoric gave confidence to the adult generation that survived the depression and the war.

In political histories, youth rarely is allowed the opportunity to carry the reigns of power. Kennedy's narrow triumph over Nixon was a repudiation of youth over age. But to maintain the balance of appeal to both required a dialectic of contradictory signs. While anti-communist rhetoric and policy may have satisfied the anxieties of the war generation, Presidential fashion and entertainment were two means to maintain a connection to the young. Kennedy's boyish eyes and toothy grin, his almost Elvis-like coiffed full head of hair, his narrow black ties and tightly fitting black suits were as close to the uniform of a Catholic high school boy as they were to an ascending senator from Massachusetts. Contrast Kennedy to Nixon's receding hairline, his blue suits and minimalist smile, and the polarity between youth and age could not be more sartorially apparent. Even after Kennedy's assassination, the British Mods reflected his style, as it was emblematic as a uniform for youth who were entering and mocking adulthood and professional life.

The fashion image of Kennedy surfaced most vividly in his fickle relationship with Frank Sinatra. While Kennedy may or may not have engaged in election rigging arranged by Sinatra in the 1960 campaign (Adinolfi, 2008: 82), Kennedy and Sinatra seemed to have visited the same tailor before they shared a table at the Sands Casino that Sinatra partially owned. And despite the cold shoulder that Attorney General Robert gave Sinatra at the urging of his brother John after he won the election, the narrow black ties and simple black suits remained in the Sinatra wardrobe during the Kennedy presidency, and in the years after both Kennedys were assassinated. The Rat Pack look changed little.

During performances at the Ceasar's Palace hotel in the Spring of 1969, Sinatra performed the title song of the album "My Way" (Turner, 2004: 154 – 55). Just a few months before, Sinatra believed that he was quitting the entertainment business. Paul Anka's adaptation of the Claude François song, "Comme d'habitude," became a fitting song for his farewell Vegas performances. "My Way" was itself a cover song with a not-so-hidden personal message of farewell. So then, what "way" might Sinatra been referring? The 1960s saw his career manipulated by mob influences where he was forced to perform or participate at the mob's bidding (Adinolfi, 2008: 82–3).

The "My Way" Vegas performances were a symbolic personal vindication for years of manipulation by politicians and the mob. But while the context of "My Way" may have personal significance, several pictures were taken that are worth noting that suggest a wider cultural meaning. A close look at Sinatra during that time presents the signifiers of haircut and wardrobe, black suits, narrow ties on white shirts in the same thread of conformity from 10 years before. This schema of syntagms signifies an orderliness and uniformity that was established a decade earlier in the late 1950s and early 1960s by young men whose self-image was still shaped by a manhood their parents projected. But these images were taken from 1969, nearly a year after the Summer of Love, when some youth had already chosen to go their own "way" with haircuts (none), and had traded in their mod and urban sports jackets for suede with indigenous designs and fringe. The *way* that Sinatra fans were hearing was as much a comment reflecting on the last four years of civil unrest in the United States (war protests, civil rights protests, political assassinations) that divided youth, as it was Sinatra's personal message.

A decade before the "My Way" record was released, the sustaining aesthetic of the Kennedy presidency was especially visualized during his jaunts to Las Vegas. The venue was a shift from previous ideas of the *presidential* imaginary—the depression and World War II required ascetic leadership. Truman and Eisenhower both fit that bill. Salacious song and dance in the party of Hollywood personae, such as other Rat Pack members as Marilyn Monroe, Shirley MacLaine and Lauren Bacall, suggested that the electorate permitted its leaders, and therefore itself, to indulge. And with this permission, a curious mutation and subsequent validation occurred.

The Rat Pack personae of the 1960s that allowed Kennedy to connect power to youth, was by 1969 waning into a critical stage where some youth, the hippies, had lost faith in suited titans of power. The 1969 run at Caesar's Palace was a performance to a divided generation between those who were disavowing the image of power, getting high and "dropping out," and those who kept some faith in institutions, and used the lubricating and self-medicating martini as a means to endure their disappointments and anxieties.

The style of youth embodied in the British Mods was a sartorial and ideological parallel that likened itself to Kennedy throughout the mid-1960s. Like Sinatra and his Rat Pack comrades in the US, the Mods came from the British working class and typically achieved a modest secondary education. As you can detect in Anka's lyrics from "My Way," he embraced a work ethic where hard work, despite hard knocks, should be rewarded, and probably would be. But, despite the forces that impose ideological and behavioral conformity (the workplace for instance), Sinatra's recording incites the listener to proudly self-determine one's personal destiny.

According to sociologist Dick Hebdige, the Mod accommodated, embraced, stylized and fetishized the ideological and semiological systems of bourgeois culture. A Mod's daily life was banal employment. His nightlife, however, was a covert exploration of amphetamine enhanced, individual expression. The mod, somewhat like Sinatra himself, rode the fence between accepting institutional norms, while indulging in private forms of personal expression (Hebdige, 1979: 52–3). Similar to the Mods in style, but not in class, the American Swinger also maintained an ambivalent attitude between respect for, and rebellion against authority (Adinolfi, 2008: 81). However, neither the Rat Pack members of 1960 nor John Kennedy were actually as young as the Mods. The Rat Pack had in common with its presidential candidate fleeting youth (as opposed to actual youth). Joey Bishop was already in his forties by the time of the 1960 campaign. And, the wealth implied by their prodigious partying reputation implied a privilege unattainable to the Mod or the Swinger. What the Rat Pack embodied was youthfulness, its attraction for play, its manifest tendency to do things differently than the past generation, to look like they belonged to the establishment, but were rebels within it. The identification with youth, through the acquisition of its behavioral signifiers, is what allowed the Rat Pack and Kennedy to captivate the mood of a nation that had not for a long time bestowed nor trusted youth with the seats of power. Certainly the closeness of the Kennedy-Nixon election demonstrated a nation's ambivalence to trust the tense reigns of the geo-political sphere with unwrinkled hands. And, as the decade came to a close, Sinatra's reticent attitude toward complying with the machinery of political and criminal cultures was wearying.

The United States in the 1960s and early 1970s, despite significant political instability, experienced the height of wealth for its working class, a condition that has never since been repeated. Britain went the other direction, and consequentially its youth culture also changed its attitude toward the hegemonic bourgeois ideology. Domestic economic policy in Britain failed miserably at maintaining economic parity with the working class across the Atlantic. Generational deprivations in England diminished the hopes of economic participation among its working class youth. The optimism of the neatly kept suit and haircut of the mod is thoughtfully revisited in the images of Johnny Rotten that presented the Sex Pistols to the world in their first iteration of 1976.

Rotten's sports jacket was torn, then pinned together, the picture of Queen Elizabeth was also safety-pinned through his jacket, if not his flesh. His arrival was a scream, a demand for inclusion within "England's dream" of a future (Pistols, 1992). These are acts of resistance not against the host nation and culture of the UK, but against exclusion from it. Johnny Rotten, and Sex Pistols manager, Malcolm McLaren, sought to return rock to its folk-local origins by humiliating those that treated popular music as sacrosanct (Marcus, 1989: 57–60). The Sex Pistols embodied the most basic impulses of consumerism without the mystification. They were "bodies" ready to consume, "not" bodies to be consumed or treated like "animals" (Pistols, 1992). And as their lot dwindled from generational unemployment, they wanted "salvation" and deliverance from the Queen, that they prayed, "God" would "save" from the "fascist regime" that had kidnapped her along with "hope" for England's future (Pistols, 1992). Through the vomit and despite the obscenities, ideologically they were typical Britons invested in the system: consumeristic, entrepreneurial and even branded (thanks to their manager, Malcolm McLaren). What they lost faith in was the ethic of work and its rewards that the Mods thought would be theirs for the taking, however marginally. And as the Pistol's message took on a nihilistic tone, attractive to those who also had lost that faith, theirs was a chance to claim some vindication by pronouncing no regrets with a parting song like "My Way."

In the last months of the Sex Pistols, as the creative effluvia began to dilute and diminish with the drug use of Sid Vicious, and the hunger for music-industry recognition expressed by Glenn Matlock and later Steve Jones and Paul Cook, resistance from exclusion lost its meaning as it tried to make a trans-national adaptation. Their tour in the USA in the late summer of 1978, while disguised as an attempt to rile the proletariat of smaller cities across the United States (from Atlanta to San Francisco), its very concept was a contradiction of meaning waiting to implode. How can one incite resistance from exclusion or marginalization, when the audience is not so excluded or marginalized? Their *way* failed in America. Working class youth in the United States at that moment had not yet shared the experience of their British counterparts. 1978 was barely the beginning of an economic decline that would not ravage rural and urban United States until the recession of 1981–82, not coincidentally the peak years of West Coast and New York Punk.

Preceding a tour that precipitated the collapse of the Sex Pistols, the band sold records, hundreds of thousands of records. Newspapers and television programs had covered not only their subversive music, but also the excretions of their very orifices. Their fame, however tainted, still lit the hopes of venue owners to make their margins until such a point that Punk ceased to be a public interest, or hazard. It became a part of the cultural landscape, another fauna born from the viral transmission of ideological mutation, made now safe by its rampant and repeated representation. With repression against class markedly acknowledged and forgotten, and with as much personal resentment for being out-smarted and manipulated as Sinatra was, Sid Vicious put together a new iteration of the Sex Pistols for what would be one show in Paris with some of his band mates. They performed, on a similarly extravagant television set that likened François's original performance of the ineffable song, "My Way." It was another cover not only of a song, but also of an exit from a famed career.

As referred earlier, the Sinatra and François versions of "Comme d'habitude" and "My Way," speak of a man who not only embraced his culture's work ethic, but also is willing to endure the punishment of original "ways" or choices with "too few regrets to mention." We are left wondering if at this moment in this man's existence (Vicious's, Sinatra's, François's, which?), he has succeeded in achieving his life's ambition. But from the song, we learn that he is proud to have spoken original words, and not those of a rote prayer. The Sid Vicious version of "My Way," resents his listener, insults him even. It brags of disloyalty, "no devotion." It rationalizes violence and drug abuse to counter boredom (a curse of the unemployed). The "lack of clothes" is the consolation—anything is possible when one has nothing to lose. While the earlier versions of Sinatra and François suggest a private message to a woman to whom the singer is giving an affectionate farewell, Vicious's character in the song offers a public declaration, offensive and disturbing. Vicious expurgates his personal truth openly, and justifies his cynicism and impoliteness for his lack of clothes, manners and hope.

This cover song, through its slight adjustments to the lyrics (obscenities), its change in instrumentation (three-chord electric guitar), rhythm (4/4 time) and tone of voice (drunkenly confrontational), among many musical attributes, becomes a historical critique of the cultural myth of the working man. Both songs personify a subject telling his story of punishment for originality and the failure to earn fair reward for his efforts. The earlier Sinatra and François recordings invest the listening subject (French or Anglo-American) with hope for eventual prosperity, loyalty to socially established ideals, and respect for the listener as judge. The Vicious recording however, disparages those past ideals for failing to deliver, and as a victim of failure, his character wants vengeance. The promises of the Labor Party to its constituents were not kept. The notion of playing the game of life by the rules of the state and the ethics of class difference were now perceived as laughable. What remains in the Vicious version are contradictory desires: to be accepted (apologetic kneeling, careful planning) for failures not in the singer's control (repressed speech, rejection), for impulsive actions that are justifiable (murder, animal cruelty), and for vengeance (he shoots a pistol at the audience at the end of the song). How does one get acceptance and vengeance from the same person? While the singing character refuses to be manipulated by elites aligned with power, he demonstrates that he is just like them, but on the losing side of the game of life. The significant difference between Vicious's version and Sinatra's is that Vicious's character emphasizes irony as performed contradiction. By overtly directing his speech at the Establishment with opposing desires, the listener experiences the irony of history, of values failed, of beliefs altered. Adding to the irony, the performance is made on a relatively lush performance space with cameras rolling before a bourgeois styled audience. The text and the context are ripe with contradiction and irony.

While I will not indulge the reader with the Elvis Presley performance and recording of "My Way," Presley's, like François's, Sinatra's and Vicious's were performed at the wane of a career. I will only offer that the Presley recording is, like Sinatra, a call to a final exit. But in Presley's utterances, his message was more about his personal failures to live up to his fans projections of his self-image. When his self-image started to fray through repeated recycling of old songs and retreat to obesity and drug addiction, the "My Way" performance seems a personal plea for forgiveness from the fans that he believed he disappointed, and whose values he allegedly shared. The voice in Presley's 1977 recording is filled with remorse and regret, contrary to the defiant words that he sings. In all versions of

"My Way" that I have mentioned, ideology and history, both personal and public, are intertwined and transient. I will explore more deeply the historiographic relevance of this observation.

The Phenomenology of the Cover Song

Earlier in this essay we looked at a generational notion of the cover song. And through an analysis of one song that has been covered many times over, we have looked at how signification manifests and adjusts over time from one recording to another, and from one performance to another, by parsing meaning inter-textually across simultaneous historic events and conditions. We should also consider the possible intent of the song's performer (as much as one can find or trust it), and also the function of the song's and the performer's genre. Following Mosser's notion of the "interpretive" cover song, memory and knowledge between performer and listener of a previous performance and/or recording must be shared. Contemporary recording stars both small and large create a recognizable acoustical and visual signature that bonds the performance to the performer in memory in an impressionable way. This memory has both historical and ideological associations. We might speak of the 1970s recording of Led Zeppelin covering Willie Dixon's "I Can't Quit You," a trans-national, trans-genre and trans-cultural cover. The Zeppelin version expresses as much about the culture of transcendental rock spectacle as it does about Dixon's guilt-ridden lament on addictive love. Similarly, we think of the 1980s band X covering the Doors' "Soul Kitchen," a trans-generational cover that expresses as much about the anxiety of Los Angeles white youth in the early eighties, as we might think about the carefree youth culture of Los Angeles in the late 1960s.

In these two examples I have given, at least one of the syntagms in the schema of the music and performance changes. This change either facilitates the conjuring of equivalent signifieds in the listener's mind (as in the case of "I Can't Quit You," that intends to express ideas about ambivalent love: guilty versus transcendent), or it purposefully conjures new signifieds with the intent of altering the meaning of the original song (as in the case of "Soul Kitchen" that begins with an original invitation by the Doors to psychedelic intimacy, and transforms to X's frustrated attempt at neurotic and addictive love). Even when a performer re-performs and/ or re-records her own song, if the resulting work conjures new meanings, she has "covered" herself (as in the case of Annie Lennox, whose song "Little Bird" she has recorded and released many version throughout her career, each laden with a shift in meaning reinforced both musically and sartorially). The variations of covering by changing an acoustical or visual syntagm, therefore become a matrix of possibilities that beckon an obvious question. Is a change in signifiers all it takes to create an "interpretive" cover? What if the change in signifiers does not manifest a different signified? Would not the result then be a "reduplication" cover? How will the resulting performance or recording qualify as a cover if the memory of it is altered by every subsequent version? The answer is not precise, and subject to debate since we cannot know the intimate signification process of each listener, nor each performance. The listener is subject to experience multiple performances, and might be constructing meaning more from latent signification rather than from stimuli experienced in the present. Meaning may also be drawn from mis-remembered stimuli when a listener recalls the original and her experience of it quite inaccurately when compared with the cover version. There is also a correlated question. When a recording artist attempts to re-perform in the present precisely like it was done in the past, does that experience constitute the same meaning? If the sign requires a signifier affix to a signified, if the musical signifier is identical, is it not impossible for the signified—that which resides in the mind of each listener—to remain unchanged? Do not the ravages of time affect every cognitive being? Might every re-performance then carry some degree of "interpretive" expression?

Despite the uncertainty of determining the experience of a cover's intra-personal signification, I offer two conditions to test for when distinguishing between a cover song that intends "interpretation" of its antecedent, and one that intentionally "reduplicates":

1. Does the signified conjured from an original performance become unrecoverable for either the performer or the listener in a subsequent performance—un-recoverable, despite manifestations of context such as published critiques, other simultaneous music, fashion, style, other art forms?

2. Does either performer or listener distinguish between the memory of an elapsed signified (with *its* unique historical moment in a particular cultural consciousness) and the recognition of a new signified (and *its* unique historical moment) that alters or replaces the old one.

To demonstrate the test, play the two versions of "Soul Kitchen," one as recorded by the Doors of the 1960s, and as recorded by X. Note the tempo of the music, slow and lulling and then changing up with John Densmore's percussive bridge into a more forceful rhythm. Note the instrumentation and arrangement that suggests through its use of Ray Manzarek's organ, the psychedelic drugs of their time. Hear the stream of consciousness meandering of Jim Morrison's hallucinogenic voice that enters as a muse or a demon.

Then, listen to X's version. Note the increased tempo and altered use of the organ that suggest a more stimulating drug, a more urgent condition, a more impatient desperation, rather than a calm surrender to the unconscious. Its chord structures are cramped and hurried. The voices, this time Exene Cervenka and John Doe's, dare you to enter the "Soul Kitchen", rather than seduce you as Morrison tries. Interestingly, in both performances, Ray Manzarek performs his organ part on both recordings. He was also X's producer on their recording of the song (X, 2001). This writer has personally heard Manzarek comment sympathetically with the Punk generation's disdain with the political impotence and narcissism of their hippie parents. The musical syntagmatic alterations to "Soul Kitchen" reinforce his intentions in the X recording. But so as not to be fooled by the fallacy of trusting an artist's intentions, might it have been phenomenologically impossible to achieve the same signified as the original recording if the context of white youth in Los Angeles had so dramatically changed from the carefree abundance of the early 1970s to the recessionary anxieties of the early 1980s?

The philosopher Edmund Husserl writes: "… every Now of the mental process also has its necessary *horizon of After*, and that is also not an empty horizon … even if it is the end-phase of duration … it is of necessity a fulfilled one" (Husserl, 1982: 195). Husserl's notion of fulfillment describes the experience of the imagined or remembered as either referenced through language or experienced through the senses. For the band X, where the organist of "Soul Kitchen" has both a memory of recording the original version and an imagination of a new version, he is experiencing what Husserl calls "noetic intentionality," where a conceptualization of the "the latter includes in itself, the former as its consciousness-correlate" (Husserl, 1982: 247). And with the new version, the signified of the first version becomes encapsulated by the signified of the second. The Manzarek consciousness of 1980s became the "horizon After" for the Manzarek of the 1960s. And while his "intention" (for as much as we may not know it) may have been to critique the youth of his generation, he can only do so by recognizing that a complete understanding of the critique requires that he and his listener hold both the signification of the first recording as contained referenced through the signification of its cover.

But how might this be accomplished either acoustically or visually? The syntax of a song (the weaving of chords, melody, rhythmic signatures and lyrics) is often what associates it to a genre. A particular arrangement of syntagms evolves a code that indicates a genre. In the contemporary historical moment, The Doors' "Soul Kitchen" is typed as "classic rock," not just for its historical appearance in the timeline of rock music, but also for characteristic arrangements of musical elements that fit the generic code of "classic rock" as it is known today. For example, the guitar solo of Robby Kreiger in some versions of "Soul Kitchen," goes on for several minutes, the single-voiced narrator subject of Jim Morrison tells a story intended for an attentive listener lauded for her inspirational cooking and psychedelic inspiration. Guitar solos and vocal soliloquies both are elements of "classic rock." The X cover of "Soul Kitchen" has no such intention or design. It is typed today from its musical codes as "Punk" because its tempo is faster. Its dual-voiced melody create nearly a monotone drone as both Cervenka and Doe sing the chorus in closely registered harmony with hardly more than two notes across all syllables, and nearly out of breath. There are no guitar or organ solos. D.J. Bonebreak's drums pound a more minimalist beat that conjure a "kitchen" wrought with confusion and danger. The two versions of "Soul Kitchen" express ideas about spending idle time for distinct generations of Los Angeles youth: one from the late 1960s, self-absorbed and drug addled, and the other from the early 1980s, ridden with anxiety and abandonment, looking for desperate relief. While each generation may use the cover song to reflect the economic and political conditions of their times, the meaningfulness of their references require a persistence of memory and process of selecting signifiers that will simultaneously trigger the signifieds of the past while constructing new ones. This process of referencing and reconstructing meaning is markedly similar to the task of the historian.

The Cover Song as Meta-history, the Cover Singer as Historiographer

The next question concerns the cover song's function as an act of historical interpretation. For the trans-generational cover song, the choice of song intends to tease meaning out of perceptions of the past, to take what residual signification exists in memory, and either "idealize" and/or "naturalize" it through its re-presentation and re-performance. One might question the necessity of either action. While an essay can create distance from, and/or reflection on a text to persuade the reader with its rhetorical style, for a song to succeed at drawing in its listener, the performer must internalize the text so that its expression seems to "naturally" emanate from the psyche and body. But cover songs are more complex than original songs. While the listener may "idealize" the myth of original expression from an original performance or recording, a cover song does not really allow for this. The listener usually knows quite consciously that the performer has appropriated and adapted himself to the song with the premise that the listener and re-performer will connect through a common memory of an original recording into a shared experience of re-performance that synthesizes remembered stimuli with live stimuli, hence transforming the signified of a song.

In reference to the writing of history, Hayden White in his volume, *Metahistory*, examines how historians in the nineteenth century used narrative structure and literary devices to conjure the historical imagination. White draws from Nietzsche to deride those historians that attempt to "naturalize" history and hence their own "objective" interpretation (White, 1973: 45–6). These Romantic historians of the nineteenth century gave an "idealized" reading of history's heroic characters. "Naturalizing" and "idealizing" lends an ideological justification of the apparent outcome of historical events. Cover songs are a form of historical writing; but rather than resist the tendency to identify and self-consciously animate the writer as a sentient being with subjectively altered facilities of cognition and expression, the cover song often instead entreats the performer-subject and the listener-subject to both become personalized fallible witnesses to common memories of the past and experiences of the present.

The versions of "In My Time of Dying," also recorded with alternate lyrics and arrangement as "Jesus Make Up My Dying Bed," are both traditional blues recordings whose songwriting authorship goes un-attributed. While the song was first recorded by Blind Willie Dixon (1927) and later by Josh White (1933), its most extensive popularization occurred in the late twentieth century with two recordings by Bob Dylan and another by Led Zeppelin. The Dylan versions are a curious pair. The first that the public heard was released on his debut album in 1962.

It is a simple studio recording with guitar and voice. The acoustics are controlled, and the textures are smooth in that Dylan sounds as if his song was written and recorded contemporaneous to his rise in public fame. Later, a bootleg version was released. That recording is tinny, the voice and guitar are both coarse and worn. The recording sounds as if it were pulled from the tornado-strewn wreckage of a depression era basement. It sounds more like the last words of a dying hobo then a popular musician riding the wave of folk that crested in the early 1960s. Then, listening to the Willie Dixon version, his singer-subject scratches out a confession with a gravelly voice for sins too dark to admit, while the guitar elides as an angel listening and waiting to take his "body home." The Josh White version, whose lyrics are closer to Dylan's choosing, is more sedate, and much closer to an Evangelist's apology for much more private transgressions. As the literature and music of Folk and Beat peaked in popularity to Dylan's advantage, he curiously made his presence without a direct reference to either version, as if his debut album recording was the first, as if his own life and persona were transported from the depression era past to the present of the early 1960s. The bootleg version, released after Dylan's authenticity was put into question, seems like a footnote, justifying his authentic affiliation with an imaginary vagabond musician culture that roamed the countryside like gypsies on the landscape. His gamesmanship with his fans about authenticity and presence is flippantly referenced with the film title *Don't Look Back* (which is a challenge *to* look back, but to where, if not the past?) and the song title "I'm Not There," which extends an existential question about being and time (How can one comment on one's existence in a place, if one is not in it?) Dylan is not an accidental genius. He consciously used the cover song, both its re-performance, re-recording, and re-release ("covering" Dixon, White and himself at the same time) as a provocative instrument to tease our thinking about history, truth and authenticity in the age of recorded popular music. Dylan gives us useful examples of how the recorded cover song is a form of meta-history through its referentiality, its reliance on memory, and the existence and decay of historical traces, both in the physical and mental realms.

The cover song performer can function to some degree, like a historian. He inherits a song from the past, namely lyrics and/or music, and with these come an array of signifieds wedded to the collective memory of the past. And from these, he must make or re-make its meaning in the real time of performance or recording, choosing to illustrate that path using musical style, acoustical and instrumental textures, to create a song object that references the present to the past. The lyrics and music of a song, as well as the grain of its recording, may recall that past, but they eventually reside in the memory of the listener. Therefore the body of the performer and the listener who exist in the present may experience a momentary disturbance between the authentic memories of the original, now compared by the stimuli of the covered version. The memory of the original is never the same once the trans-historical cover has been heard. This memory ultimately becomes the repository of a historical signified, and the embodiment of meaning transforms the performer into a historical object, a text himself, representing the past during the moment of performance. But simultaneously he must decisively interpret that past for consumption to the listener of the present, as he becomes historian and history, subject and object at the same time. The cover song performer enlivens Husserl's considerations of "world sense" where the world of consciousness (imagined and remembered) and the world of objects (sensed) are simultaneously exposited and contained (Husserl, 1982: 344–8).

This very problem of writing history while pretending to be detached to an objective point of view, is why White contextualizes Nietzsche's critique of the historian philosophers who were "disinterested spectators of the world" who brought into existence history as a thing of "beauty" without the will of a historian… as if that were possible (Husserl, 1982: 368–70). The cover song performer, at least as managed by Dylan, becomes the historian that uses his own subjectivity, and creates a past born of the will, of "self-expression" where the self is the subject aware of its temporal existence as well as an object bound to its physical appearance and the recorded trace it leaves behind. These are deliberate expressive modes quite opposed to the nineteenth-century historians that White critiques through Nietzsche.

A "History" that Erases the Past

But as a kind of recorded history, the cover song is still consumed. The cover song entertains and educates the subject of the present, that contemporary subject, the "I" of this moment. This consumption manifests the signification of the cover song through a constant reliance on access to both the material traces of the past (when available) and those memories of that past. But "In My Time of Dying," like "My Way," has been covered so many times across so many generations, that perhaps it has lost most of its original signified in the cultural consciousness, and hence its value as history is more representative of its reference to covers and their historical moments, than to any experience of original meaning and performance.

The historicity of the cover song relies not only on memory, but also on access to material traces. And, like memory, the trace is subject to decay; these traces – the surviving material objects – diminish and disappear in time. Posters and handbills to the bands of youth past are thrown away and lost as the young grow older and move from one domicile to the next. Even in reproduced formats, there is a reduction in form and physical space. Some vinyl albums with their twelve inch dimensions have disappeared only to reappear digitally re-mastered, re-compiled and with the five inch CD cover art redesigned to the taste of the contemporary moment with the intent of targeting the dollars of either new youth curiously looking to discover the past, or the leisure funds of older buyers looking to "remember." The material traces of the past, either original or reproduced, fade into the "*After horizon*" of contemporary media spectacle.

The Led Zeppelin version of "In My Time of Dying" is most exemplary of that spectacle that erases. Emblematic of virtuosic rock performance through the extraordinary performance abilities of guitarist Jimmy Page and drummer John Henry Bonham, their version of "In My Time of Dying" uses the historical reference as a stitch that sews their own super-spectacular presentation to a more antiquated source. Their recording of the song is the longest in their ouvre, completing its final note at nearly eleven minutes; and it is rich with guitar and vocal improvisations, structured and re-structured chord progressions, alternate rhythms, alternate choruses, electronic and acoustical effects, and a transformative characterization of the dying man. The recorded versions released on several albums consistently project the operatic characteristics of Led Zeppelin's cover. The story of the dying man in the song is personified as a man carried away to heaven or hell by angels or demons. The dying man remorsefully pleads for salvation at the end of his life, and forgiveness from Georgina, Saint Gabriel or Jesus, whomever would give comfort. The reference to the song itself becomes a mantle on which to present the ornate artistry of each band member. Like opera, a simple human event is dramatized spectacularly; it is drawn out for emotional effect, and uses references to religious myth. And also like opera, the spectacle as a signifier, replaces others through sheer magnitude of scale. In one bootleg recording from 1977, singer Robert Plant precedes the song with a footnote calling the song "a blues based thing from the turn of the century … with a *little bit* of Zeppelin." The "little bit" is immense. And the blues that remain comes from the opening guitar chords that slide under Page's fingers as he repeats the lick several times throughout the recordings. The rest of the song is vintage 1970s rock spectacle in its ear splitting glory. But what is left of the memory of Willie Dixon?

The memory of the post-industrial subject-listener is eroded by the modern event, and by its ideological forces. The constant stream of packaged events, sometimes proto-historical and usually entertainment-derived, gradually disables the agency of the subject. The blitz of media pushes the listener to a position of spectatorship and consumption, rather than one of contemplation and re-collection. As experience becomes more mediated by electronic forms, and less connected to material objects, the stream of representations, such as the television or Internet, becomes an uninterrupted and unending performance. In the constancy of dissemination, there are fewer invitations for reflection, for access to personal memory; there is an abundance of new and infinite transmission, even if that transmission is a retrograde reference to the past. The consequence is a gradual amnesia; the signified becomes eternally dynamic, adjusting itself every time a sign reappears altered and re-contextualized to new signifiers. The result can be Orwellian psychic erasure, where yesterday's history is systematically re-written by the magnitude of new texts, but with falsely yellowing paper and purposefully arcane typefaces to make the revised historical text appear as if it were never re-written at all. When history becomes spectacle, the listener becomes a "will-less" spectator, to borrow Nietzsche's description (White, 1973: 368–9).

The Ironic and Satiric Covers: Acts of Resistance

It is easy to slip into a cynical malaise when the cover song, like the movie remake, seems like retrograde regurgitation. Resistance to forgetting is reinforced by the impulse to actively reconcile the contradictions of the past with the present. There are recording artists who assume the ironic voice, that is a presentation of the opposite result from what is expected or previously associated. White, through Nietzsche, refers this kind of historical writing as taking the ironic attitude. It describes a history written self-consciously, with attention to foreground ideological contradictions (White, 1973: 41). Such was the strategy of the band, Black Velvet Flag. Their cover songs used historical references as signifiers to contradictory signifieds (those of the past that contradict the present). Such a creative approach proved timely. Their rise to almost-fame concurred with the rise of the Internet and access to more abundant resources of cultural information. A thread of an inherited reference found its way in most every song they recorded. And, nearly all of their songs were covers. Black Velvet Flag was a post-modern band that accessed and used the cannon of punk music, the musical lexicon of lounge jazz, and the fashion and style of the early 1960s.

Black Velvet Flag looked critically at the history of punk culture and its gradual demise—that of reconciliation after abandonment of ideology. "Punk's not dead, it's only resting," was one of the monikers of the band.[3] One might ask, what have punks been doing for the last twenty years to need a rest? And, why do middle-aged ex-Punks spend any time or money consuming reissued culture? The answer is not just that Punks eventually found jobs, and therefore had families, careers and mortgages, but that the satiation of bourgeois culture does not mandate a backward look in the way working class cultures do. The promise to the working class, and to the youth of any class, is that the reward of power, wealth and happiness is earned with hard work. Un-kept promises invite the backward glance of accountability. Punk lyrics are rich with ironic accusations of failed accountability. The titles of the songs make their point: "New York's All Right (if you like saxophones / getting pushed in front of subway trains)," by Fear, "Suicide's an Alternative / You'll Be Sorry," by Suicidal Tendencies, "Holiday in Cambodia," by the Dead Kennedys. These are just a few of the many ironic and incendiary songs.

A more complete answer to the question concerning the rise and fall of Punk is that punks regained faith in ideology, and lost faith in their own punk ethos. Punk was born in times where political and economic circumstances contradicted the promises offered by their parents' generation—in the United States, that of post-Vietnam War America embracing Ronald Reagan in a time of recession, and in the UK, that of the British Labor Party who failed to deliver economic

---

[3]   *Punk's Not Dead*, was the title of a 1981 hit album by The Exploited. The phrase was lifted by Black Velvet Flag, who added the additional sentence to their moniker. "Punk's not dead. It's only resting," implying that aging Punks were still nurturing the "ironic" attitude.

improvements after a decade of steadily declining manufacturing industries. And with that loss comes a sense of betrayal to unrealized promises and ideals. But when the perception of the economic and political realities changed, then the need for sharpening the ironic lens on history diminishes. Punk became less relevant as economies and politics favored the bourgeois dreams of youth. The mid-1990s was a period of exceptional employment opportunity for young people in the urban centers of much of the United States and Europe. As information technology changed the employment prospects of educated middle-class youth, so too did it seem to alter the need to assume the ironic historical voice. The revival of martini lounges, lounge music and fashion that hail from the Kennedy era were greeted with a variety of bands that made their way as early 1960s retro-bands.[4] But when the fuel for ironic historical expression diminished—fear of poverty and an attitude of hopelessness—then the ironic voice gave way, back to the romantic voice as a vehicle for bourgeois ideology, as White implies (White, 1973: 422–5).

But the ironic voice can also thrive inversely, primarily through satire. Black Velvet Flag realized that their former punk peers, many gainfully employed with families, were feeling the inevitable pull to surrender to bourgeois culture. That surrender was an impetus to question the values of their youth—that of distrusting and cynically criticizing a system that at least for a time, was providing a livelihood. That Jeff Musser and Fred Stesney were both employed in the advertising industry was not coincidental to the skill by which they executed the satire of their cover songs. And the schooled musicianship of their guitar player, Jason Zasky, was also effective at delivering an authentic, musically complex lounge jazz sound. Among their most satirical, "Group Sex," by The Circle Jerks, "Amoeba," by the Adolescents and "Code Blue" by T.S.O.L. – all are played as glib anthems to adults who grew up damaged and unrepentant and became bourgeois. Black Velvet Flag's cover songs hit a nerve in the New York music scene of 1994 as they went from obscurity to fame within New York circles in a matter of six months.

With regard to the satirical historical voice, White sees satire as irony progressed to ridicule and loss (White, 1973: 376). When Black Velvet Flag exploded on the stages of southern California in the late 1970s, the band's expression and critique of culture was triggered by their despair at being excluded from the cultural imagination of sanctioned creativity. Music and culture for youth was dominated by a few record companies whose monopolistic control of music production, dissemination and promotion excluded most local music communities (Bennett, 2001: 59–60). But at the core of American Punk was a "do-it-yourself" aesthetic and attitude. Henry Rollins and Greg Ginn of Black Flag, Lee Ving of Fear and Jello Biafra of Dead Kennedys were all entrepreneurial in their creation of small record labels and the dissemination of recordings of punk music that, throughout the 1980s and early 1990s, provided an alternative venue for "unheard music."

---

[4]   These are some of the neo-lounge bands of the 1990s that performed with Black Velvet Flag: Combustible Edison, Love Jones, and Friends of Dean Martinez.

But where did the will to express and resist go? Many new labels were born that followed their paths, and the majors began to co-opt the DIY strategies.

One of those labels was GoKart, which produced Black Velvet Flag's satirical album, *Come Recline with Black Velvet Flag*. The album's cover design shows a photograph of tuxedo-clad Fred Stesney, laid out on a stage in the exact position as the shirtless and razor-sliced Darby Crash of the Germs. The graphic design of the album is itself simultaneously an "interpretive cover" with carefully selected "reduplicated" elements. The album cover directly copies with color, typeface and composition, the poster and album design for the Penelope Spheeris documentary, *The Decline of Western Civilization*, and its soundtrack. The film featured chapters on many of the bands that Black Velvet Flag covered, and was a film that documented punk, but whose viewing provided an affiliation rite for punks in the years that followed. To satirize this deified film in graphics, Black Velvet Flag chose a satirical design for the cover of the album of cover songs.

White connects the ironic portrayal of history as symptomatic of the condition of "the self-satisfaction of the bourgeoisie." Irony represents the passage of the age of heroes and of the capacity to believe in heroism" (White, 1973: 232). The choice to satirize the most known punk hero/martyr Darby Crash, who died of a drug overdose on December 7, 1980 (Marcus, 1989: 327), with Fred Stesney appearing in his place on the *Come Recline* cover, could not better indicate "the passage of an age [of believing in] heroes." This intra-generational cover image is an act of reconciliation with that loss of belief; it is an act of signifying to exonerate punks from its guilt for failing to keep the faith, and allowing themselves to be seduced by bourgeois culture.

As a farewell song, at a performance at Tramps in New York City, in June of 1998, Black Velvet Flag played a cover of Jacques Brel's "Season in the Sun." Their version was done in English with a heavy Parisian accent as an impersonation of Jacques Brel. Singer Stesney performed as if he were drunk and in his final days as a performer, completely consumed by the indulgent trappings of bourgeois culture (not unlike François, Sinatra and Presley's choice to exit with "My Way"). Even as Green Day, Limp Bizkit and Sonic Youth were still recording new songs, Punk, through Black Velvet Flag, had transformed as a generation of his adherents were making their exits. Black Velvet Flag demonstrated their loss of belief through the re-signification of a cover song that drew from the distant past, so as to re-position Punk into a bourgeois future. Its ideology had changed, and like the transient ideology of every culture that re-performs and re-records its past music, it would never be the same again.

Chapter 4

Cover Up: Emergent Authenticity in a Japanese Popular Music Genre

Christine R. Yano

Cover versions hold a respectable position in Japanese popular music, and particularly within a song genre called *enka* (literally, "performed song"), sentimental ballads with the reputation of singing "the heart/soul of Japanese." In this chapter I discuss ways in which the prevalence of covering practices in *enka* helps define that "heart/soul"—in terms of both culture and the Japanese music industry (Yano, 2005). In *enka*, singing the song of another connotes not a paucity of expression, but ties of sociality, respect, and hierarchy. A cover performance may be both a tribute to the original singer, as well as a test of a neophyte singer's accomplishment. Furthermore, the song itself gains credence through multiple performances by multiple singers in practices of mimicry and repetition. In this, imitation is indeed the sincerest form of compliment. Imitation is also the highest form of accomplishment for cover performers of top-ranked singers. What results is a triangulated relationship between song, original singer, and cover singers that generates what I call "emergent authenticity"—that is, authority and validation accrued over time through processes of imitation, repetition, and tribute. Rather than conferred automatically in the act of invention or creation, this form of authenticity emerges with each successive performance. Furthermore, authenticity emerges in successive performances if—and only if—these include cover versions. One may cryptically describe hit-making in the *enka* world as a song in search of its covers.

The title of this chapter expresses the centrality of cover songs in *enka*. In Japlish (that is, Japanese reconfiguration of English), "*appu*" (English, "up") may be appended to any noun to suggest an increase or emphasis. Thus, "cover up" is my own catch phrase alluding to the abundance of repetitive performances of the same song in the Japanese commercial music world, both by the original singer as well as by others. Covering occurs at the professional and amateur levels, in contexts of tribute and training, for purposes ranging broadly from sales promotion to entertainment to pedagogy. Both the breadth and depth of practices of covering in *enka* remain noteworthy attributes of the genre itself.

At the same time, I use "cover up" in the more standard English sense to suggest something hidden—co-playing the multiple meanings of covering to include imitation (cover songs) and concealment. Covering may be idealized as a cultural norm, but it also conveniently functions as a smart business practice amid an economic climate of shrinking profits and limited market share. In the case of Japan, I argue that because covering mixes time-honored practices of tribute with business decisions to repackage old songs, the multiple functions and uses help gloss over the difficulties of the times. The ideological convenience of covering rests in the fact that processes of imitation and repetition are not negatively regarded, but parts of longstanding cultural practices that form the basis of emergent authenticity.

Enka as Context for Covering

Let me begin first with a brief discussion of *enka* as a genre in order to better contextualize the role of covering in it. *Enka* carries an inordinate place in the Japanese popular music world that far outstrips its perennially poor sales record. Garnering less than 1 percent of the market share in the 2000s, it nevertheless secures a major spot in institutions of the music industry such as awards ceremonies, where it is retained as a category, and the annual Nihon Housou Kyoukai Uta Gassen (NHK Red and White Song Contest), a multi-hour televised New Year's Eve extravaganza by the Japan Public Broadcasting Corporation in which *enka* constitutes as much as half of the programming. The question remains, why is the music industry and the public so heavily invested in a genre that relatively few choose to purchase?

The answer to that lies in *enka*'s reputation as the site of a significant national-cultural imaginary, as a pop music component of government-supported Japanese identity. That identity embeds old-fashioned values of loyalty and spiritual strength, attachment to hometowns and mothers, and highly codified gender roles, juxtaposed with melodramatic expressions. In *enka* terms, to be Japanese is to suffer—longingly and tearfully (Yano, 2002).

If one asks young people in Japan today about *enka*, the great majority will dismiss it vehemently as old-fashioned music of their grandparents. And indeed, it is widely known as generational music, its heyday arising in the 1970s and 1980s, even then as old-fashioned music. Yet, even those who profess to hate it, acknowledge the industry's claims, recognize many of the songs, and know the names of top singers—even as they may distance themselves from the genre. The Japanese public regardless of age, generation, class, gender, and ethnicity has minimally an awareness of *enka*, both by reputation and sound as what I call "music overheard." Sites for this overhearing include bars, karaoke venues, and particular radio and television programming, such as NHK and certain other commercial networks. "Overhearing music" follows vectors of social structure, cultural capital, and power: it is the music of the mainstream disseminated broadly—in this case, through government-supported media channels, such as NHK, and particularly networks—that may be heard, if not listened to, by others. Although the perception is that *enka* is the music of mainstream Japan, its actual fans fill particular demographic niches: blue collar (particularly truck drivers), rural, and older adults (fans today notably give the age of forty as the turning point in their listening biography when they shifted their preferences from more Western-derived "pops" to what is perceived as Japanese-derived *enka*; the question remains whether this turning point will continue for younger people). In this demographic, record purchases may not be the most common way of consuming music; thus the low record sales may not fully reflect the level of *enka* listenership. Nevertheless, *enka* fans do buy recordings. The record industry characterizes *enka* sales as slow and steady, rather than peaking at a high volume and then dropping off precipitously.

What is most significant in tying *enka* to expression of the "heart/soul of Japan" is the link between the genre's specific demographic of fandom—blue collar, rural, older adults—and the notion that therein lies the symbolic source of mainstream sentiment. Therefore, even if fans may occupy the margins of Japanese society, what they represent constitutes the reputed backbone of the nation. By this same logic, even if *enka*'s low record sales suggest a marginal genre in business terms, the music industry, media such as NHK, and much of the general public configures that margin as foundational to Japanese popular music. *Enka* derives this foundational status through its associations with the early days of recorded music in the late 1920s when a genre known as "*enka*" was among the earliest recorded popular songs. It matters little that these songs do or do not share musical characteristics with today's *enka*. What matters is that the term *enka* became a dividing line between popular music considered indigenous and that derived from Western genres (labeled generically *poppusu*, "pops"). The utility of *enka* as a genre developed through the 1970s music industry, which dubbed *enka* the "sound of tradition," expressive of the "heart/soul of Japanese." With Western imports and influences perceived as an immediate threat to musical and thus cultural identity, *enka* became that which could be considered "quintessentially Japanese."

This status holds true as well in *enka*'s approach to cover versions. The ways in which a greater proportion of people consume *enka* is not through record purchases as much as singing in karaoke. Even those who purport not to like *enka* may occasionally be heard singing *enka* songs in karaoke, in part because of the historic associations of the genre with the origins of karaoke as entertainment in bars. If *enka* is the music of bars, then karaoke originated as the musical accompaniment to amateur singing of that music. This says as much about karaoke as a space of performativity and patterned mimicry—in other words, cover versions—as about *enka*. Because of *enka*'s links to hyperemotional expression and characteristic staginess that is part of its performance style, the genre is the perfect means for amateurs to embrace the opportunity to over-emote in the name of song, losing themselves in the highly stylized performance of another. Performing an amateur cover version of *enka* in karaoke means seizing the star turn and relishing the melodramatic moment.

Kata (Patterned Form) as Fundamental Cultural Principle

That star turn holds particular place as a type of *kata* (patterned form). In fact, *kata* informs not only the *enka* world, but may be considered an ordering principle in Japanese society. Borrowed from the world of the arts, *kata* is a fundamental principle of teaching and learning, social structure, knowledge, evaluation, and aesthetics. In the martial arts, for example, basic movements are broken down into *kata*, taught to students, combined in on-the-spot sequences as constituent elements of sparring, and evaluated as a means of promotion. In the field of kabuki music, *kata* of drumming patterns may signal the type of precipitation in a scene, providing information not only regarding the season of the year, but also to the affective backdrop. *Kata* constitutes the language of expressivity and emotion. In the field of tea ceremony, *kata* are taught in a hierarchy of learning so that observing the *kata* of a pupil gives an accurate indication of her level in the art form. In these ways, *kata* in the arts creates order, precision, narrative, emotion, replication, and hierarchy.

As Keiko Clarence-Smith is careful to point out, *kata* should be differentiated from the closely related, but more rudimentary *katachi* (outer patterned form) (2008). Whereas *katachi* refers strictly to the superficial form, *kata* includes both the outer and inner patterning in a hierarchy of learning. As a student, one proceeds from the outer *katachi* to an understanding and mastery of the interrelationship between the outer and inner patterning (i.e., *kata*).

In the katachi stage, copying is essentially a mechanical, physical act indicating the replication of a fixed movement, form or position. If the learner is successful in this they go on to the next stage, kata, when what they have learned is internalised [sic] and an individual understanding of the meaning of what has been imitated is achieved. (2008: 55)

Clarence-Smith positions *katachi* and *kata* as both following principles of imitation and repetition, but with different intentions and results: "The significance of learning *kata* lies in the fact that by copying an external, physical form—that is, *katachi*—you recreate the internal *kata*—that is, the feelings and emotions of another" (Clarence-Smith, 2008: 56). She may, however, overstate her case. In fact, the deeper meaning of the patterned form (i.e. *kata*) may emerge gradually and unintentionally through the repeated action of *katachi*. It is the very lack of intention that allows the body to lead in this process.

A close *kata*-based analogy with architecture helps clarify the position of covers in the *enka* world. In Japan's Shinto religious system, the highest status accrues to the sacred shrine complex at Ise, which was established in the late seventh century. Every twenty years, beginning in the year 692 with the first ceremonial rebuilding, the shrine is dismantled and reconstructed, in accord with belief in the power and natural processes of death and renewal. The result is a set of buildings that are constantly and simultaneously new and old, imparting the teaching of ancient construction processes and handling of materials to new student builders. The "authenticity" of Ise Shrine does not exist in the original, first building or the event of its construction over 1300 years ago. In fact, that first building is of far less consequence than its successive iterations, continuing for centuries. Thus, authenticity and authority emerge through time-honored practices in the process of continual renewal. In short, Ise Shrine grows in stature and profundity as it continually "covers" itself. I contend that covers songs and singers function in similar ways, establishing and extending the life of the original—in fact, defining the authenticity of the hit song.

Whither creativity? The Ise Shrine rebuilding process places little emphasis on newness or innovation. So, too, in a music industry that embraces covers wholeheartedly, creativity may be far less important than recognizing one's position in relation to the past. A system of *kata* situates innovation within a hierarchy of knowledge: in a pyramidal scheme of learning, the many beginning students of an art form must replicate the teacher's *kata* (what Clarence-Smith would call *katachi*) as precisely as possible. Ideally, the *kata* of a proficient student replicates the *kata* of one's teacher, one's teacher's teacher, and a further vertical panoply of teachers. *Kata* thus narrates both history and hierarchy. In this system, creativity— as the deliberate breaking of *kata* (*kata-yaburi*)—remains the purview of those who have ascended the hierarchy, taking place in the progressive development of an art form. Japanese Noh theatre dramatist and theorist Zeami identifies three stages based in *kata*: 1) preservation of past teachings; 2) breaking of the patterned form (*kata-yaburi*); and finally 3) establishment of one's own *gei-fuu* (artistic style) (Clarence-Smith 2008: 56). Although the third stage may be the overall goal of the process, few reach that pinnacle of the art form. Innovation here is not a right, but a time-dependent, effort-filled privilege. Creativity rests in the hands of only those few who have themselves gone through years of diligent training in careful observation, precise imitation, and endless repetition. The three-step process of *kata* development does not only weed out the unskilled and uncommitted, but it also critically shapes the result. One can trust that *kata-yaburi* and even *gei-fuu* rest in processes of highly informed creativity.

Understandably, in spite of all efforts to retain the *kata*-based system, the above scheme is an idealized one. Although replication may be a student's goal, it is not always achieved. The inadvertent slippage of *kata* transmission may thus result in accidental innovation—a function of different bodies, voices, technical means, contexts, and even temperaments. The exactitude of the *kata* system may emphasize detail and technique, but it is ultimately a system with human "failures." That some of these "failures" may become resources of future innovations demonstrates some of the flexibility appended to the system.

When applied to the popular music world such as *enka*, one may easily see some of the limitations and possibilities of *kata*. What the *enka* world shares with much of the commercial production of music in Japan and elsewhere is the Taylorist assumption that rationalizing production to its constituent, replicable elements— in other words, *kata*—results in streamlined efficiency and productivity. In pop music terms, hits beget patterns to which future hit-makers strive. This principle structures culture industries in many countries. However, in those same countries, the marketplace imposes a lid on the success of the pattern, as the public reaches a saturation point in imitative hit-making. In short, a song must not only follow past hit-making principles, but also brand itself as distinctive in some way. Without the element of distinctiveness, the public has little need to purchase the next newest thing on the market.

It is exactly in the element of relative distinctiveness that the *enka* market differs from that found in other countries, or even in other pop music genres in Japan. According to an industry insider, what characterizes the *enka* market is the principle of "*ki o terasazu ni*" ("without showing anything new"). In other words, the level of distinctiveness by which hits in other genres or contexts may be made remains low in *enka*. Listeners and fans select *enka* specifically because they want to hear "old-sounding" music, rather than a brand new sound. Principles of covering—that is, replicating a song or sound from the past—thoroughly informs and even defines the genre. The aesthetic appetite for redundancy, therefore, shapes the genre as an industrial product. Even when young singers are selected for grooming and vocal training, managers take pains to ensure their connection to pastness with music that sounds old, even nostalgic, and an image by which they may be perceived as old-fashioned in values, if not in hairstyles or clothing. New *enka* singers thus show strong adherence to the *kata* of not only patterned song-making, but to the very ethos of the genre. In effect, they are cover versions of past singers.

Migawari (surrogacy) as Substitution and Hierarchy

Besides *kata*, another principle important to understanding the prevalence of cover versions in *enka* is that of *migawari* (literally, "body exchange;" the person, act, or state of substitution; self-other exchange; surrogacy). In Japanese culture, *migawari* assumes particular credence as the legitimate—and sometimes necessary—substitute for the original. Whereas in Euroamerica, a surrogate carries little real power, in Japan the surrogate principle allows stand-ins considerable leeway in decision-making. The distinction between *honnin* ("real" person) and *dainin* (surrogate) may be clear, particularly in linguistic terms, yet the division of power may be far less so, with *dainin* taking over *honnin* responsibilities, duties, and even auratic presence. According to Takie Lebra, the *dainin* may stand in for *honnin* in the following ways: 1) as a form of protection; 2) as amplification of the actions and sincerity of *honnin*; 3) as part of rectifying a status-role gap (1994: 112–18). It is the second of Lebra's explanations that applies most closely here, the rebounded actions of *dainin* contributing to the emergent authenticity of *honnin*.

This principle of *migawari* paves the way for a close relationship between original singer (*honnin*) and cover singers (*dainin*). As Lebra discusses *migawari*, cover singers' performances amplify that of the original singer, beyond the scope of what one person could produce. Here, covering is not mere imitation, but instrumental to the growing power and establishment of the original. Covering confers and reaffirms authenticity. Pointed examples of this occur frequently on the *enka* stage. Not only are there many instances when *dainin* appear in tribute fashion, singing the hit songs of *honnin*, occasionally *honnin* and *dainin* share the stage, even singing the same hits together. In one televised performance I witnessed two female singers—both stars in their own right, but one far senior to the other—performing senior star's big hit. They emerged walking stage center together, in nearly identical kimono, their hair in similar upswept fashion, with similar bodily form of height, weight, and facial features. At a glance, it was difficult to tell them apart.

The camera embraced and reinforced the *migawari* nature of the performance, framing the two and their relationship with one another continually. Whereas a front center camera captured their joint entrance, once they began singing, camera angles shifted to feature one and then the other as they performed alternating verses of senior singer's hit song. The most typical camera angle framed both women from a position slightly off-center: performing singer in the foreground, non-performing singer in the background. With a tight depth of focus, the camera kept performing singer in focus, while non-performing singer remained a distinct, but fuzzy image. The point here is that the camera itself displayed the *migawari* principle, framing the triangulated relationship between *honnin* singer, *dainin* cover singer, and the hit song's performance.

They sang shot gun, trading off verses in tandem, holding off a unison moment until the last line of song when even their wide vibrato matched precisely. In fact, both singers performed continually. When senior singer sang, junior singer could be seen in the background smiling and swaying to the music. When junior singer sang, senior singer mouthed the words and sang along, out of microphone range. By mouthing the words and singing along, senior singer performed her emotional and musical support for junior singer. This sing-along could be seen as a practical measure: should junior singer falter, senior singer would be there at the ready, providing words and melody. However more than a practical measure, senior singer's mouthing of words could also be viewed symbolically as *honnin* ownership of the song, as well as her maternalistic conferral of that song upon another. In effect, mouthing the words to the song reclaimed part of the stage for senior singer, asserting *honnin* rights even while being covered.

What is clear in this and other performances is that *honnin* and *dainin* are never equal. Junior singer performed her *dainin* status well, glancing deferentially at senior singer, casting her eyes downward just prior to her turn, and revealing in interview later in the program just how nervous she was to be performing on the same stage singing the hit song of such a senior persona. She carefully never upstaged senior singer, but also demonstrated respectful tribute appropriately by performing senior's hit extremely well. At the same time, senior singer showed gracious motherly approval of junior singer's performance. The two performed their *migawari* covering relationship precisely, with a calibration that demonstrated their interdependence. Although *dainin* occupies a lower rung in the music world's prestige hierarchy, the critical role of the surrogate ensures an enduring place in the scheme of things. Clearly, the reputation of *honnin* is established and enhanced through the presence of *dainin* in the popular music world. The relationship locks both in an interdependent dyad: neither can survive without the other. In the case of the televised *migawari* moment that I analyze, senior singer's "authenticity" (here, power, confirmation, prestige) expanded because of the star status of junior singer. The higher the cover, the more might be accrued to oneself. Undoubtedly, even covers work within a hierarchy.

The Legitimizing Act of Covering

Yamada Shouji "contends that the value of an original can only exist relative to its copies, and it is the dissemination of copies which increases the value of the original" (quoted in Clarence-Smith, 2008: 53). Herein lies the emergent authenticity of cover versions. The *enka* industry builds upon this assumption of the mutual and relative value of original and copies when it explains: "An *enka* song must not only be sung by the original person, but also by other [professional] singers and in *karaoke*" (Anonymous, 1992: 24). Each time a professional or amateur "covers" a song, that song gains credence through sheer repetition. Furthermore, these are not covers as reinterpreted through the idiosyncratic lens of personality or style of each new singer, but versions that stay remarkably close to the original, including musical arrangements and vocal inflections. In this, imitation serves as more than "the sincerest form of flattery," and becomes part of the very process of legitimation. What this also suggests is that the details of arrangements and inflections are considered constituent parts of the song itself, alongside lyrics and melody. By definition, then, a song includes the details of its performance. Therefore covering the song assumes replicating those constituent parts.

Songs, singers, and covers are bound together in a web of redundancy. Michael Taussig's by now well-known discussion of mimesis is worth quoting to add to our discussion: "The wonder of mimesis lies in the copy drawing on the character and power of the original, to the point whereby the representation may even assume that character and power" (Taussig, 1993: xiii). The case of covers in Japanese popular music, however, defies Taussig's neat analysis. The copy/cover may be "drawing on the character and power of the original," but just as critically, the original gains "character and power" through the processes of copying.

It is more than just "character and power" at work here. Covering—that is, redundancy, imitation, mimicry—circumscribes what Rupert Cox calls an "aesthetics of repetition" that can devolve into kitsch (2008: 264). In fact, this is not the only way in which *enka* and practices surrounding it are linked to kitsch, especially with the genre's reliance upon melodrama, as well as musical, textual, and visual formulas. Furthermore, *enka* fans seem not the least bothered by the prevalence of formulas—especially if one follows the principle expressed earlier of "not wanting to show anything new." The oldness of the formulas, repeated in detail through cover versions, represents nothing less than an ethos of comfort and familiarity. Sam

Binkley analyzes redundancy as a style that "employs the thematics of repetition over innovation," expressing "a preference for formulae and conventions over originality and experiment" (2000: 131). *Enka* follows these lines exactly: originality and experiment find little reward amid a genre that seeks covers.

Shu-mei Shih contends, "The important point here is that the copy is never the original, but a form of translation. It may desire to be the original, or to compete with the original, but this desire always already predetermines its distance from the original as a separate, translated entity" (2007: 5). *Dainin* cover singer's performance, then, is that translation: "not an act of one-to-one equivalence, but an event that happens among multiple agents, among multiple local and hegemonic cultures, registering an uncertainty and a complexity that require historically specific decodings" (Shih, 2007: 5). It is these decodings that I draw here, providing cultural and historic interpretations of covering practices that saturate the *enka* industry.

Linking these decodings and covering practices to the "heart/soul of Japanese"—that is, to a story that at least some Japanese may tell about themselves to themselves—suggests the place of repetition in that heart/soul. It is difficult to write of this using English words: redundancy, imitation, mimicry—these words carry too many negative cultural implications of deficiency and lack to do the concept justice. The honorable implications of imitation and repetition in Japanese culture stand as a rejoinder to the stereotype of Japan as a "copycat nation." Through our discussion of covering, "copycat" may be taken as a compliment, embedded within a hierarchy of learning and thus given a position of respect. Mimicry in the *enka* world is not a denigrated practice—linked to monkeys and primitive peoples—but a technical skill imbued with history and achievement. That technical skill intertwined surface learning with profundity, the outer forms indelibly shot through with inner content. Thus, cover versions in the *enka* world represent the legitimation of the copycat principle as achievement within the musical "heart/soul of Japanese."

THE SONG REMAINS THE SAME? SONG AND ALBUM

Chapter 5

From Junk to Jesus:
Recontextualizing "The Pusher"

Andrew G. Davis

Whatever their other functions, narratives represent a method of communicating the complexities of personal experience as constitutive of social reality. Narratives originate, issue forth, and receive their meaning from individual participation with the social, economic, and ideological systems manifest in a particular society and its culture (Barthes, 1966/1977). Through the discursive process of narrative, individuals and groups are able to explain and understand not only their own subjective experiences, but also how such experiences are determined by, comprise, and relate to the societal realm. As such, narratives are "means by which reality is actively constructed" in which "both the subject and subjectivity are brought into being through the discourses comprising the system of representation of a particular period and culture" (Martin and Stenner, 2004: 398). Within this "nexus of social relations and meanings" (Brake, 1980: 7), individual identity manifests as a particular condition of and response to dominant cultural practices and the issues that gain societal importance through such practices. The communication of individual identity and practices as they relate to the dominant culture represents this particular function of narratives as methods for making sense of the social world.

The significance of discursive narrative, then, is located in how it communicates a particular *representation* of the reality of subjective interaction with society and culture, rather than how effectively it communicates reality as an objective construct. This is due to the fact that narrative "accounts are communicative constructions articulated in specific contexts and located within particular discursive formations" (Martin and Stenner, 2004: 399) and, as such, remain embedded within the subjective experiences of individuals or groups for which a particular narrative holds import. Because subjective experience results from the interaction between individuals, groups, and the society in which they reside, the narrative communication of experience is entirely dependent upon cultural context. As a result, narratives serve to represent the negotiation between individuals, dominant culture, and the social issues arising from this interaction. Such a perspective enhances Barthes's (1966/1977) earlier assertion that the function of narrative is entirely dependent on historical circumstance and development, and the social milieu thereby created. Barthes also notes one further factor upon which the function of narrative is contingent—the genre through which a narrative is expressed. While Barthes was concerned primarily with narrative expressed through literary genres, such assertions can also be applied to the operation of narrative within song (i.e. words sung or spoken to musical accompaniment).

The analysis of song lyrics as a narrative discursive formation presents several unique challenges not posed by other narrative forms. As noted by Booth (1976), "lyrics are of course subject to the pressure of their accompaniment all the time... They must contend with the positive distraction threatened by their accompaniment" (242). Although subject to their own internal discipline, lyrics and the narratives they offer are often subservient to or obscured by the musical content of a song and its interplay with lyrical content—a relationship made ambiguous by the concurrent cooperation and competition between the two. Additionally, song lyrics must necessarily (due to the constraints of form) propagate a simplified narrative lacking the more nuanced and complex presentation of literature or storytelling. The clarity and unity demanded by the song form requires that a song must "be the imagining anew of some simplification of life that is more or less in our possession already" (246).

Despite (or, perhaps, because of) these constraints, analyzing song lyrics as narrative presents unique opportunities for detailing the potential of a song to become recontextualized within the progression of historical circumstance and cultural development. The narrative created in song is made imminent and immediate by the music, which attracts the listener's attention, "and as the story ends, the mind is reaching, and will return for another try, not to 'interpret,' most likely, but to get close to the stories our music tells us" (Marcus, 1969/1972: 127). From this perspective, strict interpretation of the intentions or meanings of a song is not as important as the potential of a lyrical narrative to reveal social issues and how individuals navigate the boundaries between personal experience and dominant cultural attitudes toward such issues. These opportunities for detailing recontextualization become particularly pronounced when comparing a cover version of a popular song to the original or preceding versions.

By removing a song from the original context of its authorship and placing it in a different social/historical milieu, cover songs can express a discursive relationship between different eras (Gracyk, 2001). This dialogue enables the consumer of music to discover the historical progression in a society of the negotiation between individual identities and dominant cultural attitudes from the perspectives of both the original and the cover version(s). If a particular song is recorded (and rerecorded) by a variety of artists, then "a genealogy unfolds" (Plasketes, 1992: 13)—a narrative genealogy whose representations (although arising from the same text) provide insight into the ever-changing relationship between individuals, groups, social issues, and the dominant culture that informs them all—without negating the subjective understanding of reality presented by any of them. Depending upon how strict or relaxed its interpretation of the original material, cover songs contain the capability to "render new meanings by placing the original song in a different musical, or perhaps social, historical, or stylistic context" (Plasketes, 1992: 11).

In this way, we are able to view songs not merely as constructs of personal creative musical expression, but as social texts that "embody always snippets of the myths we hold... By myth here is meant myth as giver of identity, as template for self" (Booth, 1976: 248). Directly related to this notion of song as the expression of culturally bound myth fragments, Booth further notes that song is a social ritual for the expression of common patterns of thought and emotion, as well as the affirmation of personal experience as an extension of the teller of such lyrical narrative. What arises from this ritual is (ideally) identification by the audience with the attitudinal subjectivity of the narrative identity, thus providing the space for engagement with the dominant culture through a text that is contextually bound to societal and historical circumstance. Thus is located the basis for Chye and Kong's (1996) assertion that popular music is the result of individual and collective action. More than this, however, popular music results from the operational interplay between individual and collective realities. As noted by Shepherd (1991), because people create music, music contains basic qualities of the cognitive processes of the musician/composer. Because cognitive processes are socially mediated, different styles of music are socially mediated and, consequently, socially significant. Thus, the "meaning of music is somehow located in its function as a social symbol" (13).

While the above statements are applied to music generally, their relevance to rock-and-roll is of particular interest here. Wicke (1987/1993) iterates the connection between cultural milieu and the functional context of music by applying the concept of music as a social text directly to the development of rock-and-roll as a fundamental "cultural system of reference" (11) for the youth culture which gained prominence (ideologically and economically) in America in the 1960s. This development represents the first era in which popular music served a central function for the conveyance of meanings, pleasures, and problems of everyday collective experience. Thus rock-and-roll represents a complex cultural process of leisure that is constantly active and dynamic due to its origins in "concrete social experiences and cultural contexts" (73). As cultural texts rather than simply constructs of individual creative expression, rock songs provide an open-ended discursive formation that allows for the articulation of multiple meanings in regards to social issues. Such ambiguity is further enhanced by the simple narrative demands of musical accompaniment and song form. For the youth culture of the 1960s, this method of cultural expression represented a means to move beyond the traditional thematic concerns of popular music—entertainment, courtship, and dance—and, consequently, the dominant culture of the 1950s. Therein arises the potential of rock-and-roll to address social concerns from perspectives that often deviate from the dominant culture, a potential once reserved exclusively for the fine arts (Wicke, 1987/1993).

One such social issue that was of particular concern to the youth culture of the 1960s was the use of psychoactive substances. Although the connection between drugs and artistic expression can be traced back through centuries of cultural developments in a number of societies (Smale, 2001; and Wolf, 2005), rock music of the 1960s represents the first mass cultural expression of drug use as a leisure activity. This is not to imply that earlier forms of American popular music did not address the issue of drugs. On the contrary, accounts of drug use have appeared intermittently throughout the history of American popular music. Shapiro (1988) provides a particularly detailed and illuminating account of the connections between drugs and popular music in America. Drug references in American popular music arose primarily from the working relationship between travelling musicians and travelling medicine shows during the nineteenth century. Musicians were employed by medicine shows to provide entertainment for crowds of potential customers. These performances also served as advertisements for the various patent medicines offered by pharmaceutical companies. As such, travelling musicians often served as drug pushers through their role as entertainers. Many of the substances offered by travelling medicine shows were churched-up concoctions consisting primarily of opiates (e.g. heroin, laudanum, opium) or cocaine. Musicians were frequently paid in trade and, as a result, would often develop drug habits or addictions. References to drugs in the lyrics of popular music came about for one very simple reason—musicians write about what they know.

Narrative depictions of drug use continued to occur until (as noted by Shapiro, 1988) the 1950s, when references to drugs almost entirely disappeared from American popular music. Reasons for this disappearance, though interesting, are beyond the scope of the present argument. What is relevant is that the resurgence of drug references in song lyrics only came about when rock-and-roll became a fundamental system of reference for the youth culture that developed (in part) as a reaction against the dominant culture of the 1950s. The narratives (i.e. rock songs) produced by and for this youth culture are illustrative of a sea change within 1960s American society. The reappearance of drug lyrics as a "recurring musical motif" (Markert, 2001: 194) in American popular music reflected the shift in social attitudes towards drug use brought about by the emergent youth culture and subsequent counterculture of the 1960s. Drug stories within popular music lyrics are not simply endorsements or confessions, but can also serve as a discursive narrative framework for positioning an individual or group within society—a method for making sense of the world and one's position in it (Campbell, 2005). Furthermore, they represent a way for people to "reach 'alternative understandings' rather than those provided by the official" dominant culture (Campbell, 2005: 331). For a primarily middle-class youth culture consumed with the concerns of leisure, alternative understandings regarding drug use became a prominent social issue and, consequently, a central narrative theme within rock-and-roll—a theme which persists to this day.

It is not sufficient, however, to merely state that the past four decades have seen an increase in the number of narrative representations of drug use/abuse in popular music lyrics. A study conducted by Markert (2001) indicates that although there has been an increase in the number of popular songs that portray drug use, this does not mean that such songs glorify or promote the use of drugs. On the contrary, most drug depictions in popular song lyrics are decidedly negative. The only drug to receive consistently positive representation is marijuana (as opposed to hard drugs such as heroin, hallucinogens, cocaine, and amphetamine). This fact runs counter to the dominant cultural assumption that musicians' depictions of drugs indicate an endorsement or glorification of drug use. Markert's (2001) study shows that "drug use, social context, and song lyrics are interconnected and each interacts with and influences the others. Drug lyrics are often rooted in a specific time frame and/or social group and tend to reflect the values of that group" (196). It is crucial, then, to examine song as a discursive narrative method of positioning personal experience in relation to dominant culture, taking into account the social and historical (as well as personal) contexts out of which songs arise. Furthermore, it is equally crucial (as asserted by Diamond, Bermudez, and Schensul, 2006) to analyze *how* drug use is portrayed in a song, not simply the fact that it *is* portrayed. To understand how song operates as such a narrative formation, then, it becomes necessary to examine the lyrical content of a specific song or songs. In particular, "The Pusher" by Hoyt Axton stands as an exemplar of drug depiction in popular song lyrics.

"The Pusher" is exceptionally pertinent to the argument at hand for a number of reasons. First, it was written and initially recorded in the 1960s during the emergence of youth culture as an alternative to dominant American culture. As such, it is representative of the changing attitudes regarding drug use from the authoritarian *Reefer Madness*-inspired anti-drug hysteria of post-war America to the more accepting and experimental attitudes characteristic of 1960s counterculture. Second, at least nine different musical artists and/or bands recorded versions of "The Pusher" between 1968 and 2007. Spanning four decades of historical and cultural development, the most notable of these versions offer vastly different narrative representations of the same social issue while working from the same basic text. While minor lyrical variations occur in each version, two versions in particular significantly altered, deleted, or added lyrical content as deliberate commentaries on the original version that reflect the changes in social context in regards to dominant cultural attitudes toward drug use. Third, the narrative genealogy created by the recording and rerecording of "The Pusher" highlights the potential of cover songs to not only express a musical heritage or tradition, but also serve as frames of reference within the ever-changing discursive formation that is popular music—a contextually bound discourse in which the discussion of social issues serves to form and express individual and group identity in relation to dominant cultural attitudes.

Songwriter Hoyt Axton originally wrote "The Pusher" in 1963. It was not recorded, however, until Steppenwolf included a version on their 1968 album *Steppenwolf*. This version of the song reappeared the next year on the soundtrack to the movie *Easy Rider*. As such, authors (even some of the scholars cited in these pages) often misattribute the song to Steppenwolf. Since its initial recording and release, "The Pusher" has been rerecorded at least eight times. Ironically, Hoyt Axton himself provided the first cover of the song on his 1971 album *Joy to the World*. Since that time, Nina Simone (1974, *It Is Finished*), S.W.A.T. (1994, *Deep*

Inside a Cop's Mind), Blind Melon (1996, *Nico*), Cowboy Mouth (1998, *Half Baked* soundtrack), Sons of Otis (2005, *X*), the Ron Evans Group (2006, *65 to 97*), and the Substitutes (2007, *When the Money Runs Out* single) have all covered "The Pusher." The following pages will consider only those versions recorded by Steppenwolf, Hoyt Axton, Nina Simone, S.W.A.T., and Blind Melon. This is due to the fact that each of these recordings provides a significant recontextualization of the lyrical content in such a way as to alter its meaning and perspective. Such recontextualization represents a narrative genealogy of the changing social attitudes of individuals toward drug use/dealing through the negotiation of identity in relation to dominant American culture. Exclusion of other versions of this song is not intended to downplay their worth as individual musical expressions. However, those versions offer no significant narrative recontextualization and, as such, are not pertinent to the argument at hand. They are covers in the strictest sense—"new performance[s] or recording[s] of a composition written and/or previously recorded by another artist" (Leyland, 2007, p. 62). As such, they more closely represent the "creative convenience" or recognition of musical influence described by Plasketes (2005: 148), rather than a significant recontextualization of narrative in the negotiation between individual or group identity and dominant cultural attitudes.

Thematically, "The Pusher" examines the complex relationship between drug users/addicts and drug dealers through the presentation of two crucial narrative distinctions: 1) the distinction between marijuana and "hard drugs" (Markert, 2001: 199) such as amphetamine, cocaine, and heroin; and 2) the distinction between a drug dealer and a drug pusher. In regards to the first distinction, "The Pusher" follows a tradition within popular music lyrics of taking a favorable attitude towards marijuana, referring to this particular substance as "love grass" that provides "sweet dreams."[1] Such characterization stands in opposition to the characterization of hard drugs as responsible for "people walkin' 'round with tombstones in their eyes." As noted by Shapiro (1988), this distinction between marijuana and hard drugs is a traditional theme in American popular music extending back through early rhythm-and-blues, jazz, and traditional blues. The rhetorical stance of "The Pusher" (and, indeed, many popular music lyrics) regarding marijuana stands in direct opposition to dominant American attitudes. The often-favorable view of marijuana among musicians is symptomatic of a more general condition of social positioning. "Bohemianism is the musicians' 'natural' ideology; the values of leisure—hedonism and style—are elevated above the conditions and routines of 'normal' society" (Frith, 1978: 170). Such a deviant and self-appointed stance that generally favors marijuana use carries with it certain social repercussions. "The drug connection was central to the creation of the jazz (and later, rock) musicians as outlaw figures. From the earliest concern about marijuana, musicians were implicated" (Shapiro, 1988: 47). Whereas the

---

[1]   Lyrical content was obtained through transcriptions by this author from audio recordings by Steppenwolf, Hoyt Axton, Nina Simone, S.W.A.T., and Blind Melon.

rhetoric surrounding drug legislation and the dominant social attitudes regarding marijuana use focused blame on musicians for corrupting American youth, "The Pusher" rejects the stigma commonly associated with such behavior by extolling its virtues and markedly distinguishing between marijuana and hard drugs.

This distinction is further noted by Markert's (2001) claim that the one constant in drug lyrics from the 1960s on is that hard drugs are destructive and to be avoided. Whereas marijuana represents (for the narrative voice of "The Pusher" and many other popular songs) a socially beneficial substance, hard drugs are almost exclusively portrayed in negative terms. Marijuana may cause "sweet dreams," but hard drugs represent a force that one's "spirit [cannot] kill," leaving the body in ruins and causing the "mind to scream." Their destructiveness is related not only to this physical and psychological damage caused by the substances themselves, but also to the fact that these substances (e.g. opiates, cocaine, and amphetamine) originally came to prominence through the advertising "push" of pharmaceutical companies and travelling medicine shows (Shapiro, 1988). Such correlation leads to the second crucial distinction contained in the narrative reality of "The Pusher"—that between drug dealer and drug pusher.

Within the narrative genealogy of popular songs containing depictions of drug use, the distinction between dealing and pushing drugs is as traditional in popular music as the distinction between marijuana and hard drugs. For musicians involved in the drug subculture, drug dealing is typically "a family affair rather than a hard-nosed business deal" (Shapiro, 1988: 36). In fact, Shapiro provides numerous examples of professional musicians who also sold marijuana—only to friends and only to support their own habits. Marijuana use, though illegal, represents an acceptable social ritual to the groups responsible for such narratives—particularly jazz, rhythm-and-blues, and, later, rock-and-roll musicians. Likewise, those who provide marijuana to these groups are portrayed in an equally positive or at least tolerable light. Conversely, hard drugs represent self-destruction of the body, mind, and community. While the dealer is simply a man, the pusher is "a monster... he's not a natural man." At the time "The Pusher" was written, amphetamines were commonly associated with the publicly destructive behavior of Southern musicians such as Hank Williams, Sr., Jerry Lee Lewis, and Johnny Cash. Cocaine served as a reminder of the racist origins of drug legislation and dominant cultural perceptions concerning both African Americans and drug use. At the farthest end of the hard drug spectrum, heroin served as a stark reminder of the tragic deaths of such jazz luminaries as Charlie Parker (Shapiro, 1988).

By the time Steppenwolf recorded "The Pusher," another shift in the relationship between drugs and popular music had occurred. Heroin and cocaine "became seemingly mandatory for the burgeoning white rock elite, as musicians took over from film stars... as the new aristocracy... They also became the focus of attention for social revenge as the white pop star toppled the black jazzman as public enemy number one" (Shapiro, 1988: 99–100). Rather than accept the personal stigma of habitual hard drug use, popular song narrative allows rock musicians to refocus blame onto another culprit—the drug pusher. This stance is by no means unique to this particular song. Shapiro (1988) points out that blaming the pusher for one's drug addiction is a recurrent motif in drug lyrics. Whereas earlier social condemnation of drug use targeted African American jazz and rhythm-and-blues musicians, the cultural context surrounding the writing and original recording of "The Pusher" refocused the concern over hard drugs onto rock musicians—mostly middle class white youth. These musicians were now being supplied to a large extent by the record industry itself. Whereas marijuana could be obtained through friendly dealers, hard drugs were available almost exclusively from profit-driven record company executives or profit-driven criminal organizations who operated akin to and were motivated by the same goals as pharmaceutical companies and medicine show hawkers—earlier narrative incarnations of the pusher.

Firmly rooted in this cultural struggle over meanings of drug use, "The Pusher" operates as a protest song—a popular song that places primary importance on its lyrical content as a means of exposing to the audience a particularly problematic social issue in the hopes of propagating the awareness that such an issue illustrates a condition in society that is in need of correction (Denisoff, 1983). Protest songs express a "consciousness of dysfunction" (10)—the perception that social reality is flawed in some sense. Protest songs utilize the emotional power of song to act as a weapon, often in the form of first-person put-downs. More specifically, "The Pusher" operates in a narrative capacity as what Denisoff (1972; 1983) terms as a rhetorical song of persuasion—one which identifies a problematic social condition without proffering a solution based in ideological or organizational commitments. Rather, a rhetorical song of persuasion posits or infers a solution that lies on the margins of or deviates from socially accepted standards of behavior. Such a protest song "stress[es] individual indignation and dissent but [does] not offer a solution in a movement. The song [is] a statement of dissent which [says], 'I protest, I do not concur,' or just plain 'damn you'" (Denisoff, 1972). As will be discussed below, "The Pusher" offers such dissent in suggesting that drug pushers be stabbed or shot—murdered outright, as it were. Such a rhetorical stance is summed up neatly in the song's oft-repeated chorus of "Goddamn the pusher man."

As with narrative in general, the function of a protest song relies profoundly on historical and cultural context. As noted by Robinson, Pilskaln, and Hirsch (1976), protest rock (as "The Pusher" can certainly be classified) represents a particular strand of rock-and-roll that deviates from traditional lyrical concerns in popular music. Typical narratives of romantic pursuits or imperatives to dance are discarded for lyrical concern over politics, business practices, and, of course, drug use. Such deviation is not just indicative of personal habits or thought processes, but rather serves as a cultural indicator of the burgeoning youth culture of the 1960s. This is particularly true for "The Pusher," which (as stated above) was written in 1963. Viewed as part of this cultural development, "the relation between popular music and drugs thus appears as part of a larger network of shared attitudes and behavior, of which a key element was an openness and willingness to explore new ways of looking at the world" (Robinson, Pilskaln, and Hirsch, 1976: 134). As the authoritarian attitude of the 1950s abated, protest rock was one of the first cultural indicators of this openness by highlighting (as noted by Shapiro, 1988) that the issue of drugs in society invariably rests on the control of money within the drug trade *and* the cultural significance of drugs for users of such substances. Therein lies the contextual basis for the fundamental distinctions embedded in the narrative of "The Pusher"—the distinction between drug dealers and drug pushers, and the distinction between marijuana and hard drugs—distinctions not normally considered in mainstream discourse about the role of drugs in American society.

Although the thematic concerns discussed in the preceding pages remain constant throughout all versions of "The Pusher," those by Hoyt Axton, Nina Simone, S.W.A.T., and Blind Melon differ by varying degrees from Steppenwolf's original version in the attitudinal subjective stances towards drug use/dealing they express through these themes. In order to trace the narrative genealogy of "The Pusher," each of these versions are briefly discussed in chronological order. This discussion begins with a comparison between Steppenwolf's and Hoyt Axton's versions, working from the perspective that these two versions represent different attitudinal stances engendered by the same social/historical context. Next, Nina Simone's version is examined separately because it represents a social/historical context that differs radically from any of the other versions. Finally, versions recorded by S.W.A.T. and Blind Melon are considered in comparison as a counterbalance to the comparison between versions by Steppenwolf and Hoyt Axton.

Steppenwolf and Hoyt Axton

Musically, Steppenwolf's version is a mid-tempo malaise reminiscent of hangover and comedown. Languid guitar rhythms replete with reverb and echo effects place this version firmly in the category of psychedelic rock. John Kay's vocals seem urgent yet disjointed, undergirded with the ferocity of withdrawal. The narrative voice admits to having smoked copious amounts of marijuana as well as having ingested "a lot of pills." The people in the social world inhabited by this narrative voice exist in a somnambulant despondency of addiction. Rather than accepting personal responsibility for its own addiction, the narrative identity instead blames the pusher for providing substances that the spirit cannot kill. The solution to the problem of hard drug addiction offered in this version is consistent with this shuffling of responsibility onto a scapegoat. No sense of personal responsibility is offered. Instead, the solution offered to the social issue of drug addiction is to "declare total war on the pusher man." No specific organizational or ideological solution is offered, however—just "god damn, god damn the pusher man." This stance represents the subjective reality of a drug user who has gone beyond habitual use into the rock-bottom dejection of addiction attempting to wrest some sense of resolve from an excessiveness that is as much societal or cultural as it is personal.

By the time this version was recorded, several important developments had taken place. First, psychedelic rock and other expressions of the counterculture had been transformed into a commercial ideology (Allen, 1969/1972; Gleason,

1969/1972). What had begun as an organic expression of subculture was transformed into a marketing tool aimed at a group of middle-class youth becoming aware of the reality that popular music and drugs have little to no radical significance (Frith, 1978). While the youth culture initially strove to explore alternatives to dominant American culture, "the anti-work elements of rock-as-leisure [had] been reduced from their threatening collective forms to the individual indulgences of bohemian hedonism" (208). The narrative identity of Steppenwolf's "The Pusher" is a musician residing in the self-absorbed isolation of megastardom. Such disconnection from society-at-large expresses itself in admission of personal experience with a concurrent refusal to take responsibility for the results of such behavior. This attitudinal stance embodies the typical countercultural concerns of expressivity, subjective individualism, and dissociation that lack almost completely the active analysis required for meaningful discursive resolution of problematic social conditions (Brake, 1980). By the time Hoyt Axton finally recorded "The Pusher" in 1971, the excesses of youth culture had reached a high-water mark while social engagement and political activism had receded into "hedonistic apathy" (Frith 1978: 23). Inclusion of Steppenwolf's version on the soundtrack to the film *Easy Rider* the year after its initial release further highlights this shift from youth culture to youth market, a shift whose significance was fully realized almost two decades later in the recycling of cultural forms (primarily those of the 1960s and 70s) that became a defining characteristic of 1990s youth culture.

"The Pusher" as recorded by Hoyt Axton does not deviate significantly from the lyrical content of Steppenwolf's version. The pusher is still a monster; the solution is still to kill him. There are a couple of lyrical variations, however, that present a recontextualization of the individual attitudinal stance of the narrative identity. Whereas the narrative voice of Steppenwolf's version has "popped a lot of pills," the narrative voice of Hoyt Axton's version has only "popped a couple of pills." This identity represents a stance towards drugs that can engage in self-regulatory moderation without devolving into destructive excess. It admits to smoking a lot of marijuana, but claims, "I've never touched nothing that could break my will." This further distinguishes between marijuana and hard drugs while refuting the dominant argument that marijuana is a gateway drug. This narrative identity is perfectly capable of engaging in recreational marijuana use without feeling the urge to ingest harder substances. While addicts still walk around "with tombstones in their eyes," the narrative identity does not share in their subjective reality, providing distance between itself and those who succumbed to the hedonistic excess of the 1960s by noting, "If they don't quit their hard stuff, you know they're gonna die." Whereas the narrative voice in Steppenwolf's version relocates blame for addiction onto the pusher, that of Hoyt Axton's version injects a sense of personal accountability into the discourse by showing that a mature and moderate individual is perfectly capable of using marijuana responsibly. Musically, Hoyt Axton's version further enhances this distance. It is mid-tempo with a honky-tonk rock-and-roll groove that indicates an identity that, while witnessing the destruction of those around it, remains untouched, remains alive and vital. Such a stance counters not only the dominant cultural notion that all drugs are inherently destructive, but also the countercultural push toward excessive indulgence.

Nina Simone

Of all the versions of "The Pusher," Nina Simone's best exemplifies the potential of a song, through recontextualization, to engage in direct confrontation between individual or group identity and the dominant culture that is responsible for that identity's attitudinal stance—without significantly altering the original text. Here, the issue of drug use/dealing is completely divorced from the social context of 1960s youth culture and placed firmly within the struggle of black Americans to thrive in a society that consistently, systematically, and institutionally works towards their exclusion. This recontextualization is first made apparent by the version's musical structure. Although following the same chord progression and melody of the original, Simone's rendition of "The Pusher" utilizes the instrumentation, vocal style, and rhythmic patterns of rhythm-and-blues. This is significant because, as noted by Denisoff (1983), rhythm-and-blues has always contained elements of covert protest—providing an escape from harsh social conditions while concurrently "underlin[ing] the inflexible station of caste" (143) that exists for many black Americans within this society.

In terms of lyrical content, Simone's version remains a fairly strict interpretation of the original. As with Axton's version, however, there exist minor variations, the presence of which provides the discursive space for a new and radically different context. The narrative identity of Steppenwolf's version renounces claims of personal responsibility by acknowledging that its spirit is incapable of defeating the substances that the body ingests. With Simone's version, however, the narrative identity proclaims, "I never did touch nothin' that my spirit *couldn't* kill" [emphasis added]. Even though it has ingested a considerable amount of marijuana and pills, Simone's narrative identity voices a sense of responsibility by avoiding the hard drugs that more readily lead to addiction. The problem of addiction still exists, however, within the community of which the narrative identity is a member. Whereas the addicts of Steppenwolf's version are the products of hedonistic excess, the "people walkin' 'round *here* [Simone's variation indicates the specificity of urban black communities] with tombstones in their eyes" have been victimized by a dominant culture that is embodied in the character of the drug pusher. Simone consistently places the location of the narrative in a specific community by use of vocal interjections (e.g. the "here" emphasized above) that personalize as well as contextualize the problem. Besides being vocal affects typical of rhythm-and-blues, these interjections serve a number of purposes. Use of the imperative "hear me" represents a call-to-action for black communities to "declare total war on the pusher man." The phrase "the pusher don't care, *child*, if you live or if you die" [emphasis added] represents the voice of experience attempting to offer guidance to younger, more impressionable members of the community. Simone's narrative identity even acknowledges the social benefits of marijuana use by affirming that although the "pusher is a monster, good god," the dealer serves a purpose for the community because "lord knows we need lots of sweet dreams" to help make sense of the marginalized position of black communities within American society.

Such an analysis is consistent with Simone's background in radical activism, as detailed by Feldstein (2005)—an activism intensely and self-consciously "associated with the end of a beloved community and failure" (1350) to assert a meaningful identity within the dominant culture. Although Simone's version of "The Pusher" was released in 1974, Simone's use of songs as weapons to combat the racism embedded in American society stretches back to the late 1950s. As part of a cohort of influential artists that included Odetta, Cicely Tyson, Lorraine Hansbury, and Abby Lincoln, Simone expressed a "vision of black cultural nationalism... that insisted on female power—well before the apparent ascendance of black power or second-wave feminism" (1352). This attitudinal stance opposed not only the dominant culture of American society, but also the predominant attitudes of the comparatively mainstream civil rights movement. Simone operated within the vanguard of "activist cultural producers" (1352) that represented a more urban, confrontational, and commercially viable response to the dominant culture than did the gradualist, non-violent, church-based tactics employed by the civil rights movement. Simone's background in nonconventional radical activism thus represents the *personal* context out of which arose the political analysis provided by this version of "The Pusher." In order to more fully understand this, however, it becomes necessary to address the *societal* context out of which Simone's narrative identity developed—particularly in its stance towards drugs.

Shapiro (1988) recounts the history of drugs in relation to black communities in America—a history largely determined by interference into these communities by a predominantly white society. In addition to the connections between popular music and drugs described in previous sections, such interference can be traced back to plantation owners maintaining supplies of cocaine for the purposes of controlling slave populations. Out of this situation developed a relationship between drugs, black communities, and American society in which the dominant white culture is responsible for pushing drugs in black communities while at the same time producing cultural representations of drug-crazed black men. These stereotypes inculcated in white society a profound fear of the black male population. By the time Nina Simone released "The Pusher" in 1974, hard drugs (particularly heroin and cocaine) had produced an epidemic in predominantly black urban communities. Concurrently, drug legislation implemented by the white power structure ensured that these communities were further destroyed by the incarceration of black males convicted of using such substances. When considered in light of the claims by a number of spokespeople for the black nationalist movement that the United States government intentionally flooded urban black communities with hard drugs in order to neutralize their revolutionary potential, the social context out of which Simone's version arose becomes clearer. To further compound the situation, the connection between black communities and drugs was solidified in the social consciousness by the success of blaxploitation films such as *Superfly* (released in 1972), which often presented drug dealing as a viable option for escaping the poverty and oppression experienced by a marginalized black population (Shapiro, 1988).

The relationship between drugs, black communities, and dominant culture is, admittedly, far more complex than presented here. The preceding paragraph is in no way intended to stand as an absolute objective statement on the history of race and drugs in America. It is instead intended to point to certain developments within American society that directly contributed to the narrative identity expressed in Nina Simone's version of "The Pusher," and illustrate how the interrelation between personal and social context provides a discursive space for the creation and assertion of identity in response to dominant culture. Additionally, it is intended to illustrate the potential of cover songs to provide a narrative genealogy of how individuals make sense of social issues. In the hands of Nina Simone, "The Pusher" ceases to be a lament on the excesses of middle-class youth in the pursuit of leisure. It becomes instead a battle cry for the empowerment of black communities led by a strong female presence.

S.W.A.T. and Blind Melon

Twenty years passed between the release of Nina Simone's cover of "The Pusher" and that of the two versions discussed in the following section.[2] Any attempt to explain such a time lapse would be pure conjecture. However, certain changes within American society during this time can account for the resurgence in cultural relevance of this song. First, the 1980s brought with it a backlash against the drug culture of the 1960s and 1970s. This backlash was characterized by a return to the view dominant in the 1950s that drugs are (completely, inherently, and without exception) a social ill. This perception of drugs became culturally manifest most explicitly in the War on Drugs inaugurated by the Reagan administration, expanded during the presidency of George H.W. Bush, and continuing through to the present (Diamond, Bermudez, and Schensul, 2006). Second, groups such as Parents' Music Resource Center set out on a crusade to protect American society from the supposed negative influence of popular music upon the behaviors and attitudes of youth (Markert, 2001). Both of these factors are indicative of the resurgence of religious fundamentalism during the 1980s—a point that is crucial to understanding the narrative identity expressed in Blind Melon's version of "The Pusher." Third, a cultural condition referred to by Plasketes (2005: 138) as "The Cover Age" emerged during this time. This condition became characterized by the rediscovery and appropriation of older cultural trends by American youth in the late 1980s and 1990s. This youth market gravitated most heavily towards the behaviors, styles, and music of youth culture from the 1960s and 1970s. Not

---

[2]   Other versions of "The Pusher" may have been recorded between 1974 and 1994, but as of the writing of this chapter, none could be identified or located.

surprisingly, these cultural developments created a context in which drug use once again became a central thematic concern of popular song.

In 1994, S.W.A.T. released their version of "The Pusher." Musically, this version is a fairly strict interpretation of the original. Narratively, however, a vastly divergent identity is expressed. The opening lines are altered to "You know I've had a few gin rickeys in my time. Oh yes, I've had a sedative or two." These lines are spoken in the stereotyped voice of an upstanding law enforcement officer of the 1950s, placing this version of "The Pusher" in the category of what Bailey (2003) refers to as an "ironic cover," one which includes elements of ridicule as well as validation in a "process of creating dissonance" (141) between two discursive formations. The narrative identity of the original version (i.e. a habitual drug user or addict) is replaced by a voice from within the dominant culture— one who has never taken illicit drugs and wholeheartedly disapproves of drug use and dealing. Besides the lyrical variation described above, most of the lyrics remain faithful to the original version. Between the verses and chorus of the song, however, another narrative emerges—a comedic sketch of two drug pushers (one Mexican, one black) interacting with potential clients on a street corner.

As with the main narrative identity expressed in the song's lyrics, these two voices represent stereotypes of particular communities within American society. The Mexican drug dealer claims, "I'll get you high 'til the day you die, 'cause I'm so fly," in attempts to sell "cheeba," amphetamine, and crack cocaine. Exasperated with their potential clients, the black drug dealer exclaims, "I ain't got time, white boy. Go back to the suburbs." The sketch ends with police officers violently arresting and incarcerating the two pushers. In the War on Drugs, mandatory minimum sentencing is the ultimate way to damn the pusher man. What is interesting about S.W.A.T.'s version of "The Pusher" is how it expresses racial stereotypes that have always been embedded within dominant cultural perceptions regarding drugs. Shapiro (1988) notes that even in the beginning stages of social concern about drug use in America, Mexicans were demonized as the group responsible for marijuana, black males were demonized as cocaine fiends, and white youth were viewed as being endangered by both. By including this sketch with the original lyrical content of "The Pusher," S.W.A.T. places these old stereotypes within the context of postmodern America. The narrative identity expressed by this version of "The Pusher" rekindles the latent racism that has always plagued dominant cultural attitudes regarding drugs while at the same time reinforcing Shapiro's (1988) assertion that drug "laws were enacted as demonstrations against particular user groups, their lifestyles and the threat they allegedly posed to white society" (24).

Although recorded in the same year as S.W.A.T.'s version, Blind Melon's cover of "The Pusher" was not released until 1996. In terms of lyrical content, this version presents the greatest amount of variation from the original. There still remains a personal admission of drug use in regards to both marijuana and hard drugs. The narrative identity in Blind Melon's version, however, is proud of such use, rejecting any form of stigma for such behavior. Any references to declaring war on or killing the drug pusher are eliminated, replaced with an almost farcical verse about having groceries delivered at 4:30am. Such rewording serves in a capacity to subvert the original song through irreverence (Weinstein, 1998). This irreverence is further reinforced by the lyrics immediately following the reference to being cold and hungry in the early morning: "I'm oh so tired of you pushing that thorny crown down onto my head so hard, my knees are two inches in the ground." Although the narrative identity shares with the original an admission that it "walks around with tombstones" in its eyes, this voice places no blame on the drug pusher. Drug use is characterized as a personal choice, and the real culprit behind the death of the soul is made explicit in the reworked chorus: "god damn that Bible pushin' man." Such an attitudinal stance expresses the belief that neither drug use nor drug dealing are social issues, but rather a matter of personal leisure and experimentation. This narrative identity identifies religious fundamentalists as the actual source of division in society because, as noted by Shapiro (1988), "whatever the parts played by medical self-aggrandizement, international diplomacy and genuine concern about public health, *social disapproval* was central to the banning of recreational drug use" (24). In America in the 1980s and 1990s, the religious right played a significant role in the social disapproval of recreational drug use.

Beyond expressing a reaction against the resurgence of religious fundamentalism and authoritarian responses to drug use, Blind Melon's version of "The Pusher" also marks the return of attitudinal subjectivity characteristic of 1960s youth culture, but in a form infected with the materialism characteristic of the 1980s—bohemianism translated into commercial ideology. Viewed from this perspective, it is interesting to note that Blind Melon was one of the bands to perform at the Woodstock repeat of 1994. In addition to music and fashion, 1990s youth culture also appropriated an attitudinal stance towards drugs characteristic of the 1960s. Resurgence of drug use was particularly pronounced among musicians, a fact that may be explained in part by Chesky, Hipple, and Ho's (1999) assertion that musicians (particularly males) are at increased risk for drug addiction "if they believe there is a base of working musicians who currently use drugs" (8). Many of the rock-and-roll musicians of the 1960s and 70s idolized by musicians in the 1990s were notorious for their drug consumption. Keith Richards, Jimmy Page, Eric Clapton, Lou Reed, and Jerry Garcia all used/abused heroin—a drug that had considerable influence on music in the 1990s.

As noted by Colapinto (1996, May 30) and DeRogatis (1995, November 30), heroin's popularity resurged with a vengeance among young musicians active in the late 1980s and 1990s. This drug claimed the lives of Hillel Slovak of the Red Hot Chili Peppers, Bob Stinson of the Replacements, Skinny Puppy's Dwayne Goettel, Layne Staley of Alice in Chains, and Hole's Kristin Pfaff. Scott Weiland of Stone Temple Pilots, the Breeders' Kelly Deal, Kurt Cobain of Nirvana, and Blind Melon's Shannon Hoon all struggled with heroin addiction. Hoon in particular had been forced into rehab twice for heroin abuse before his death of a cocaine overdose in New Orleans on October 21, 1995 (DeRogatis, 1995, November 30). Blind Melon's version of "The Pusher" was released after Hoon's death, serving as a macabre reminder not only of the destructive potential of hedonistic excess,

Chapter 6

David Bowie's *Pin-Ups*: Past as Prelude

Stuart Lenig

I very rarely have felt like a rock artist. I don't think that's much of a vocation, being a rock-and-roller.

—Ferris, 1972: 94

David Bowie's enigmatic approach to rock was to restart it in the middle. He decided he would rechristen rock/pop with a new guise known as glam, an acidic, campy, glittery, superficial approach to rock tropes and clichés. Bowie saw nothing unusual in this, since like his mentor, pop artist, Andy Warhol, he perceived art as a series of superficial poses, guises to be adopted or dispensed with at will. He said, "I feel like an actor when I'm on stage, rather than a rock artist" (Ferris, 94). Warhol was a good place to start. The Prince of Pop looked at the sixties as a time of superficiality. He chose subjects, Marilyn, Elvis, or comic strips for their surface qualities rather than any depth. He said, "during the 1960s, people forgot what emotions were supposed to be. And I don't think they ever remembered" (Warhol, 1975: 27). For Warhol, film with its flat images and pop stars with their vacant faces and manufactured images were the ultimate art.

Like Warhol, Bowie sought the secret to surfaces in sixties culture, territory he knew from his own struggle. Bowie had spent ten years in the pop wasteland trying on different guises in an endless and fruitless bid for fame. When he achieved it, he revisited his roots in an album called *Pin-Ups*, a tribute to the bands of mod, mid-sixties Britain. But he wasn't content with looking back, he also wanted to recreate the past in his new image, the guise of glam rocker, a strutting peacock, the ultimate image *sans* content. Glam was Bowie's vehicle for producing fame and for creating a style of rock that emphasized look, image, and glitz over depth. Through the device of *glam*, Bowie could make musical styles serve his career and shed them just as quickly. *Pin-Ups*, was just such an experiment in style, and Bowie used it to illustrate the commonality between sixties pop art transparency and seventies superstars adorned in rhinestone costumes and glitter make-up. For Bowie the juncture was clear, but for others it was a puzzling grafting of glam sensibilities onto the venerable mod movement of the sixties.

Bowie's approach was complicated. *Pin-Ups* had a variety of meanings, and his esoteric strategy to the cover song puzzled critics. Usually, covers fall into three categories. First they exist as a monument or tribute to the past and prime innovators, like Lennon playing Elvis songs in *Rock and Roll*. They are a form of homage.

Second, they restate influences, reference images, and make explicit connections between artistic generations, like Oasis quoting The Beatles in "Wonderwall." Beyond paying homage, these artists acknowledge their progenitors. Finally, at its most creative, the cover song re-creates reality, it's a reworking of the material to produce a new product, a synthetic reconstruction of the past, such as Moby's retreaded samples. In this way, covers can be both past and prelude, both original and reactionary. At its heart, rock and roll, is a continuing cover project, reuniting blues, bluegrass, euro-art song, and pop elements into endless combinations and new styles of American popular music.

Bowie's Objectives: Influences, Images, Rewrites

First, *Pin-Ups* is a statement of influences. Bowie was clearly a fan of the recent past and before his twentieth birthday was plowing the pop-rock trade in a succession of bands and solo configurations striving for the magic combination that would make him a star. Stardom eluded the young musician for a long time and his significant apprenticeship made him acutely aware of how time and tide influenced musical tastes, casting marginal performers into the limelight and casting aside some other very deserving bands. Bowie wrote, in the linear notes to *Pin-Ups*, "these songs are among my favorites from the 64–67 period of London. Most of the groups were playing the ricky-tok (was it a 'y' or an 'i') scene club circuit." Bowie had been there and seen the wreckage and felt a need to do something, to say something about the previous sixties British pop. Indeed, Bowie thought it might all fade away. A year before the breakthrough of Pink Floyd's *Dark Side of the Moon*, and some twenty years before Van Morrison's canonization as the master of celtic soul style, Bowie worried that this vital sixties music of his youth could be lost. Fortunately Bowie and his mentors were survivors.

As influences, the artists of the era provided various templates for Bowie's own work crafting the glam style. Each artist in their own way gave Bowie ideas that he reworked for his own distinctive seventies form. First, there was the idea of self-ridicule and self-deprecation through the jaundiced eyes of camp. Susan Sontag described the form, saying, "to perceive camp in objects and persons, is to understand 'Being as Playing a Role.' It is the farthest extension, in sensibility, of the metaphor of life as theatre" (Sontag, 1982: 109). Bowie's idea was to theatricalize rock, and make it self conscious, but that idea had already been planted in the 1960s. The Kinks were the decade's masters of the droll send up, and Bowie strategically reanimated these hard rocking wits with Ray Davies' opus, "Where Have All the Good times Gone?" This joking reference to introspection and questioning the partying rock lifestyle contains typical Ray Davies mockery. ("Wondering if I'd done wrong, will this depression last too long?") *Camp* as Susan Sontag pointed out was a rarified style that depended on the awareness of performer and audience to be in on the same joke. She wrote, "the whole point of Camp is to dethrone the serious. Camp is playful, anti-serious" (Sontag, 116). Bowie shared Davies' understated horror at pop stardom because they had both endured it.

Another key influence was Bowie's fixation on acid rock, a strongly hallucinogenic, drug-inspired, form that preached a sort of zen spirituality. Think John Lennon's "Tomorrow Never Knows," as a cornerstone of pop/ acid/asceticism. Acid rockers merged august insights and lush soundscapes of ambience and atmosphere. Bowie absorbed that sixties exoticism blending sharp cutting guitar sounds, (forged with helpmate and music director, Mick Ronson) strings, exotic instrumentation, musique concrete, and a healthy mixture of sound effects into a potent brew. Bowie borrowed The Yardbirds corrosive "I Wish You Would," and "Shapes of Things," and assumed Pink Floyd's psychedelic 'See Emily Play," a cornucopia of canivalesque whimsy and menace, and one of their earliest singles. This robust acid rock left an imprint on Bowie. The Yardbirds were the most experimental blues band featuring the great triumvirate of guitarists Clapton, Beck, and Page. Syd Barrett's Pink Floyd were cosmic troubadours under the tutelage of a manic poetic. These songs offered strange tonalities, exotic riffs, and an incandescent energy proving that psychedelic rock was still vital.

But as a young Sixties mod, Bowie was often perceived as a pop crooner, not a rocker. His initial record company, Deram, tried to sell him as a young Anthony Newley or Frank Sinatra, and that aspect of Bowie's early career appears in his rendition of The Mersey's "Sorrow." Here Bowie's masterly plaintive vocal, low key arrangement, charming sax solo, crisp string arrangement, reverb guitar, and theatrical fade out focus the entire *Pin-Ups* project. Here mod and glam sensibilities merge seamlessly, suggesting that glam was merely an extension of the previous ten years.

Bowie layered mod with the incipient heavy metal movement that debuted in the sixties but had become mainstream in the seventies. Bowie attacked the The Pretty Things "Rosalyn" and "Don't Bring me Down." As screaming rockers, "Rosalyn's" slurred acerbic vocals and reverb fuzz guitar produced a flaming rave-up, and "Don't Bring me Down," combined staccato rhythms with Elvis swagger as Bowie warbled, "I'm On My Own, Nowhere to Roam." He nailed the surly punk aspect of songs with just enough satiric bite to suggest a note of parody. By now, The Spiders from Mars had become a very tight little rock ensemble, and *Pin-Ups* was the band's swan song. Here Bowie's over the top vocals make them every inch the Sixties mod band.

Bowie's idea of poses, and his stylist approach from the mods, the most important style group in the 1960s was significant. Nicholas Schaffner said that, "for the Mods, style was substance; image was everything" (1983: 115). The Mods stylized codes dictated clothing, hair style, and attitude to everyone from the Beatles to the ultimate mod band, the Who. Bowie's version of The Who's "Anyway, Anyhow, Anywhere" acts both as a manifesto of the Mods and the Glams. "I can go anyway, I live anyhow, I can go anywhere." Bowie's arrogant defiance and insolence gives a blistering attack to the material. Even more cathartic is Bowie and the Spiders' approach to "I Can't Explain," another Who mod anthem expressing that rebellion is about *the act of rebellion*; it doesn't have to mean anything. Bowie and the band tackle the song at half speed milking the rough metal side of the track. This time Bowie whispers, hisses, and insinuates the lines, "A new feeling inside, it's a hot certain kind, I feel hot and cold, down my soul, baby." The heavy beat, Bowie's tortured vocals, Ronson's ripping guitar, and Bowie's soulful sax mark this as two minutes and seven seconds of threat and menace.

Together, *Pin-Ups* melds camp, acid pop, crooner, hard rock and mod influences as a codex to Bowie's glam style. All the dark visual elements are embedded in these mod tunes marking mod as the wicked bastard father of glam. Glam suffered with identity problems because Americans hadn't experienced Mod, they didn't know how to decode glam. *Pin-Ups* provided that missing secret code that defined and identified Bowie.

But *Pin-Ups* operated in a visual sense, conjuring 1960s images that Bowie wished to appropriate. The title, "Pin-Ups," is tongue in cheek. All the album's 1960s groups were immaculately tailored—The Yardbirds, The Who, and The Floyd were fashion trend setters. *Pin-Ups* meant there were visual codes to the era as well as sonic ones. Twiggy shared the cover with Bowie, and remained one of the principle icons of the era—a model, a beauty, slightly vapid, and totally androgynous. Visually, the Mods already were a transgender movement; boys as pretty as girls; girls as curve-less as boys, and styles that could adorn either sex. It's as if *Pin-Ups* re-hung all of Bowie's Mod posters from the sixties. The album operates as a collective of media images that existed in Bowie's mind as the exciting sixties scene, a mental *Hard Day's Night* as psychic template. Bowie seems to be saying that the attractively costumed images of the model thin sixties pop stars were simply a prelude to his glam revolution. This ties Bowie to some messianic image of himself as uber-rock star, the fruition of the Elvis dream turned on its head and trans-gendered. By the mid-seventies, even Elvis, the ultimate hetero-rocker had embraced the trappings of glam, glitter, styled hair, tasseled costumes, and sparkly jump suits.

But finally, *Pin-Ups* isn't just a series of influences, a portrait of digestible media images, it also functions as a transformative album. Bowie is rewriting the 1960s in terms of the seventies glam culture that he helped to create. By recalling his influences, arranging his media images, Bowie reorganizes the media world in his own terms. In a way Bowie rewrites rock history re-categorizing sixties items of import. He re-prioritizes British pop away from the Beatles/Stones axis towards a more eclectic set of identity codes and influences that focus on Bowie's core concerns of style and image.

Pin-Ups Critical Reception

Pin-Ups received a lackluster reception. Cover albums were rampant in the early seventies. During that time, Bryan Ferry, Bette Midler, Manhattan Transfer, the Band, Bob Dylan, Don McLean, were all engaged in cover projects. Television like *Happy Days*, plays like *Grease*, and films like *American Graffiti* celebrated a culture of past worship. Musicians were confused in the post-Beatle period as they were desperate to evaluate where they had been and where they were going. The music business was in a state of shock, genres were all over the map, there was no single coherent trend or band, and cover albums were likely to at least rally some sales in a precarious and uncertain market.

Bowie puzzled the critics and the public. For one thing, he chose music less than ten years old. These were hardly oldies, let alone classics, so why bother to revive them? No one really understood Bowie's idea. They knew he was a prolific songwriter who worked frantically and was releasing albums at a rate of two per year. People asked: "why a cover album?" The response seemed to be a disinterested, ho-hum attitude. Most people still felt they remembered the originals, at least in England. The situation was different in the US where Australian imports, The Easy Beats ("Friday on my Mind") were little known, and bands like The Merseys ("Sorrow") had hardly made a dent on American audiences. For the most part, many of these songs received a virgin hearing in the States through *Pin-Ups*. At a basic level, Bowie's *Pin-Ups* was a crash course in British pop/mod culture of the last ten years, and it was significant for Americans who were unaware of Britain's youth sub-cultures. Unfortunately, particularly in the American press, the album was ignored in between bigger Bowie releases (*Aladdin Sane* and *Diamond Dogs*). Others dismissed it, and almost no one critically analyzed it as a real aesthetic project.

Reviews criticized every aspect of the work. Greg Shaw for *Rolling Stone* suggested that the original songs were offhand pop trash, but then, he turned to criticizing Bowie's vocals for not equaling the material. 'Bowie's vocals float carelessly above the music, and his excessively mannered voice is a ridiculously weak mismatch for the material" (1973). Even the partisan, MOJO Magazine wrote that "most of his tributes to 1960s British beat boom were faintly embarrassing" (Du Noyer, 2002: 80). Shaw wrote that "none stand up to the originals." Again since most American audiences had never even heard of these tracks, it seemed a moot point to mock them as less than the originals. The fact that they were taken from the period of 1964–67 prompted some people to dub Bowie's effort "instant nostalgia." If the tracks were so recent and not ready for such reverence than could Bowie's efforts commit a sacrilege on them? Such was the trend of media in the seventies. Everything was moving faster and the recycling of pop culture was accelerating. Christopher Sandford, author of *Bowie, Loving the Alien*, was more upbeat and said, "*Pin-Ups* celebrated Bowie's reason for being: raw sometimes mawkish R & B with few overdubs or edits and even fewer stylistic departures." (Sandford, 1997: 115). Probably most of the people listening were missing Bowie's deeper purpose, that is, to focus on and capitalize on those 1960s influences in some meaningful way. In the *Music Scene*, "R.G." wrote that Bowie had a "total lack of sympathy for the songs" (1973). What the artist was after was elusive to critics, but he came close to explaining himself in a 1974 joint interview with writer, William S. Burroughs. Bowie said, "a song has to take on character, shape, body and influence people to an extent that they use it for their own devices" (Copetas, 1974: 109). That is a key to his songs on *Pin- Ups*. These tracks were so influential to Bowie that they spurred his own work, and the similarity of Bowie's work to the originals serves to illustrate that in many ways, glam existed as simply a hyperbolic form of sixties mod pop. In much the same way postmodernism often merely extends and expands the experiments of modernism. To Bowie, the *Pin-Ups* experiment was about re-purposing the music. The only reviewer who appeared to grasp Bowie's underlying concept was Bruce Eder for the *All Music Guide*. With the benefit of years of hindsight, Eder wrote, "*Pin-Ups* was an artistic statement, of sorts, with some thought behind it, rather than just a quick album of oldies covers to buy some time, as it was often dismissed as being" (Eder, 2008).

Other artists were annoyed with the record. Sandford reports that Bryan Ferry who was working on the nostalgia drenched *These Foolish Things* felt that Bowie was just cashing in on a craze and demanded his record company take action against Bowie. In the end, both Bowie's and Ferry's albums were released on the same day.

In his text *Bowie, Changes*, Stuart Hoggard argues this is the music Bowie wished he had had a chance to perform in the 1960s. He called it, "a complete departure from the star seeking Ziggy image which Bowie had created out of nowhere to take himself beyond the mediocre straitjacket Decca had pushed him into in the sixties" (Hoggard, 1980: 38), Sadly, many saw the album as simply a personal remembrance by a new star, and not particularly meaningful. Bowie not only viewed it as a way to rekindle his influences, but as a respite from the work of topping his last achievement in a flurry of albums that had raised expectations on each new release. For Bowie, *Pin-Ups* was, at least partially, a relaxing look back.

Certainly, accounts of the recording suggest an intellectual sabbatical and a vacation spirit. Bowie boarded a train at Victoria Station and crossed to Paris to record the album at the Chateau d'Herouville. There, Bowie and the band recorded and lived together for the month of July. While there, Bowie and the Spiders also recorded British pop singer, Lulu (famous in America for the tune, "To Sir, With Love") who assailed two Bowie tunes, "The Man Who Sold the World," and "Watch that Man." By the end of the month, Bowie, his wife, and son had left to vacation in Rome. The album had been mostly completed. By all accounts it was a pleasant and idyllic period.

Later Aesthetic Reception of *Pin-Ups*

But as a series of cover songs, *Pin-Ups* meaning has continued to grow as the 1960s pop canon has gained importance. Horne and Frith's *Art into Pop* suggested that much of the British pop of the sixties was a direct result of the collision of pop art ideologies imbedded in young artists at art and design technical colleges and the impetus to produce a new form of art through pop music. Horne and Frith wrote, "media practice was… modernized art practice, dissolving the work/leisure distinction: there were no Positions Vacant columns in the underground press" (Frith/Horne, 55). Artists like Bowie would simply take the ideas of the early twentieth-century avant-garde artists and apply these notions to the topical world of pop music. They perceived no difference in their use of mediums. They were artists working in pop culture. Whether it was music or art made no difference to them. For Bowie and artists like him, the objectives of pop art and pop music was similar, to explore new and popular culture territory.

The same impetus to fuse art and music practice also served to make *Pin Ups* an early example of postmodern tendencies to collage eras, negate histories, reinvent the past, and refashion previous consumer products to conform to current aesthetic needs. Bowie wasn't satisfied to simply restage the past, Bowie wished to recreate it in light of what came afterwards. In this regard, glam was a very postmodern phenomenon wishing to combine different styles. Throughout *Pin-Ups*, Bowie applies various stylistic forms to sixties material. His take of Them's "Here Comes the Night" combines Bowie's crooning falsetto with the original's soulful rock. Bowie's version of "Sorrow" laces the sixties tune with strings and a pop undercurrent that links it to seventies glam ballads. Bowie's version of "See Emily Play" mixes the surreal psychedelics of Floyd's original with Bowie's more progressive rock inclinations. Everywhere Bowie is mixing the seventies hard rock style of the Spiders with the various lighter forms of sixties pop. In a way, he remakes the sixties into songs that sound appropriate for seventies glam. Despite his auditory surgery on the tunes, his fans demanded Bowie play in a style that conformed to glam aesthetics, and sadly much of the material from *Pin-Ups* went unperformed during the era. The last appearance with Mick Ronson and the Spiders was the Midnight Special segment Bowie produced on October 18–20, 1973. Bowie in transition to a new phase and at work on the *Diamond Dogs* project quickly called back the Spiders for a brief weekend gig at the Marquee Club in London. The show was jokingly called, "the 1980 Floor Show," a pun on *1984*. He had wanted to do a musical revue based on Orwell's 1984, but he could not secure the rights to the property from Orwell's widow. There in this venerable old dance hall of the British invasion bands, Bowie and the band blasted through "Sorrow," "Can't Explain," and "Everything's Alright." Sadly, the rarely seen *1980 Floor Show* stands as Bowie's most complete statement of a glam musical revue performance genre. But after that performance, Bowie's *Pin-Ups* picks rarely appeared in his live performances. They had done their work, reviving his personal muse and connecting him to his aesthetic childhood. In this way Bowie both embraced and rejected history, arguing that to some extent, what was in the past was just as effective in the present.

Finally, *Pin-Ups* can be seen as Bowie's prelude to punk. When punk broke out, Bowie was detoxing in Berlin, and producing his late seventies trio of albums, *Low, Heroes* and *Lodger*. *Pin-Ups* was played rough and fast, and allowed Bowie and the band to express their rock roots. *Rolling Stone* critiqued the album as under produced, but part of Bowie's plan was to produce a raw album with a minimum of overdubs. The rough and aggressive playing spoke to Bowie's desire to play at a more elemental level. Not only Bowie, but the punks themselves were strongly influenced by the aggressive playing of the British invasion bands. By 1975, The Sex Pistols and Elvis Costello were seeking to recapture that Brit pop spirit, only Bowie started the movement towards such elemental simplicity and rage two years earlier.

Pin-Ups as Reinvention

Pin-Ups, despite its confused initial reception, has served as a model for reinventing an era. First, Bowie wanted to comment on what were the key areas of British pop and how that energy, enthusiasm, and spirit had been lost by the leaden beat of heavy metal, the baroque excesses of progressive music, and the trivial banality of the new pop. Bowie wanted a return to freshness, spontaneity, and a cultural vigor that seemed mired in excesses of technical splendor at the expense of innovation.

Bowie also used *Pin-Ups* as a goodbye to one era (Ziggy and the Spiders from Mars) and as a signal of changing directions. In particular, the dark tonalities of "See Emily Play," the piano glissandos of Mike Garson, the slowed thundering power of "I Can't Explain," and the spacey mellotron ambience of Bowie's version of "Shapes of Things" signaled a change to darker and more disturbing messages. These tracks reflected Bowie's interest in a grim science fiction-influenced sound that led him to pursue the idea of a *1984*-themed stage production (abandoned), and a post-apocalyptic dystopia album (*Diamond Dogs*).

Yet at the same time *Pin-Ups* established the flip side of Bowie's personality, at once dark and foreboding, and yet on the surface bristling with light, enjoyable, pop tonalities. The lighter aspects of *Pin-Ups*, "I Wish You Would," "Sorrow," and "Everything's Alright," predicted the happier post-*Diamond Dogs* sound of *Young Americans* and *Station To Station*. In a way, *Pin-Ups* predated two Bowie evolutionary steps, one from band to soloist, and another from Eurocentric to a more American-centric sound.

Meaning in *Pin-Ups*: Beyond the Music

Bowie was the epitome of the successful rock artist in the early seventies, but he was also miserably aware of the vile aspects of the music business. He had suffered a succession of bad managers and poor dealings with record companies. In a way, *Pin-Ups* was Bowie's revenge on the industry, placing musical values and music that was important over the marketing men who proclaimed what were hits and what were unimportant records. *Pin-Ups* also addressed that issue of a commoditized record buying public. If a buying audience could be manipulated to buy mass produced product, Bowie assumed they could retrained to recognize quality. In a way, *Pin-Ups* served as a surrogate fan's perspective of what was really essential and sought to overwrite the official record of what was great music of the mod era. In essence it was revisionist mod history.

Bowie predated the democratizing influence of the web by several decades. His act of revolt was necessary. He was commenting on the complacency and dullness of music in the mid-seventies. He suggested that by selecting an uplifting series of songs from an earlier era that music need not be so limited or co-opted. Bowie was suggesting that music had more to offer than the trivial (Abba), soft rock (James Taylor), or heavy metal (Deep Purple). Bowie commented to *MOJO Magazine* on his aspirations at the time. "You have to kill your elders. We had to develop a completely new vocabulary, as indeed is done generation after generation" (Du Noyer, 80). Sadly demographics predominated media in the seventies slicing markets into neat groups. This helped savvy marketers segment the populace carving the audience into ever smaller consumer niches. Bowie was keenly aware of this cultural merchandising even at an early age, and he told Charles Shaar Murrey for the *NME* in 1973 (while recording *Pin-Ups*) that, "I knew being a mod meant that I had to wear clothes that no one else was wearing" (Cann, 1984: 115). He understood the codes of fashion. To Bowie, the *Pin-Ups* experiment was about re-purposing the music. Bowie was looking to restore the musical gestalt of the sixties and reverse the fragmentation that was demanded by the business. He was seeking a glam consensus and accommodation with sixties pop. He saw intrinsic links and commonalities between the two forms that he wished to make explicit through *Pin-Ups*.

This bridging of barriers of time marks Bowie as working in a postmodern mode deconstructing indicators of time. For Bowie, time, like style, required elasticity. Remember Bowie's early model was Warhol who appropriated time, image, and style and repurposed them to his own agenda. Bowie sought something similar. He said, "my key 'in' was things like *Clockwork Orange*, that was *our* world, not the bloody hippy thing" (Du Noyer, 2002: 80). Bowie literally reworked his material to fit the style of glam and felt that glam could be a universal style that could carry this older material to a present day audience. Bowie saw a unification of pop, crooner vocals, Jacques Brel art song, and hard rock rolled into a new synthesis. Bowie believed he could transform all music into a contemporary idiom. He had proven in the past year (1972) that he could take diverse sixties artists (The Velvet Underground, Mott the Hoople, Marianne Faithful, Iggy Pop, and Lulu) and transform them into viable seventies artists, why couldn't he do the same with the music of artists from the era?

Finally, Bowie the cabaret performer and artist wished to use hard rock stripped of its original context and situate it in this new theatrical setting. Bowie felt that he could redefine rock and pop saving the best of the rock music in a pop context. Bowie neatly anticipated the end of rock, the exhaustion of the form, and planned for a post rock era. In a sense he de-contextualizes the rebellion of the mods and moves the battle to the new zone of identity politics. Bowie is placing mod rebellion in the context of gender and identity politics and illustrating that these battles are both struggles against a form of conformity. It is a canny revisualization of the sixties mod rebellion and was meant as a way to refocus attention on the British music scene that had lately been eclipsed by the rise of new American pop.

In all, *Pin-Ups* is a complicated approach to the cover song as art work. Bowie in his apprenticeship to Warholian principles saw pop as simply source material, much as Warhol found the rough Velvet Underground and reshaped them to his lightshow/total theatre concept. *Pin-Ups* serves to redefine the era of the past as a proper antecedent to the glam era, and suggests a commonality between the two forms. What better way to show that common thread than by doing the older songs in the latter day style. Bowie still believes in following the Warhol aesthetic to redefine his work. This year, the *Sunday Mail* newspaper in Britain released a hand-picked compilation by Bowie, entitled, *I-Select* that included a revamped version of Bowie's greatest hits, or at least hits that Bowie now thinks are superior works from his past thirty-five years. For Bowie the act of re-selecting, literally, re-designates what is important and refocuses our attention. The idea was taking the recent past and restructuring it in a way that we felt we had authorship of (Du Noyer, 80).

LOOK WHAT THEY'VE DONE TO MY SONG: GENDER, IDENTITY, MEDIA MAKEOVERS

Chapter 7

Queering Cohen:
Cover Versions as Subversions of Identity

Erik Steinskog

In Zadie Smith's novel *On Beauty* (2005) one of the characters, Kiki, remembers how her husband Howard used to describe Leonard Cohen's song "Hallelujah" as "a hymn deconstructing a hymn." Her reflections, however, are related to a "far more beautiful 'Hallelujah' by a kid called Buckley" (173f). Here, then, are two kinds of repetition; firstly, between two versions of hymns, and secondly, between Cohen's original and Jeff Buckley's cover version.[1] There seems to be an original hymn, something akin to the secret chord, which Cohen's "Hallelujah" deconstructs. And there is also a difference, an increase in beauty, in Buckley's version. Thinking about "Hallelujah," Kiki contemplates one of Cohen's most covered songs.[2] But what if these rather loose thoughts also tell something about repetition and cover-versions? It might be that the two kinds of repetition have something in common, what Howard calls to "deconstruct."

In this article I will discuss several covers of Cohen songs, taking Liam Lunson's movie *Leonard Cohen: I'm Your Man* (2005), as well as its soundtrack album, as points of departure. Here a wide range of artists—Antony, Nick Cave, Jarvis Cocker, Beth Orton, Teddy Thompson, Martha Wainwright, Rufus Wainwright, and others—contribute.[3] Related to one of the earliest concerts in this project, "Came So Far for Beauty" (Brooklyn, June 28, 2003), Rufus Wainwright, commenting upon his cover of "Everybody Knows," stated that his intention was "to fag it [the song] up."[4] This rather campy comment simultaneously underlines dimensions of gender in the practice of cover versions. There is, I want to argue, a possible queering taking place in cover versions, a queering pointing to possible subversions of identity. And perhaps those subversions are similar to what Howard, in *On Beauty*, calls deconstruction.

---

[1]   Leonard Cohen, "Hallelujah" (*Various Positions*, 1984); Jeff Buckley, "Hallelujah" (*Grace*, 1994).

[2]   For an updated list of Cohen covers see "The Leonard Cohen Files," http://www.leonardcohenfiles.com/coverlist.php

[3]   *Leonard Cohen: I'm Your Man* (Lunson, 2005), *Leonard Cohen: I'm Your Man* (motion picture soundtrack, 2006), soundtrack produced by Hal Willner.

[4]   Cf. http://www.leonardcohenfiles.com/brooklyn.html; Cohen's original of "Everybody Knows" is found on *I'm Your Man* (1988).

The theoretical dimensions of this argument are inspired by Judith Butler's groundbreaking work in feminism and queer theory, and my subtitle is meant to evoke her book *Gender Trouble: Feminism and the Subversion of Identity* (1999). Combined with its companion volume, *Bodies That Matter: On the Discursive Limits of Sex* (1993), Butler contributed substantially in altering theories of gender, with a focus on gender as something being done, instead of something one is (or has) as a stable identity. This activity does not, she argues, imply that there is any doer behind the deed. Rather, the doer is constructed in and through the deed, and this construction is an ongoing process depending on repetition. Gender, then, is also repetition, ways discourses and practices repeat in an on-going negotiation of what used to be called identity. In these repetitions, however, there are also inbuilt possibilities of subversions. And I take this mode of thinking as comparable to how cover-versions work, as repetitions of the same but with important differences, a process questioning both the way songs are perceived and the interrelations of the different versions. Not only can cover versions become new "originals"—in the sense that they become the matrix for future covers—they may also question the presupposed "original's" originality. In this they resemble how Butler discusses gender in relation to repetition. "The replication of heterosexual constructs in non-heterosexual frames," she writes, "brings into relief the utterly constructed status of the so-called heterosexual original." Only to add that, "thus, gay is to straight *not* as copy is to original, but, rather, as copy is to copy" (1999: 41).

Such an understanding immediately makes sense in the context of Jeff Buckley's cover of "Hallelujah." His cover illustrates the relation between versions, as it is built on John Cale's cover rather than on Cohen's original. It is, that is, a second-degree cover, a cover of a cover, and thus establishes Cale's version as point of departure for several others.[5] The major difference is that whereas Cale's version is with piano-accompaniment, Buckley's being guitar-based presents another sound. In Lunson's movie, Rufus Wainwright performs the song, reinstating the piano and thus coming closer to Cale's version. This says something about how cover versions might obtain a life of their own, while simultaneously echoing Butler's description of a copy of a copy, or a copy without an original.

In his article "Anti-Orpheus: narrating the dream brother" Oliver Lovesey clearly finds this problematic. Describing Buckley's musical practices he even writes "covers" in inverted commas, pointing out something seemingly wrong in these "covers of covers" (2004: 341). In his interpretation Buckley's covers

---

[5]   John Cale's version was recorded for the tribute album *I'm Your Fan* (1991). It was also featured on the sound-track to the movie *Basquiat* (Julian Schnabel, 1996) as well as on the sound-track to the movie *Shrek* (Andrew Adamson and Vicky Jenson, 2001). On the sound-track album to *Shrek* (Universal, 2001), however, it is Rufus Wainwright performing it. Another version closely related to Cale is k.d. lang's, found on *Hymns of the 49th Parallel* (2004) thus nicely referring back to the notion of hymns.

become "postmodern pastiche," devoid of a certain "authenticity."[6] But, as Shana Goldin-Perschbacher writes, in "'Not with You But of You': 'Unbearable Intimacy' and Jeff Buckley's Transgender Vocality," this is primarily due to his standards (in Jamrmen-Ivens, 2007: 216). Her article describes how Buckley's voice, despite being the voice of a "straight" man, may seem queer to many listeners (213). The vulnerability of his voice, and him singing songs either associated with female singers—and in a high-pitched range—or from the point of view of women without changing the text, opens up for different ways of hearing his voice, not least for hearing it beyond the simplified binary gender system found within normative culture. Being on the receiving end of such a voice, as listeners, this might be uncomfortable, and might be seen as threatening to normative heterosexual manhood. This point, however, is not the whole story. There are different kinds of queering. As Stan Hawkins argues, in "On Male Queering in Mainstream Pop," male queering in pop culture is entering mainstream culture through acceptance as well as resistance (in Whiteley and Rycenga, 2007: 279). And important aspects of queer identities have already entered mainstream pop culture, making the traditional binary partly a thing of the past.

Buckley's vocal delivery contains an intimacy or private dimension, making his performances into an almost sexual encounter between singer and listener. With Buckley being understood as "a straight man who queered his gender" such an encounter opens up for the listener to question her or his understanding of identity.[7] Identification with the person he is singing to seem inevitable, primarily due to the intimacy of his vulnerable-sounding voice. His songs embody a wide range of gendered personae, all coming out in his ever-changing style(s) of delivery. His performances are not limited by the heteronormative scheme; most of the time he deliberately challenges such norms, showing another kind of strength than a classical macho one.

In Goldin-Perschbacher's use of the term "transgendered" she acknowledges that Buckley never had to face "the everyday oppression and dangers of living in between genders," but in his address he challenges the listeners, opening up for their conceptions of identities (215). From a totally different angle, Lovesey sees some of the same features as becoming narcissistic and mannerist. He understands Buckley's "iconic voice" as an "inherited signature from his father" and the "shape shifting" of this voice is interpreted in a quasi-Oedipal sense (Lovesey: 333), But, as Goldin-Perschbacher shows, he fails to consider the possibility of Buckley's performance as identifications with the different singers. Indeed, camp mannerism have for a long time also served to accentuate an opposition to gendered stereotypes, and Buckley's "hetero camp"—if that is what it is—

---

[6]   Lovesey is here explicitly following Frederic Jameson. See Jameson's *Postmodernism, or, The Cultural Logic of Late Capitalism.* London: Verso, 1992 (1991).

[7]   The quote is from Goldin-Perschbacher, "'Not with You But of You'," p. 214.

underlines a playfulness in the midst of the vulnerability.[8] Vulnerability is one part of the game, and one part queering might contribute. But rather than interpreting it as provoking or threatening one might consider it a destabilizing move. In such a destabilizing process the plurality of masculinities might come along in a different, and supplementary, way to more political projects of resistance.

Butler's interpretation of the relation between a copy and a copy simultaneously questions the very idea of "originality." Following this it may be more precise to speak of Cohen's "version" than of his "original." Within the culture of repetition cover versions illustrate there are in a sense no originals.[9] Butler's statement that "the parodic repetition of 'the original' [...] reveals the original to be nothing other than a parody of the *idea* of the natural and the original" (1999: 41), thus opens up for another way of interpreting the relation between different versions. It is not as if all the covers on *Leonard Cohen: I'm Your Man* participate in what Wainwright called fagging up, even if they all to a greater or lesser degree participate in rearticulating the songs and as such in the questioning of originals. In this article, however, I am primarily occupied with those versions where gendered identities also might be said to be at stake.

Born with the Gift of a Golden Voice

Let us for a moment return to Buckley's version of "Hallelujah." A key dimension in any discussion of both this version and Cohen's own is the voice. A singer's voice is, in so many ways, a signature, marking her or him as musicians and performers. But describing voices or vocality is notoriously difficult, and not only when these voices challenge normativity. Cohen's take on his own voice is famously stated in "Tower of Song": "I was born like this, I had no choice. I was born with the gift of a golden voice" (2007: 252).[10] But obviously, it is only "the gift" of this voice—as a kind of promise—he was born with. The alterations of any voice, from childhood through adolescence, are important in how voices are gendered. The deep ringing bass of Cohen, heard somewhere between singing and speaking, is important for his sound. It might be described as "golden," and is often heard as patriarchal or priestly. It is also eroticized, as perhaps the most important part of

---

[8]   The notion of "hetero camp" is found in Lovesey's "Anti-Orpheus," p. 340. For an interpretation of camp and playfulness, cf. Hawkins, "On Male Queering in Mainstream Pop," p. 282. A not dissimilar project, but done very differently, is arguably found in Jarvis Cocker's performance of "I Can't Forget" on *Leonard Cohen: I'm Your Man*. Cocker's mannerism, very recognizable in his quirky movements, alters the song, and also in relation to masculinity.

[9]   I lift the phrase "the culture of the copy" from Robert Fink's book *Repeating Ourselves: American Minimal Music as Cultural Practice*. Berkeley: University of California Press, 2005.

[10]   Leonard Cohen, "Tower of Song," from *I'm Your Man* (1988).

his fascination. The line from "Tower of Song," however, have an ironic ring to it, and within a normative vocal culture, his voice could be described as "unmusical," an understanding Cohen seems to share, as Ira B. Nadel tells in *Various Positions* (2007: 252). From another perspective such "unmusical" voices are understood as "authentic" opening yet another layer.

Hearing Buckley's voice, on the other hand, Kiki calling him a "kid" makes sense, as his boyishness is often underlined. Equally important is challenges to the gendering of his voice. Kiki also describes it as "ethereal," a term Lovesey too employs, as a category for describing what he calls Buckley's "pure voice" (332). Calling a voice "ethereal," however, also brings up the possibility of hearing it as gender-less. As of lately this has not least been a case regarding Antony Hegarty (of Antony and the Johnsons), where there seems to be a possible non-human dimension to the voice.[11] Daphne A. Brooks, in her book on *Grace*, writes about Buckley's "oceanic" voice and his "red velvet passion," but she also references "Jeff's Mahalia-like cadences" and that he dared to "flaunt gender and racial conventions" (Brooks 2007: 2-4, 24). Here gendered—as well as racial— dimensions come to the fore. But this gorgeous voice is simultaneously visceral, embodied and with a powerful effect on the listeners' bodies. Buckley described himself as a chanteuse or, even better, a "male chanteuse with a penis." This is what Goldin-Perschbacher follows up in her discussion of "transgendered" vocality, where "transgender" partakes in the transgression of any clear-cut divisions between male and female, heterosexual and homosexual. Judith Halberstam argues, in *In a Queer Time and Place*, that: "the term transgender can be used as a marker for all kinds of people who challenge, deliberately or accidentally, gender normativity" (Halberstam, 2005: 55). The term, then, does not necessarily signify any transperson; it describes any challenge to normativity, and, of course, the normativity is in the eyes and ears of the beholder.

Buckley's examples show how gendered understandings of voices are part of the discourse of cover versions. Relating it to the more traditional gender divide, the "problem" would be related to male and female voices, and then Martha Wainwright's cover of "Tower of Song" from *Leonard Cohen: I'm Your Man* is a good case. How do we hear her singing "I was born with the gift of a golden voice"? Given that Cohen in this particular phrase intones one of his deepest pitches ever, the song changes radically when sung by a woman. And pitch is the most explicit parameter in our usual division of vocal labor. In addition to pitch, the lyrics too are important for our understanding of the gendered positions in singing. Interesting cases are found when an artist so to speak changes the gender of a song, as when a female artist performs a song associated with a male perspective, expressing love or desire for a woman, without changing the lyrics. As Simon Frith writes, in *Performing Rites*, "we hear voices as male or female and

---

[11]   I have discussed some possible problems with such an interpretation in my article "Voice of Hope: Queer Pop Subjectivities," in *Trikster: Nordic Queer Journal* nr. 1, http:// trikster.net/1/steinskog/1.html

listen to what they say accordingly—according to our own sexual pleasures and preferences (which is why gay and lesbian singers can subvert pop standards by *not* changing the words […])" (1996: 195, italics in original). What Frith describes here would be even more open for interpretations if the singers are not openly gay or lesbian or if the artist is an open queer.[12]

In *Leonard Cohen: I'm Your Man* this happens in Martha Wainwright's performance of "The Traitor."[13] The band intones the song in a loose, murmuring sound. And Martha sings beautifully with a country flavor to the song, taking another waltz. But it is when listening to the lyrics, and the way she delivers them, that the gender-bending dimensions come to the fore. When she sings "She said at last I was her finest lover," "I touch her here and there, I know my place" and "I kiss her open mouth and I praise her beauty," the song turns into a queer (or lesbian) love-song, no matter any sexual identity of the performer. If this makes the song's "I" into a traitor, so be it. This performance is an even stronger moment of gender-switch than the examples from Suzi Quatro that Philip Auslander discusses (2004). The text has hardly any innuendoes; here everything is in plain sight. But Martha sings with such an intense longing, that the intimacy becomes obvious to anyone, and any member of an audience might start to wonder whether it is her or him she is singing to.[14]

The understanding of the voice as an expression of one's identity might also be challenged. Suffice to remember that "person" comes from Latin *per sonara*, meaning the voice coming out through a theatrical mask. The persona is intimately related to masquerades, to metaphors taken form the theater, to a play of and with the personal as a voicing of some kind of persona. Personality is, in this specific sense, a masquerade. From this and in reference to Judith Butler again, one might understand subjectivity as a staging. It is about presentation, about making present—not least through the voice—a role, rather than some kind of essential being behind the mask. In his book *Performing Glam Rock*, Philip Auslander distinguishes between three layers in any musical performance: "the real person," "the performance person" and "the character" (2006: 41). These layers of course interact, and the division between them must be understood as heuristic. This might, however, cover up for the play of ambivalence at stake in the performances. The division so to speak "normalizes" the ambivalent subject position, making it in one particular sense "straight." The queer position I am after complicates this

---

[12]   I acknowledge that "open queer" sounds kind of paradoxical, but think it is pretty close to the position described by Fred Maus in his article "Intimacy and Distance: on Stipe's Queerness," *Journal of Popular Music Studies* 18/2 (2006), pp. 191–214.

[13]   Cohen's original is from *Recent Songs* (1979).

[14]   Compare this question with Judith Butler's comments related to Aretha Franklin's "(You Make Me Feel) Like a Natural Woman": "But what if Aretha were singing to me?" (Butler, "Imitation and Gender Insubordination," in Diana Fuss (ed.), *Inside Out: Lesbian Theories, Gay Theories*. London: Routledge, 1991, pp. 13–31, p. 28).

whole picture, making it necessary to introduce either more personas or combining the different layers in different ways.

Cover versions necessarily question identity on several accounts. Firstly, they are both a copy, while at the same time being something different. They deviate from the original; copying it, they add something while still being similar enough for the audience to recognize. Hearing the same with a difference changes the meaning of the song as well as how we perceive it. But secondly, the cover-versions question identity as a performed version. In the performance, the "original" is present—as a kind of shadow—in the background. And it is in this play, these interactions, cover-versions simultaneously are subversions; they are subversions in questioning any straightforward identification with the original, but also subversions in different layers of desire being part of the performance as well as the reception of the song. And as with the song—its poetic personae, its structuring of desire, the identification between the song and the singer. Discussing normative, or stereotypical, understandings of gender any other performance might be seen as deviance. The copy—or rather, the repetition—at the same time questions the one script assigned as the (back)ground from where the different performances of gendered identities are taken. Not that there are homologies between a song and its cover on the one side and the normative and the performed/deviated gender-identification on the other. Rather, they can be seen as intertwined in a complex negotiation of desire—the desire being crucial to popular music lyrics and music alike.

The "I" of any song is an important dimension of the play of identities. Not altering the text, but with a change in the perceived gender-identity of the singer, changes the song substantially. If identity is, as Judith Butler discusses, an effect of discursive practices, this opens up important questions for any discussion of identification (1999: 24). There are several dimensions of identification found in popular music. The first is between the singer and the persona in the song. The singer performs in the voice of another, giving voice to a character in the song, but this performance is always already doubled. The intimacy of the voice, the way it communicates to us is in one sense independent of the text and character. It opens up for us hearing another person. We hear a voice, and it becomes the voice of another in a more particular sense. We are hit or caressed, hear it as vulnerable or viscera, but we hear the voice as much more than a detached object. And this simultaneously draws us into the song. We become the "You" any "I" sing to. We become intimate with the song as well as its singer. This opens up another layer in the challenges of the queer positions in popular music. Even if we are used to think along normative dimensions of representation, that is to say, even if we know that it is "only" a performance, any song can challenge this act, but in particularly cover songs in their making explicit the acts of repetition and the play of genders.

I'm Your Man

One of Cohen's songs where the relationship of an "I" and a "you" are staged very explicitly is "I'm Your Man," a song giving direct access to discussions of masculinity, primarily through its lyrics.[15] It is an iconic Cohen-song, as demonstrated by Lunson using it as the title of his movie. The tagline of the movie was "Poet. Songwriter. Ladies' Man," underlining one image of Cohen, a heteronormative one, despite—or perhaps because of—his album *Death of A Ladies' Man* (1977), an album containing what is his most homoerotic rendition of any song, when Allen Ginsberg and Bob Dylan sing backing vocals to "Don't Go Home With Your Hard-On" (Nadel: 214f).

But then there are the cover versions of "I'm Your Man," speaking directly into questions of masculinity, and not least to subversions of any normative masculinity. In the different versions the idea of "man" is deconstructed. In other words, by the different repetitions, quotations, citations, found in the covers of this song, the idea of the original begins to crumble; the copies obtain a life of their own. In this, the very process of citation, so strongly related to the idea of performativity, points toward a dimension of appropriation suitable to problematize the notion of original. On *Leonard Cohen: I'm Your Man* Nick Cave is doing "I'm Your Man." His cover exists in two versions, one in the movie and another on the sound-track album. But to really bring out what happens with Cave's version, I also want to discuss Elton John's cover, taken from the tribute-album *Tower of Song*.[16] These versions are very different, but both arguably queer the song, but they do so in different ways.

Cohen's lyrics are clearly directed towards a woman, but the singing "I" is still not your average tough-guy. The man singing will do anything the "you" asks; be a lover, wearing a mask if another kind of love is wanted, be a partner, a boxer or a doctor, a father to her child, or simply a companion for a walk. And even if, in the bridge, the "I" singing claims that "a man never got a woman back / not by begging on his knees," this is pretty much what the singer is doing. And so, this male is close to begging, and is a passive position towards the woman's agency. It is she who decides what will happen next; the man will do anything he is asked to. All this is delivered in Cohen's regular quite flat voice, and there are passages where the voice is close to breaking. The "please" in the bridge almost breaks, before he pulls himself together assuring that "I'm Your Man." The musical arrangement of the song has not aged well, and is perhaps even more timely than the Phil Spector-produced *Death of A Ladies' Man*, an album kind of an embarrassment to lots of fans, and one which Cohen himself, in the movie, describes as a "kind of

---

[15]   Leonard Cohen, "I'm Your Man" (*I'm Your Man*, 1988).

[16]   *Tower of Song: The Songs of Leonard Cohen* is from 1995, that is just a couple of years after Elton John's *Duets* (1993), where John and Cohen sang a duet of Ray Charles' "Born to Lose," and where their different voices are highlighted.

a failure." But perhaps *I'm Your Man* was never timely either, no matter how big a success it was.

It is not least in the interaction between voice and arrangements that the differences between the versions are brought forward. The covers bring out the differences by vocal delivery as well as arrangements. When Elton John is doing his version, the song must be transposed up in pitch, giving it a lighter or higher sound. At the same time is his flamboyance very different than Cohen's. That Elton John is openly gay, however, is what opens up for questions. What happens when an openly gay singer sings "I'm Your Man"? Does this alter the song? And which masculine positions are staged in this cover-version? This is similar to the discussion of Martha Wainwright's cover of "The Traitor," but not identical. Remember how Frith discussed "gay and lesbian singers" subverting by not changing the text. The openly gay position of Elton John could then be considered differently than Martha Wainwright's perceived "straight" one, even if Martha's delivery speaks in a "lesbian" tone.

In Elton John's cover there are also different genre-codes in play. His version resembles his own songs and is played in a style the audience would recognize as his. He changes the accompanying figures, and the piano becomes more important. In addition changes are done by him camping up the original. This dimension of camp is one of the new features in this version, but whether it is heard as camp or not is another question. The codes of camp are there, but they are on the side of the interpreter. This also opens up a question related to queering, and to the relation between camp and queer. In one sense is camp queer too, but perhaps queer in another way than more explicitly queer expressions. It is almost as if one would like to see Elton John performing as well, given that important dimensions in the performance of gender come more easily through in visual codes than in aural ones. The visual display and the uses of the body inscribe politics of representation (Hawkins: 282). This is not to undermine the importance of the voice in such a politics, also when it comes to queering. But what a queer voice is, is still not easily determined, and is so far more difficult to define than different codes of dress and other visual signs. When Judith Butler, in *Gender Trouble*, famously discussed drag, the effect seems in particular to have gone into dressing and the visual domain (1999: 179ff). What about the aural? How do we discuss voices in this sense? And what would vocal drag be? These questions have not gone unnoticed, and points to important dimensions for the discussion of queering related to popular music.[17]

A focus on the aural does not, however, mean that the visual is unimportant. Suffice to see Rufus Wainwright perform "Everybody Knows" in Lunson's movie. His campy, over-the-top, performance, and perhaps not least his top—and

---

[17]   See in this context Elizabeth Wood, "Sapphonics" and Joke Dame, "Unveiled Voices: Sexual Difference and the Castrato," both in Philip Brett, Elizabeth Wood and Gary C. Thomas (eds), *Queering the Pitch: The New Gay and Lesbian Musicology*. London: Routledge, 1994.

jewelry—quite obviously is part of him fagging Cohen up. He dances while singing and is slurring the syllables on a lot of the words. And then, on the chorus, we find long-held tones, with a cheeky smile on his face. The third verse begins in low volume and swells into an opening of the whole song, and towards the end of the song he holds a caesura, and when the backing-singers come in too early, he cannot let go of a pretty goofy smile. His cover-version of "Everybody Knows" queers Cohen's song, also by making it into a tango.[18] And this queering is not least found in the combination of vocal performance and visual display, in the playing with different signs, where Wainwright performs a certain gayness related to the song. The signs are there for those who have eyes—and ears—to see and hear them. His statement about wanting to fag Cohen's songs up, underlines the perspective from an openly gay artist. As such there are arguably nothing subversive about this. But his performance has effect on Cohen's song. The songs change, perhaps nowhere as clear as in Wainwright's version of "Chelsea Hotel No 2."[19] Here too the change is primarily due to the lyrics. In addition there are some biographical dimensions surrounding the song. Cohen's encounter with Janis Joplin being the basis for the song—making an indiscrete exception as it were—is coupled with Rufus having lived at the same hotel for quite some time (Nadel: 144). But the line "giving me head on the unmade bed" simply must sound differently coming from Wainwright than in Cohen's own version. Wainwright sings quite lovely, and without the campy dimensions of "Everybody Knows." Instead there are strings, guitar, and a close-to-country feel to it, but the phrase "I need you" does sound different coming from him, opening up for various positions of masculinity.

Nick Cave's version of "I'm Your Man" opens the movie. He is crooning, and the version resembles the kind of torch-like songs found in his own repertoire. There are jazz-elements, and it is performed in a nonchalance manner. The version on the sound-track album, however, is better that the one in the movie. The arrangement is the same, but Cave's singing is heard better, and not interrupted by the documentary-part, as the performance is in the movie. The musical dimensions are very different than in both Cohen's and John's versions; the sound is different and the orchestra plays a "dirtier" version, adding a cabaret-like dimension. There is a long saxophone-solo, which contributes to associations of genres. And, finally, there is Cave's voice. Cave has covered other Cohen-songs as well, and his version of "Tower of Song" is particularly interesting.[20] Being a song "about" voices, Cave performs a polyphony of voices and stylistic dimensions, where the song moves across a huge spectrum of genres, and where Cave's voice is not even identical with itself.

---

[18]   At the Brooklyn event he sang it together with his mother in what he called "the Leonard Cohen meets Doris Day version."

[19]   Cohen's original of "Chelsea Hotel No. 2" is from *New Skin for the Old Ceremony* (1974).

[20]   Nick Cave, "Tower of Song" (on *I'm Your Fan*, 1991).

But back to "I'm Your Man." Which figures of masculinity are staged in Cave's version? My claim is that the changes here are less obvious than in Elton John's version, but this does not mean that we have to do with a straight version. On the contrary. There is something in Cave's performance, his ways of using the voice, and how he underlines single word—not least "every iiiiiinch of you"—showing a different figure of masculinity. In heightening the sense of ambivalence, in playing with the voice and doing voices in different ways, Cave's version is, in this particular sense, queerer than Elton John's. In addition to the play with voices, this relates to how he plays with the audience's expectancies, as well as how his performance underlines that he is performing.

What are the arguments for claiming that Elton John's or Nick Cave's versions are queer? Is it, in the case of Elton John, enough to fall back on biography? (McNair, 2002: 136). The reading of three versions of "I'm Your Man" seems to indicate a movement from a more or less normative—heterosexual—masculinity, by way of a more gay version, to a more ambivalent queer one. In one sense such a scheme makes sense, but within such a linear understanding of figures of masculinity much of the bigger picture disappears. Working through these versions, in a movement towards queerness, has consequences for all versions. We find that the possibility of a queer reading was there already in the point of departure, or, more concretely, if Nick Cave's version of "I'm Your Man" is a queer version of Cohen's song, it at the same time shows the possibility of queering Cohen. But this at the same time mean that a "neutral," non-queer, reading of Cohen is almost impossible after having gone through this process. One can, so to speak, never go back to the point of departure: the interpretation, or rather the process of interpretation, leads us to a point of no return, in the sense that the point of departure disappears; it is no longer there, and as reader we start to doubt whether it ever was. The way we hear Cohen—that is, the way we hear the "original"—is as an original after the copy, and as such questions the original's originality. The cover version is thus so to speak inherently subversion, in the sense that it covers over the original, and shows the original to be of less interest. The original has potential only the covers—as copies—can bring out. And here Cave's version is superior to Elton John's. Even if queer theory always is anti-normative, it is not neutral, and here the opening up for ambivalence, differences, and potentials, in this case in different versions of masculinity is the basis of the judgment. And even if there might be some threatening and unsecured dimensions following from it, this opening up shows that masculinity by necessity exists only in the plural, as different versions of masculinities. Such an opening up challenges normativity. In a similar way to how Halberstam defines "transgender" as a marker for "all kinds of people who challenge, deliberately or accidentally, gender normativity," a similar definition could be made for "queer" (Halberstam: 55). As Alexander Doty argues, in his book *Making Things Perfectly Queer*, "'queer' is touted as an inclusive, but not exclusive, category," and is as such different than "straight," "gay," "lesbian" or "bisexual" (Doty, 1993: xiv). As the examples discussed in this article hopefully make clear, the queering of Cohen's songs are much more complicated than assigning a fixed gendered identity to the performer. The possibility of queering Cohen arises from several different angles, but all having in common a challenge to any straightforward reading of Cohen's songs as hetero-normative. No matter how much Cohen perhaps have been seen as a "ladies' man," his songs open up a site for multiple readings or hearings. And, as he says himself in the movie, "My reputation as a ladies' man was a joke."

That There is a Voice

This article began with Jeff Buckley's version of "Hallelujah," and related it to Goldin-Perschbacher's discussion of the transgendered vocality. On *Leonard Cohen: I'm Your Man* another transgendered voice is heard, when Antony performs "If It Be Your Will."[21] Here it is perhaps *the* hymn being sung, or, probably better, this is a prayer, but a "prayer deconstructing a prayer." Antony takes on the soul-dimension known from his own recordings, and shows an emotional depth where you have to be made of stone not to get goose bumps. In Antony's performance it is as if the voice strives to get out of the body, to leave the body behind. And the orchestra builds up, with a gospel-like drive—hearable also in the backing vocals—and Antony lifts the song up, but to a "you" of semi-divine proportions. After the last "if it be your will" the orchestra sounds almost as intoning "amen." But it is not this passage of closure that captures the listener. It is the on-going building-up in orchestra and voice, where Antony sings, and repeats, "If it be your will" moving loosely around the beat, and with an insisting delivery. Insisting on "the voice," a voice Simon Frith famously described when Antony received the 2005 Mercury Music Prize: "He's got such an extraordinary voice—it could be black, white, male or female."[22] This voice in-between, this transgendered voice—transgendered in the sense underlined both by Goldin-Perschbacher and Halberstam—is intoning the lyrics: "If it be your will, that there is a voice, from the broken hill, I will sing to you [...] from this broken hill all your praises they shall ring, if it be your will to let me sing." This you is a you drawing us near, not only to Antony's voice, but to this song, a song changing everything. Antony (deliberately?) changes the text. Cohen's version reads "If it be your will, that a voice be true," whereas Antony sings "If it be your will, that there is a voice," and there is a poetic justice to this change. That "there is a voice" is crucial for

21 Cohen's original is found on *Various Positions* (1984), the same album containing his "Hallelujah."
22 Simon Frith quoted in Adam Sherwin, "Antony and the Johnsons win the Mercury Prize," Times Online, September 7, 2005 http://entertainment.timesonline.co.uk/tol/arts_and_entertainment/music/article563734.ece The statement is also quoted in Richard Middleton's "Mum's the Word: Men's Singing and Maternal Law," in Freya Jarman-Ivens (ed.), *Oh Boy! Masculinities and Pop Music.* (London: Routledge, 2007), pp. 103–24, p. 103.

humanity. Humanity consists of voices. And if ever there was needed an argument for the humanity found in Antony's voice—and it seems to be, not least given the vast amount of commentators always needing to underline the voice of this "creature," the angelic, ethereal, and thus (close to) non-human voice—here it is. Antony's performance is by far the emotional highpoint of the movie (the possible exception being Martha Wainwright's version of "The Traitor"). And it points towards a voice beyond clear-cut categories and identities, while simultaneously queering Cohen. At the same time he shows queering to be a process, and on-going process, of transgressions and transformations.[23]

Ira B. Nadel writes about the Jewish dimensions of this song: "'If It Be Your Will' was also borrowed from Jewish prayer, originating in a phrase from the Kol Nidre service on Yom Kippur eve where, just before the listing of sins, the petitioner cries, 'May it therefore be Your will, Lord our God, and God of our Fathers, to forgive us all our sins, to pardon all our iniquities, to grant us atonement for all our transgressions'. The melody for Cohen's song is derived from the synagogue song" (239). This dimension, even if at first sight at quite some distance from the subject of queering, might still throw light on Antony's version. Along with Richard Middleton's article it can also bring back memories of Al Jolson's performance in *The Jazz Singer* (Alan Crosland, 1927) (in Jarmen-Ivens: 107). Jolson was Jewish but performed in blackface. Antony's performance contains a similar transgression of perceived boundaries, his voice echoing, as the quote from Frith makes clear, black and white as well as male and female voices. Middleton refers to Jolson's queering of normative masculine vocality, but at the same time underlines that this is enabled by way of a mask. There is no mask in the case of Antony, and somehow it seems that he is not asking for atonement for his transgressions. Here then, we are in a similar context as in the discussion of "Hallelujah" as a "hymn deconstructing a hymn." Daphne A. Brooks employs a somewhat different designation, calling Cohen's "Hallelujah" "a fractured hymn of emotional, spiritual, and sexual confluence and revelation" (Brooks: 138). Along similar lines, and thinking of "If It Be Your Will" as a prayer, I am tempted to call it a fractured prayer. But at the same time a prayer directed towards a beyond—a place beyond clear-cut racial and gendered categories and a place hinted towards in Antony's performance. In *The Autograph Man* (2002) Zadie Smith has a passage entitled "The fundamental goyishness of Leonard Cohen" (2003: 85f). Categories are difficult to handle, and attempting to subvert them is politically important. Cover versions may uncover the normativity attached to well-established categories, and in the repetition something different arises. In

---

[23] For another argument about transformations related to Antony, see Eva Hayward, "More Lessons from a Starfish: Prefixial Flesh and Transspeciated Selves," *Women's Studies Quarterly* 36: 3 and 4 (Fall/Winter 2008), pp. 64–85, where she discusses Antony and the Johnsons' "The Cripple and the Starfish" (from *Antony and the Johnsons*, 2000). A somewhat different version, entitled "Lessons from a Starfish," is found in Noreen Giffney and Myra J. Hird (eds.), *Queering the Non/Human*. Aldershot: Ashgate, 2008, pp. 249–64.

Thinking in Jewish, Jonathan Boyarin writes about a "general Jewish tendency to view citation as more authoritative than originality" (1996: 142). Perhaps this is what happens in these repetitions, cover versions that in their citations and repetitions uncover the original's status as another copy, while simultaneously showing the joy—and the power—in repetition.

Chapter 8
Covering and Un(covering) the Truth with "All Along the Watchtower": From Dylan to Hendrix and Beyond

Russell Reising

In 1994, the Fox television network aired an episode of their sci-fi classic, *The X-Files*, entitled "Beyond the Sea," in which, during their investigation of the abduction on two college students, Agents Mulder and Scully interview Luther Boggs, a prison inmate who claims to have psychic powers that enable him to interface with all human life, past and present. Mulder rejects Boggs's input, wrongly sensing him to be nothing more than a skillful humbug. Disgusted and oddly incredulous, Mulder tells Scully, "after three hours [of his "channeling"] I asked him to summon up the soul of Jimi Hendrix and requested 'All Along The Watchtower.' You know, the guy's been dead twenty years, but he still hasn't lost his edge!" Mulder's claim remains true, both for Dylan's song, for Hendrix's interpretation, and for many other cover versions of it today as it was over a decade and a half ago when "Beyond the Sea" aired. Mulder alludes to, though the soundtrack doesn't actually play, one of the most important songs in film and television soundtrack history. That he does so in doubting the truth of Luther Boggs's claims, moreover, situates "All Along The Watchtower" squarely within the history of how it is most usually sampled in the electronic visual arts: as a musical/lyrical reminder of the "many among us who feel life is but a joke," and "fate," "talking falsely" and that the "hour is getting late."[1]

Indeed, if he *is* talking falsely, Boggs jeopardizes the lives of two young people for whom, since the killer is known to murder his victims within a predictable time frame, "the hour is getting late."

To some extent "All Along the Watchtower" has achieved mythic proportions in Anglo-American and Western European popular culture. Well over 150 cover versions of "All Along the Watchtower," either recorded and/or performed in concert, although some of these include multiple versions by the same performers (Neil Young and John Cougar Mellancamp, for example, are both credited with three versions).[2] While Jimi Hendrix was clearly the first, there's clearly something

---

[1]   All lyric citations in the text from "All Along the Watchtower" (unless otherwise noted) are from: "All Along the Watchtower," words and music by Bob Dylan, 1967.

[2]   See http://www.bjorner.com/songsa.htm#_All_Along_The_Watchtower

about the Dylan original that not only continues to inspire performers but resonates with the socio-political events of our culture. For one thing, it's difficult to listen to any FM radio station for an extended period of time without hearing those thunderous notes kicking off the Jimi Hendrix Experience's cover. With only one possible exception, the Hendrix's cover of Dylan's song has arguable usurped the original; only Elvis's cover of "Hound Dog" might challenge for this feat, although anyone who's ever heard the Big Mama Thornton original would probably argue strenuously otherwise. Consider the relationship between other originals and their covers, and it's hard to imagine anyone actually preferring the cover. When Pat Boone covers Little Richard's "Tutti Frutti or Jay and the Americans cover the Drifters' "The Magic Moment," the anemic results are almost a textbook case of what "covering" is all about, a "white bread" denaturing of the soul and passion of the originals. Even such well known examples from early in the so-called British Invasion as the Beatles' versions of Chuck Berry's "Roll Over Beethoven, the Marvellettes' "Please Mr. Postman," the Shirelles' "Baby It's You" or the Rolling Stones' covers of Otis Redding's "I've Been Loving You Too Long," of Muddy Waters' "I Just Want to Make Love to You," or Rufus Thomas's "Walking the Dog" continue to interest us primarily due to their position as early songs in these super groups' repertoires and as attempts by British bands to import some of the soul from their American heroes. Not that the Beatles' cover of Buck Owens' "Act Naturally" or the Rolling Stones' version of Robert Johnson's "Love in Vain" aren't, in themselves, crowning achievement of cover versions, but that they exist primarily as covers, perhaps even coequal in their appeal, but not usurping the originals in the history of popular music. The same could probably be said of most of the Animals' early hits, nearly all covers of soul and R & B classics such as Texas Alexander's "House of the Rising Sun," John Lee Hooker's "Boom Boom," or Sam Cooke's incredible "Bring It on Home to Me." Eric Burden's resonant voice could only approximate the depth and soulfulness of the originals.[3]

"All Along the Watchtower" has penetrated much more deeply into our cultural bedrock than its sheer musical significance. German filmmaker Wim Wenders' 1969 short film *Alabama: 2000 Light Years from Home* is an interesting case in point. On his website, Wenders explains the connection between his film and "All Along the Watchtower":

> The film starts with a shot of a cassette recorder, and it has a juke box in it. There's always music in it. When I was asked by some critics at a festival press conference what the film was all about, I said "it's about the song 'All Along The Watchtower,' and the film is about what happens and what changes depending on whether the song is sung by Bob Dylan or by Jimi Hendrix." Well, both versions of the song appear in the film, and everybody thought I was pretty arrogant to explain the story this way. But the film really is about the difference

---

[3]   See the website of The Covers Project for an excellent catalogue of the genre: http://www.coversproject.com/

between the Dylan version of "All Along the Watchtower," and the Jimi Hendrix Version. One is at the beginning and one is at the end.[4]

Wenders elaborates that the film, named after John Coltrane's "Alabama" (also included in the film) is a film about death: "It's more of an after-action film, or after-story film. The subject is death. You could say that much about the story: it deals at least with death" (see www.wim-wenders.com). Such deep and universal significance tends to characterize the trans-musical expropriations of the Dylan/ Hendrix classic. To some extent, Wenders' film exists as a meta-cover of the Dylan original and the Hendrix cover.

Several post-September 11th websites draw on the ethos of Dylan's apocalyptic lyrics to highlight their political commentary. On "truthout.org," William Rivers Pitt entitled his June 23, 2002 commentary on the political implications of the terrorist attacks of September 11, 2001 "All Along the Watchtower." According to Pitt, Stanley Hilton, a San Francisco lawyer and former aide to Bob Dole, believes that the entire tragedy was orchestrated by George W. Bush, Dick Cheney, Condoleezza Rice, Donald Rumsfeld and Norman Mineta, among others, "so as to reap political benefits from the catastrophe. Hilton alleges that Osama bin Laden is being used as a scapegoat by an administration that ignored pressing warnings of the attack and refused to round up suspected terrorists beforehand. Hilton alleges the ultimate motivation behind these acts was achieved when the Taliban were replaced by American military forces with a regime friendly to America and its oil interests in the region."[5] On another web news and editorial site, "The Road to Serfdom, an intermittent blog by Tim Dunlop," Dunlop entitled a poignant posting from April 13, 2003 on the plight of US military personnel on duty in Iraq "All Along the Watchtower":

> In the post below I wondered, in the light of apparent local discontent at the US presence in Iraq, how the average coalition soldier must be feeling. I mean, having been worded up about how they will be greeted as liberating heroes and perhaps even having experienced something of that very reaction, it must be disconcerting to find yourself now on the end of resentment.[6]

For Pitt and Dunlop, Dylan's lyrics and perhaps even Hendrix's treatment both resonate with the high seriousness of global catastrophes as well as with the sense that we must all maintain extreme vigilance (we, like Dylan's princes, must keep the view for whatever riders may be approaching). The titles of their websites, "truthout" and "road to serfdom" likewise draw on Dylan's sense of immanent menace and on the importance of not talking falsely.

---

[4] See http://www.wim-wenders.com/movies/movies_spec/shorts/shorts.htm

[5] http://www.truthout.org/docs_02/06.21A.pitt.watchtower.htm

[6] http://www.roadtosurfdom.com/surfdomarchives/001005.php

"All Along the Watchtower" has also been used in much lighter moments, more as comedic reference (the role of "the joker"?) and nostalgic touchstone than political and ideological beacon in a darkening world. In 1999, the BBC television played off the serious tone of Dylan's song with its six episode series, *All Along the Watchtower*, a comedy about the wacky personnel in charge of an RAF base in rural Scotland. Focusing largely on the irony of three such unlikely characters in charge of a military installation and jibes at Scottish village life, *All Along the Watchtower* had almost nothing in common with "All Along the Watchtower," aside from the ironic juxtaposition of its absurdist, comedic ethos with Dylan's apocalyptic lyricism.[7]

Thus, even in a lighthearted presentation, "All Along the Watchtower" still functions as a reference point for a world in crisis.

John Wesley Harding: Dylan's Original

Transitional and transformative both for Dylan and Hendrix, the song marks both beginnings and endings, but especially moments of truth. On his epochal 1968 album, *John Wesley Harding*, Dylan migrates from the densely surrealistic poetry of albums such as *Bringing It All Back Home*, *Highway 61 Revisited*, and *Blonde on Blonde* into a simpler, though by no means insignificant or unambiguous lyricism. *John Wesley Harding*, in other words, is Dylan's threshold album, marking a new (and different) way of engaging the world around him.[8] In spite of all the musical and social complexity of the song's lyrics and historical context, two of the more interesting commentators to situate Dylan's song in a cultural context have read it in strangely escapist terms. As David Pichaske notes, the tendencies that vitiated rock and the movement of the sixties may have been just what made Bob Dylan turn his back on artiness and professionalism and at the close of *John Wesley Harding* adopt the simplest, most hokey, most unpoetic and unprofessional music of all, country music (1989: 207).

---

[7]　http://www.phill.co.uk/comedy/allalong/prod.html See this website for production notes. In another whimsical example, the British vocal quartet Barefoot in the Park (from Devon) responded to a BBC interviewer who asked them how they named themselves thus: "All along the watchtower, princes kept the view, While all the women came and went, barefoot servants, too." 'I guess you could say it was Bob Dylan who inspired the name when Karen was learning the lyrics to "All along the watchtower", she glanced down, saw the word "Barefoot" and the rest, as they say, is history.'

[8]　In this respect, *John Wesley Harding* is something like the opposite of the Beatles' *Revolver*, the album on which they shifted from simpler rock and roll sounds and words into the bracing musicological explorations of exotic soundscapes and lyricism. See Reising, *Every Sound There Is: The Beatles'* Revolver *and the Transformation of Rock and Roll* (Ashgate, 2003) for related discussions.

For Pichaske, anything that makes rock swerve from direct social activism constitutes part of its ultimate defeat, sometimes by cooptation and sometimes by virtue of its own pretentiousness. Nick Bromell reads a slightly more nuanced drift in "All Along the Watchtower," regarding it as "another meditation on the attitude we should take toward the evils ... that dominate the world. This song understands our temptation to respond ironically, to conclude that, after all, *life is but a joke*, but it urges us to go a step further" (148). However, in addition to misreading the context of the above quote, when faced with what he regards as the song's ultimate question, "what should we do?", Bromell understands the song in terms of hopeless despair, embellishing his own defeatism with rhetorical hyperbole: "Dylan's song gives no answer, and in Hendrix's version the pain of our paralysis is sharpened by the apocalyptic winds struck from the cold strings of his guitar" (2000: 149). ... and further, "Hendrix playing Dylan represents the consummate fusion of the blues tradition with the psychedelicized hunger of white youth enmired in loneliness and looking for a new self, trapped in history and looking desperately for *some way out of here*." In other words, both Pichaske and Bromell share the sense of "All Along the Watchtower" as a song of retreat, of distance, of ironic paralysis. Both somehow elide the stress that Dylan's song and Hendrix's interpretation of it place on truth telling. Neither version might lead directly to any immediate action, but the unflinching courage and commitment to not talking falsely in the face of immediate and present dangers characterize both Dylan's and Hendrix's performances as well as critical junctures in their careers.

Like all great translations, and all great cover versions of great songs, Hendrix covers to reveal. In making "All Along the Watchtower" his own, Hendrix evokes precisely the militant essence inherent in Dylan's lyrics. In the liner notes of his *Biograph* (1985) box set, Dylan himself states that ever since hearing Hendrix's version from the 1968 *Electric Ladyland* album,

> I liked Jimi Hendrix's record of this and ever since he died I've been doing it that way. Funny though, his way of doing it and my way of doing it weren't that dissimilar, I mean the meaning of the song doesn't change like when some artists do other artists' songs. Strange though how when I sing it I always feel like it's a tribute to him in some kind of way. ... "All Along the Watchtower," it probably came to me during a thunder and lightning storm. I'm sure it did!

American Beauty (1999) may be the only film that uses Dylan's original song. Lester Burnham, played brilliantly by Kevin Spacey, registers his sense that his life has come to a crashing halt in a series of transformative realizations: "In a way," he muses, "I'm dead already. ... I know I didn't always feel this ... sedated. But you know what? It's never too late to get it back. ... It's the weirdest thing. I feel like I've been in a coma for about twenty years, and I'm just now waking up." These insights, ultimately verified, albeit problematically, by the film's twisting narrative, precipitate a rebirth in Burnham, an intense commitment to telling the truth and to recovering the energy, intensity, and dreams of his youth. The first moment in which we see Burnham spring into action, lifting weights in his garage as a symbol of his newfound individualism, the first verse of "All Along The Watchtower" plays in the background. *American Beauty* reprises this scene when, near the end of the film, it samples the beginnings of the Who's classic, "The Seeker," with its lines about "ask[ing] Bobby Dylan" about the truths they seek. That Burnham's "moment of truth" finds its origins in his infatuation with his teenage daughter's friend, and that it involves smoking pot with his teenage neighbor, buying his "dream car" (a red 1970 Firebird), quitting his advertising job, and working at Smiley Burger because he's looking for the "least possible amount of responsibility," combine to suggest that Burnham's "moment of truth," has elements of a deferred adolescent rebellion and feeling "that life is but a joke." However Burnham's metamorphosis transforms not only his life, but the lives of those around him, and even his death reveals the final triumph of his life. There was "some way out of here" for Burnham; he got relief from the confusion and anomie of a dead-end bourgeois existence, he decides no longer to "talk falsely" with his boss, his family, and himself. In fact he reveals that he has hardly spoken at all with his family, and the keenest evidence of his awakening is his voice and his refusal to countenance the falsehoods that had defined his entire life. The folkiness of Dylan's original resonates beautifully with the litotic, even banal, nature of Burnham's own transformation.

The Hendrix Cover

Just as "All Along the Watchtower" appeared on one of Dylan's most important pivotal albums and, because of that, marks a transformative moment in his early career, Hendrix's cover similarly demarcates a crucial transition for him. Hendrix's meteoric rise to fame corresponded not only with the rise of unrest and protest, globally over the war in Vietnam, and with crucial moments in African-American history, and Hendrix felt the tensions of a black guitar player teamed up with a white rhythm section acutely. By the time of *Electric Ladyland* sessions and the album's release in 1968, Black Panthers frequently confronted Hendrix about playing white music with a white band for largely white audiences, and also called Hendrix a "coconut," a derisive term for a black man who they felt was white on the inside. Commonly soliciting support and funds, the Panthers frequently tried to corner Hendrix and even pressured Kathy Etchingham at their London flat while Jimi was in the United States. Trixie Sullivan, assistant to Hendrix's manager Mike Jeffrey, recalls a particularly telling encounter from backstage at the Fillmore West: "These two black guys came in. … they were bloody heavy, I'm not joking, calling Jimi a white nigger and God knows what else. Bill Graham came in and had them thrown out" (Shapiro and Glebbeek, 1992: 368). To exacerbate matters, one of Hendrix's few published statements on his relation to African-American political radicalism appeared in *Teenset,* a "teeny-bopper" fan magazine marketed almost exclusively to white youths.[9]

The story about Hendrix's decision to record "All Along the Watchtower" is itself mixed and complex. Shapiro and Glebbeek argue that

> When *John Wesley Harding* was released in January 1968, Jimi's initial idea was to record "I Dreamed I Saw St Augustine," but as a song chronicling the passage through dissipation to redemption via guilt, he thought it too personal to Dylan and changed his mind. Instead, he chose "All Along the Watchtower," where Dylan confronts the chaos of fallen man and emerges from Armageddon chastened but intact, much as Jimi does in "1983." (320)

However, even in their own book, Shapiro and Glebbeek include a contradictory account in their appendix. There,

> Jimi, Dave Mason and Viv Price were at a small party where they all listened to Bob Dylan's *John Wesley Harding* LP for the very first time. When it got to "All Along the Watchtower," Jimi said, "we gotta record that, I gotta do that." That same evening Jimi recorded the song at Olympic. Brian Jones and Linda Keith among others attended this session. (529)[10]

So, did Hendrix immediately connect with "All Along the Watchtower," or did he settle for it after deciding that he shouldn't tamper with his favorite cut from *John Wesley Harding*?

Within the Experience, Jimi's relationship with Noel Redding had begun deteriorating and continued along that downward spiral during the *Electric Ladyland* sessions, so that Jimi himself overdubbed the bass line to "All Along the Watchtower" after Redding left the studios. Hendrix's dedication to reproducing the aural effects he heard in his mind's ear resulted in increasing hostility between him and Redding as well as with Dave Mason, who was brought in to play additional guitars on "All Along the Watchtower." Hendrix knew exactly what he wanted, remembers Eddie Kramer, and would yell at Mason, playing guitar in the studio's vocal booth, as he struggled with the song's chord changes. As a result, Hendrix cut a staggering number of basic tracks so much so that midway through the session Redding decided that enough was enough and bolted from the studio. … Mason took over bass in Redding's absence, but Hendrix would later overdub the part himself, using a small, custom bass guitar that Bill Wyman had given to

---

[9]   These examples are drawn from Shapiro and Glebbeek's *Electric Gypsy,* the best single source for biographical information about Jimi Hendrix. For another, equally fine and much more personal account of Hendrix's life by an intimate friend, see Lawrence.

[10]   Shapiro and Glebbeek indicate some of this information in the form of "NOTES" to the recording session data. They provide no sources for the quotes or stories included in these NOTES.

Andy Johns. Kramer and Chandler mixed "All Along the Watchtower" five days later on January 26, thinking the recording complete. But many months and three tape generations later, at the Record Plant in New York, Hendrix would record a number of additional overdubs (McDermott, 1992: 106–7).

Remarkably, "All Along the Watchtower" was the Jimi Hendrix Experience's only top 20 hit! And yet despite, or perhaps because of, the song's immense popularity, Hendrix rarely included it in his live repertoire. In fact, Hendrix clashed with manager Mike Jeffery about his reluctance to perform his cover of Dylan's song. As John McDermott notes,

> Hendrix loathed requests shouted from the audience and, not unnaturally, the success of "All Along the Watchtower" made fans expect the Experience to perform the song in concert. But despite its chart success, it had not been added to the Experience's live set, a decision that had caused a mild dispute between Hendrix and Jeffery. In Frankfurt on January 17, during one of their better performances of the tour, Hendrix, in an attempt to pacify steady calls for the song, finally addressed the issue. "There is something we would like to tell you about that 'Watchtower' scene," he drawled. At the mention of "Watchtower" the predominantly German-speaking audience roared with approval. "Wait a minute," he asked them. "We recorded that a year ago and if you've heard it, we are very glad. But tonight, we're trying to do a musical thing, okay? That's a single, and we released it as a single, thank you very much for thinking about it but I forgot the words, that's what I am trying to say." (163)

Apparently, Hendrix always had a notoriously difficult time remembering the words to "All Along the Watchtower," and that mnemonic blip seems to have been the primary reason for his reluctance to do it live. He does, in fact, confuse the lyrics during his rendition on the Isle of Wight concert cd and video. The Jimi Hendrix Experience never performed the song live.

To some extent, "All Along the Watchtower" has been transformed from the "other" song Jimi Hendrix wanted to record from *John Wesley Harding*, his "back up" so to speak, to become the most covered song in rock history, standing the ordinary relationship between original and cover on its head. Most of the cinematic and televisual incorporations we will consider below are either Hendrix's version or covers of Hendrix's original cover. It's Hendrix's thunderous version virtually exploding with force and menace, not Dylan's original enigmatic and provocative folk song, that has migrated from *Electric Ladyland* to FM radio, to cinematic and televisual science-fiction, animation, documentaries, reality television, farcical comedies, and high tragedies to become the song that embodies the lingering sense of mystery and intensity from an epochal period in American history.

The many visual media that incorporate the Jimi Hendrix Experience's "All Along the Watchtower" tend to do by referencing one (sometimes more) of its dominant themes. The initial line, "There must be some kind of way out of here," accompanies many stories of escape. The notion that "There's too much confusion" tends to be primary in narratives in which the complexity and confusion of an individual's life or of contemporary society in general overwhelms all senses of sanity and coherence. Perhaps most frequently, television and cinema uses the lines "So let us now talk falsely now, The hour is getting late" to suggest a moment of existential or communal crisis, one which demands the shedding of all pretense and the embracing of unbridled truth. Finally, a sense of immanent danger or destruction can be intensified with the song's final lines: "Two riders were approaching and the wind began to howl." While the other cover versions which we will examine last tend to draw on one of these typical senses, it is the Hendrix version that establishes the dramatic setting and vocabulary for Dylan's original lines. Of course many such usages embrace more than one of these categories, but I have organized them below according to what seems to be their primary dramatic function.

"There Must Be Some Kind of Way Out of Here"

The song's cinematic use frequently accompanies a moment of escape, as was the case of its popularity during the Vietnam War. Like the Animals' "We Gotta Get Out of this Place," "All Along the Watchtower" played an important role in the spirit of many GIs. During 1968, Hendrix's version of "All Along the Watchtower," with its opening line "There must be some kinda way outta here . . ." seemed to become part of the soundtrack to the Vietnam War. Since Armed Forces radio was tightly controlled, GIs set up pirate radio stations in the fields and broadcast to troops fighting in rainforests and rice paddies. Vietnam veteran Michael Kelly recalls, "I just spun the dials ... lo and behold there's Midnight Jack broadcasting: 'Midnight Jack, man, I'm deep in the jungle.' 'Oh bad news, my man,' he says. 'What can I play for you man?' He's gone for about 30 seconds and I imagine he's putting a reel-to-reel tape on, y'know, and there comes Jimi Hendrix (Robbins, 21).

A number of the films that incorporate "All Along the Watchtower" into their soundtracks do reference this intense desire to escape the hellish environment of war, but many share Nick Bromell's view, barely getting beyond the drift of the song's initial line: "There must be some kind of way out of here." For example, *Where the Buffalo Roam*, Art Linson's 1980 fuses Hunter S. Thompson's gonzo journalism and his roller-coaster relationship with his "attorney," Lazlo, with period music. The film samples Hendrix's cover of "All Along the Watchtower" just after Richard Nixon's straight press secretary throws Thompson off the airplane carrying members of the official press covering the 1972 presidential campaign and just before he doses a buttoned-down *Washington Post* reporter with acid. There's not much point to the moment, as it doesn't include the line "let us not talk falsely now" and meshes with the film's narrative only vaguely and anachronistically, Hendrix already being dead for almost two years relative to the time frame of the film. Along with Dylan's "Highway 61," the Temptations' "Papa Was a Rolling Stone," the Four Tops' "Can't Help Myself," and the Pointer Sisters' "How Long?", Hendrix's "All Along the Watchtower," like "Purple Haze" do little more than add a nostalgic touch by decorating the film with immediately recognizable jewels from late 1960s rock and soul. *Flashback* (1989), starring Kiefer Sutherland as a straight-laced FBI agent bent on rejecting his parents' hippie past and Dennis Hopper as "Huey Walker," a fugitive from 1969, plays "All Along The Watchtower" during one of the film's earliest scenes, as Walker is being transferred from a local jail to be taken to federal prison. In addition to the "way out of here" signaled by Walker's prison release and eventual escape to freedom, *Flashback* plays with the idea of finding a "way out of" the doldrums of the late 1980s and finding a way back in touch with the radical energies of the late 1960s. But "All Along The Watchtower" barely figures more importantly than this, and the rest of *Flashback*'s soundtrack similarly settles for merely setting a nostalgic tone, as in the playing of Canned Heat's "On the Road Again" when the FBI agent and Walker board a train.

"There's Too Much Confusion, I Can't Get No Relief"

Other movies sample "All Along The Watchtower" as an index to how much confusion inflames the American streets during the late 1960s, using its lyrical drift to explore larger social and political realities. Robert De Niro's directorial debut, *A Bronx Tale* (1993), illustrates this point quite nicely. An undercurrent of racial tension permeates this narrative of a bus driver father (De Niro) struggling to keep his son away from the local mobsters and his hero named Sonny (Chazz Palminteri). *A Bronx Tale* features several remarkable, largely doo wop, soundtrack moments, as when the local Italians brutally beat up some obnoxious bikers who have disrespected their bar to Harvey and the Moonglows' tune "The 10 Commandments of Love." The youths in the film react to the increasing black presence in their area with vicious racist slurs and occasional violence. Calogero, De Niro's son, never seems quite in tune with their ugliness, and he eventually falls in love with a young black girl new to his school. Racist friends of his eventually coerce Calogero into getting into their car as they head to fire bomb a black neighborhood, and Hendrix's "All Along The Watchtower" (non-diegetically) plays during his intense internal dialogue in which he agonizes about how to extricate himself from the developing disaster. The film pits his neighborhood friends against his new romantic interest, Calogero's father against Sonny, and racial (and ethnic) homogeneity against modern integration, and Calogero's moment of truth captures the unrest rampant in America's urban streets ("There must be some kind of way out of here … There's too much confusion, I can't get no relief"), but it also marks the boy's moment of truth ("Let us not talk falsely now, The hour is getting late"). Indeed, Sonny, Calogero's mobster hero, intervenes and gets him out of the car, but it was his words of advice, almost magically in synch with Bob Dylan's lyrics, that have already informed the teen's internal deliberations.

Lili Fini Zanuck's gritty 1993 film, *Rush*, uses "All Along the Watchtower" in a similar, but more limited way, marking a crisis in its character's life. *Rush* follows the careers of two undercover narcotics agents in mid-1970s gulf-side

Texas, who train, bond, fall in love, suffer, and eventually triumph, mostly to an Eric Clapton's soundtrack. The female agent, played by Jennifer Jason Leigh turns to police work because she wanted an opportunity "to make a difference," but her introduction to the corruption, betrayals, and danger of a narc's life pushes her (and her partner) into drug dependency and confusion as they pursue the man suspected of being the local king-pin, played subtly by Greg Allman. "All Along the Watchtower" plays (seemingly on Leigh's car radio and/or on the drug dealer's stereo and, non-diegetically as audio overlay) as she alone enters the speed lab, makes her purchase, and is forced to take some of the drug herself. It turns out to be a powerful hallucinogen, and, as she drives away, she hallucinates, pulls off the road, and eventually passes out, all to Hendrix's tune, some of which features remarkably distorted passages, drifting in and out of Leigh's consciousness, apparently to communicate Leigh's drugged experience of the song. Not quite nostalgic, and not closely related to *Rush*'s themes, "All Along the Watchtower" resonates primarily as a marker of "too much confusion" in the lives of the agents and of the fact that they "can't get no relief." It marks a crisis, but not any kind of final turning point; it meshes with some of the other soundtrack songs, "Knocking on Heaven's Door" and "Tears in Heaven," but doesn't constitute a coherent musical environment.

One can only surmise that Ernest Thompson, who made *1969* in 1988, had only the barest nodding acquaintance with youth culture of 1969, although he was born in 1950. *1969* tells a confused story of two college students pranking and traveling around, trying to avoid the draft during spring and summer of 1969. Scott's and Ralph's mothers come, along with Ralph's younger sister Beth, to visit the local state university campus, and, while the five are on their way to lunch, a charismatic African-American professor instigates a crowd of assorted hippies to protest the Vietnam war, asking them finally "what are you going to do about it?" Some anonymous agitator yells "Take the [administration] building," and a riot ensues to Hendrix's "All Along the Watchtower." Chaos erupts, the mothers scream, campus cops beat up anybody within reach of their riot sticks. Despite its soundtrack offerings of Cream's "White Room" (played while Scott and Ralph fight in Selective Service offices as they disagree over whether to steal, burn, or leave their draft files there), Blind Faith's "Can't Find My Way Home," the Zombies' "Time of the Season" (played the first time Scott and Beth make love), *1969* seems wildly out of touch with the 1960s from beginning to end, especially when it tries to represent hip young people. For example, during one conversation, Scott begins to suggest all the rock groups he and Ralph can be like, if they only become as free as "leaves" on a tree. After mentioning names like Dylan and the Beatles, he adds, "and the Rolling Stones," to which Ralph implausibly replies: "the Rolling Stones; yeah, they are cool cats." The only saving grace is Hendrix's "All Along the Watchtower," played as an index to the confusion of the times, and of the fact that Scott and Ralph must find "some kind of way out of [t]here" in order not to be sent to Vietnam. But *1969* stops at that usage, failing to capitalize on the song's emphasis on a "moment of truth" and on its stress on not talking falsely. In fact, Scott and Ralph meander for another hour or so, rarely deciding on any definite course of action. Even *Forrest Gump* draws more significantly on Hendrix's version among the scores of popular tunes it includes, synchronizing the initial moments of Hendrix's version with Forrest Gump as he marches into the Vietnamese jungles.

"Let Us not Talk Falsely Now, The Hour is Getting Late"

Also in line with its narrative ethos, "All Along the Watchtower" frequently figures as the soundtrack moment marking exactly the opposite of retreat, withdrawal, and detachment from social concerns. I'd like to turn now to visual moments which, however different their contexts, share a complex sense of the core of Hendrix's cover: two episodes of *The Simpsons*, *Blue Chips*, and *Withnail and I*." In each case, whether diegetic or non, the playing of "All Along the Watchtower" signals both an end to talking and a decisive moment of the character's rejecting a world of withdrawal and propelling themselves into the world of action.

Televisions' *The Simpsons* offers a pair of episodes that more or less define the uses of Hendrix's version. "Mother Simpson" introduces Simpson's viewers to Homer's long absent mother, Mona, and "My Mother the Carjacker" recounts her return after living on the lam and her eventual incarceration for terrorism. In the first of these, Homer wants to know all about why she left and what she's been doing, so Mona relates her life story to the entire family. Once her marriage to husband Abe became intolerable, Mona gets radicalized when television coverage of Joe Namath's "wild, untamed facial hair revealed a new world of rebellion—of change. A world where doors were open for women like me. But Abe was stuck in his button-down plastic-fantastic Madison Avenue scene." Mona soon links up with radical hippies from the local university, and together they plan to bomb Mr. Burns's biological warfare lab. As Mona characterizes her newfound sensibility, "We'd met the enemy and it was Montgomery Burns. Drastic action had to be taken to stop his war machine." So, one night, after kissing Homer goodnight, Mona announces to her husband: "I put Homer to bed, Abe, and now I'm going out. It could be a late night—I'm meeting my destiny."[11] She walks out the door and the scene jumps to her and her comrades blowing up Mr. Burns's plant to the soundtrack of Hendrix's "All Along the Watchtower." As in so many other visual uses, the song here represents the crucial moment in Mother Simpson's life—her choosing to sacrifice life with her son, rejecting a comfortable middle-class existence, and embracing the radicalism necessary to fight for justice.

In the "My Mother the Carjacker" episode, Homer's mother returns to visit after decades on the lam and, after being recognized and a brief chase scene, is nabbed by Springfield police culminating in Homer crashing their getaway car into the police station. During the evening news, Kent Brockman recounts her career, and, for those "too young to remember the sixties," plays the station's "stock

---

[11]   http://www.snpp.com/episodes/3F06.html

montage" with Jimi Hendrix's "All Along the Watchtower" as the soundtrack. File footage stitches together brief scenes of student protests, GI's tramping through Vietnamese swamps, hippies dancing barefoot at Woodstock, Richard Nixon flashing double V's for "Victory" (as opposed to the Peace), Batman doing the Boogaloo, Neil Armstrong stepping onto the moon, and African-American athletes protesting during the medal ceremony at the Olympics. The montage concludes with the *Laugh In* tagline "you bet your sweet bippie" and Brockman's remark, "what a shrill, pointless decade." Indeed, Brockman's "stock montage" utilizes what has become the "stock soundtrack" for such historical footage, indicating the level of transparency "All Along the Watchtower" has achieved. The two Simpsons episodes dealing with Mother Simpson's radicalism, then, suggest both the song's radical ethos as well as its level of cliché. "All Along the Watchtower" quite readily fulfills either function.[12]

William Friedkin's 1994 intense basketball drama *Blue Chips* plays "All Along the Watchtower" in a manner similar to "Mother Simpson," at the defining moment when the coach Pete Bell's (Nick Nolte) career and life turn from decency and honesty to corruption. Stressing the seriousness of its themes, corruption in college sports, director Friedkin fills his film with actual sports and media personalities, including professional players Bob Cousy, Larry Bird, Penny Hardaway, Shaquille O'Neal; players from three entire college basketball teams; coaches Rick Pitino, Bobby Knight, Jerry Tarkanian, and Jim Boeheim; and sportscaster Dick Vitale. *Blue Chips*, which actually begins with an orchestral anticipation of the opening riffs to Jimi Hendrix's cover, traces a year in the career of a passionate and scrupulously honest coach, whose recruiting has been hampered by allegations of a point-shaving scandal several years before. As a result, he suffers his first losing season and is forced to reevaluate his approach to his team, the game, and himself. His road trips to visit three "blue chip," elite high school athletes is marked by soundtrack samplings of Booker T. and the MG's "Green Onions," Van Morrison and Them's version of "Baby Please Don't Go," and other tunes resonant with the various geographic regions he visits, Chicago, rural Indiana, and New Orleans.

Nolte knows he has a great chance to recruit his "blue chips," but he also realizes, after one of them openly demands money and another's mother requires a cushy job and new house "with a yard," that he has to break the rules to get his team (and his career) back in the win column. After anguishing over the decision,

---

[12] Howard Stern's *Private Parts* and National Lampoon's silly *Vegas Vacation* provide two other examples of the obviously frivolous usages of the Hendrix version. When the young Howard Stern decides really to make something of himself in radio, his decision and determination are reinforced by the playing of Hendrix's version. Similarly, after Clark Griswold (Chevy Chase) has lost most of his family's money on the gambling tables during their vacation to Las Vegas, he makes one final, desperate trip to the casino's ATM, Hendrix's "All Along the Watchtower" nearly explodes onto the screen in mock apocalyptic fashions as Griswold gleefully withdraws a huge amount of money, intended to help him recover his family's losses, but destined, inevitably and quickly, to slip out of his hands.

he is given the tacit go-ahead by athletic director (Cousy) and finally approaches his slimy nemesis, Happy, played by J.T. Walsh, a corrupt alumnus booster who arranges various kinds of pay-offs from "friends of the program." Nolte seems to have accepted the decision as a necessary evil, but when the boosters go too far and buy extravagant cars for the recruits, he confronts their leader and demands he stop. Whereas Happy had earlier tried to coax Coach Bell into helping the players because, as he said, "we owe them," he now informs Nolte that he "owns him" (and that he "owns" some of the players) and that he has, in fact, fixed games in the past, the "alleged" point-shaving scandal from three years earlier that Nolte knew nothing about and never believed. After watching films of the game in question, he realizes that one of his favorite players actually did make enough obvious mistakes to enable the opposing team to beat the spread, while nonetheless still insuring his team's victory.

Hendrix's "All Along the Watchtower" erupts into the soundtrack at the moment Nolte proceeds to the player's dormitory room to confront him about the charges. What follows is Nolte's raging at his player, his face contorted as he screams "tell me the truth, tell me the truth, tell me the truth!", this keying on the lyrics "So let us not talk falsely now / The hour is getting late." But the scene also builds on Nolte's rage ("no reason to get excited") and alludes to the crooked boosters who claim to "own" both the coach and some players ("businessmen they drink my wine" and "none of them along the line / Knows what any of it is worth"). Nolte walks out of the player's room as Hendrix's guitar solo fades out, prior to the final verse.

The scene precipitates a cluster of realizations for Nolte, and the rest of *Blue Chips* follows the trajectory of his "moment of truth." Nolte meets with his ex-wife, and she confronts him with the fact that he had earlier lied to her when she asked him if he had broken the rules. That she questions him and confronts him in exactly the same language as he had used with his player jolts Nolte with the realization that he has betrayed his wife, his team, the game, and himself, and he decides to retire after the triumphant game in which his team eventually defeats Bobby Knight's Indiana team. This film's final scene represents Coach Bell's ultimate transcendence; in front of a wildly enthusiastic press conference following his team's victory over Indiana, the coach owns up to his failings, blows the whistle on the corruption of the boosters, and resigns. He knew his hour was upon him, and that there was no time to be talking falsely. In other words, the playing of "All Along the Watchtower" in *Blue Chips* has significance far beyond the scene it accompanies; it establishes a force field of honesty, integrity, self-knowledge, and insight capable of guiding the lives of those who know that "life is not a joke."

Bruce Robinson's darkly witty *Withnail and I* (1986) offers an interesting index to the power and endurance of "All Along the Watchtower" for visual media.[13] Set

---

[13]   *Withnail and I* is a film whose debt to the culture of popular music includes George Harrison as "executive producer" (also featuring a brief segment from "While My Guitar

in the autumn of 1969 (the film makes several references to the impending end of the 1960s, called "the greatest decade in the history of human kind") in London, *Withnail and I* follows a few days in the lives of two unemployed actors who spend their time drinking, smoking, bemoaning their fates, launching hyperbolic declarations and demands, voicing paranoid suspicions, and falling into orgies of recrimination about the most mundane facets of their trivial existences. After rambling about in the mazes of their apartments and their booze and pot addled minds, Withnail and the unnamed protagonist realize that they've been inside too long—"I feel unusual," as Withnail puts it—and they realize that "we should get out of here for a while ... rejuvenate ourselves." There follows the most parodic playing of "All Along the Watchtower" in film history. Despite their interesting differences, other movies draw on the song to indicate moments of unarguable significance and intensity. *Withnail and I* utilizes the song to highlight the absurd trivialities, not the seriousness, of its protagonists' lives. They drive out of their urban wasteland to the sight of a huge wrecking ball smashing a building and to the lyrics, "There must be some kind of way out of here ... There's too much confusion / I can't get no relief." Shortly thereafter, Withnail launches into one of his hysterical tirades to the soundtrack of "No reason to get excited," and the two finally reach the remote cottage in a driving rainstorm to the soundtrack, "Two riders were approaching / And the wind began to howl." Whereas other film characters escaped brutal prison conditions or found themselves confronting war and race riots or the dangers of war in Vietnam, *Withnail and I* simply need to get out of their rat-infested apartment and get back in touch with something akin to normalcy, if not sobriety. If not for the humanity eventually revealed beneath each's bombast and narcissism, the parodic rendering of "All Along the Watchtower' might descend into unrelieved mockery. In a beautiful reflexive moment, *Withnail and I* calls attention to the artifice of the soundtrack. After about an hour of prolonged, chaotic adventures in the country, the two get in the car to return to London while "Voodoo Chile (Slight Return)" plays in the background, reconfiguring the entire rural interlude as something that can only take place to a rock and roll soundtrack, or, perhaps more interestingly, as something that has taken place in the empty grooves separating *Electric Ladyland*'s final two songs.

Each of these borrowings responds to Dylan's lyrics, to be sure, but each act also responds more decisively to Hendrix's instrumentation of "All Along The Watchtower." "There must be some kind of way out of here ... There's too much confusion" both Dylan and Hendrix sing, but it is Hendrix's bracing guitar thunder that galvanizes each film's characters to enter some world and to problematize the issue of exactly "where" "there's too much confusion."

These moments all problematize the meaning of the seven verses, beginning with "No reason to get excited" and concluding with "the hour is getting late."

Gently Weeps" near the end of the film), Richard Starkey as "special production consultant," and a soulful King Curtis rendition of "Whiter Shade of Pale" played during the opening credits and scene.

In both Dylan's original and Hendrix's cover version, these lines foreground the contradiction of the song, one which simultaneously advocates both escape (or withdrawal) and engagement. The drift of these lines urges us to recognize that some apocalyptic moment has arrived, one which threatens life as we know it, and, in response to the immanence of this threat, to accept the inherent seriousness of life, to abandon falsehoods, and to talk truly. But in each of these examples, the playing of the song marks a moment beyond talk altogether, a moment when all talk, whether true or false, has failed and immediate action seems the only proper solution.

"Two Riders Were Approaching; The Wind Began to Howl"

Almost immediately after the album's release in 1968, Tony Palmer captured the apocalyptic essence of Hendrix's "All Along the Watchtower" in one of the most powerful and poetic tributes to the song: "Listen to the single … the sound is by Hendrix, orgasmic, sputtering, aching, as if the entire fabric of the world is being torn apart. It is an assault … which must be like the roaring one hears moments before being disintegrated by an exploding hydrogen bomb" (quoted in Roby, 2002: 95–6). I don't know of any remarks that capture so perfectly the visceral impact of Hendrix's version, combining it with a sense of the song's cosmic significance, almost as a matter of life and death. Indeed, the final two appropriations of Hendrix's classic we will examine prove themselves equal to Palmer's paean, fusing the core of the song's intellectual, philosophical, political, and even psychological impact, bundling lyrics, sound, and cinematic moment into packages of immense significance. In these films, one original and one a classic, a person's fate and the fate of entire civilizations hinge on the ways in which individuals accept their moments of truth, even against almost insurmountable odds.

Tupac: Resurrection (2003), the bio documentary on rapper Tupac Shakur directed by Lauren Lazin and deftly edited by Richard Calderon, utilizes Hendrix's "All Along the Watchtower" to highlight a moment of crisis in its subject's life, and with equally powerful force. As Tupac remarks during a general discussion of the political angle of his rapping, "I represent twenty years on this planet earth and what I've seen; this is my report. It's like my battle cry to America." However, it's Shakur's response to the Vietnam war that truly radicalizes his perspective and cements his aesthetic. As in other films, Hendrix's "All Along the Watchtower" blasts onto the screen as Tupac recounts his own moment of truth as an artist:

> Just because the reporters show us pictures at home of the Vietnam war, that's what made the war end when it did, or the shit probably would have lasted longer. If noone knew exactly what was going on, you know, they were just dying valiantly in some beautiful way. But because we saw the horror, that's what made us stop the Vietnam war. So that's what I'm going to do as an artist, as a rapper: I'm going to show the most graphic details of what I see in my community and hopefully they'll make it stop, quickly. (*Tupac*, 2003)

During the first half of this extended meditation, the film samples various shots of bombing, bloody soldiers, and death in the rice paddies of Vietnam, but, once he moves on to his feelings about his contemporary existence, the footage changes to equally graphic scenes of bloody victims, violence, and death in the Los Angeles ghettos. Just as television journalism during the Vietnam war decided to stop talking falsely when it realized the hour was getting late, Shakur redoubles the truth-telling function and political responsibility of his own art in an effort to prevent both further daily casualties of urban violence, but also to prevent the musical media from avoiding direct confrontation of such daily ghetto realities. By 2003, "All Along the Watchtower" had been routinely associated with cinematic explorations of the chaos and violence of the Vietnam war, and, to some extent, its use in Tupac: *Resurrection* merely echoes this familiar soundtrack device. However, unlike *Forrest Gump*, *The Simpsons*, and other productions, *Tupac: Resurrection* parlays it into much more than a cinematic cliché. The gripping juxtaposition of violence in Vietnam and in Los Angeles deepens the significance of Shakur's own aesthetic by placing it in a global perspective. Again, far from the avoidance and escapism possibly suggested by thinking "that life is but a joke," Shakur zeroes in on the immediate dangers of not telling the truth, whether from a journalistic or a musical vantage point.

Even so-called "reality TV" has exploited this sense of looming danger to accentuate the melodramatic appeal of its programming. The History Channel's 2008 series *Ax Men* returns to this sense of vague foreboding in its use of "All Along the Watchtower" in its opening credit sequence. As the video zooms in on various groups of burly lumberjacks (are presenting different logging companies) looking defiantly into the camera or cutting down trees in the Pacific Northwest, a voiceover declares: "Here a rare breed of men gambling with life and limb. ... It's boom or bust, with big rewards and even bigger risk for those who call themselves Ax Men." In order to underscore the immanent danger looming over each logger, the commentary continues:

> Danger is a full-time job, as these brave men put everything on the line each and every day to retrieve the timber with which we build our country. Snapped cables, runaway logs and razor-sharp chainsaws are just some of the dangers that threaten their lives daily. Even with new technology that should make the job easier, it all boils down to the toughness and perseverance of the logging crews. Anything and everything can and does go wrong. Not everyone will survive, but those who do will earn their place in a long line of men who call themselves "Ax Men."[14]

In the background plays the first several bars of "All Along the Watchtower" followed seamlessly by the final few seconds of Hendrix's guitar fadeout. From deep political conspiracies to dangers faced in Iraq to the threat of immanent

---

[14]   http://www.history.com/content/axmen/about-the-show

amputation, "All Along the Watchtower" provides the sense of importance and, more significantly, of menace.

Beyond Dylan and Hendrix: Alternative Covers

As popular and iconic as Hendrix's version has become, and as much as it virtually defines the filmic appropriation of "All Along the Watchtower," other directors have incorporated stunning alternative covers, most, but not all, of which play off of Hendrix's original. The German film *Bandits* (1997) in which four female inmates form a rock group, employs "All Along The Watchtower" for a musical accompaniment to the dream of escape from prison life, similar to films like *Where the Buffalo Roam* and *Flashback*, but it plumbs the song's depths more seriously. The film, a simultaneously touching, harrowing, and derivative glimpse at *Thelma and Louise* style bonding among the women, opens with a sizzling diegetical rendition of "All Along The Watchtower," with views of the Bandits actually playing the song juxtaposed with those depicting the brutality of prison life in the form of beatings, hosings, and many deprivations. Emphasizing "there must be some kind of way out of here" and "there's too much confusion," the scene sets the frenetic pace followed by much of the film while also communicating the desperation of each band member's life and reason for being incarcerated. Having escaped from prison during their transport to perform at the local Policeman's Ball, they run from an unexploded WWII bomb they accidentally uncover to an instrumental reprise of the song.

Michael Mann's 2001 feature, *Ali*, charts significant moments from African-American history, including the murder of Emmet Till, the rise and murder of Malcolm X, the assassination of Dr. Martin Luther King, and the contemporaneous rise of boxing promoter Don King, as it traces the boxer's roller coaster rise to eminence. During Ali's suspension from boxing stemming from his refusal to accept military induction, Ali's lawyer phones him to let him know that his case looks weak. The telephone conversation is interspersed with scenes of chaos in the American streets, including anti-war riots, race riots, and, finally, the murder of Dr. King, all to a wordless, electric version of "All Along The Watchtower" by an ensemble listed in the film's credits as the "Watchtower Four." *Ali* foregrounds the song's two dominant themes, "there's too much confusion" and, since life is not a joke, "let us not talk falsely now," in this case applied to the corrupt decisions rendered depriving Ali of his boxing privileges in retaliation to his refusing to countenance the immoral and murderous war in southeast Asia. *Ali*'s use of "All Along The Watchtower" is remarkable, for two reasons: this wordless version suggests how powerfully the song resonates with the chaos and confusion of the period of the late 1960s—it can be used, even without the lyrics, as a kind of shorthand evocation of social upheaval, and Dylan's song is the only "white" song in the entire film, one that opens with a Sam Cooke live performance and which features numerous R & B tunes and African music. However, accompanying signs of social unrest following the murder of Dr. King as it does, *Ali*'s "All Along the

Watchtower" references another song from *Electric Ladyland*, "House Burning Down," the cut immediately preceding "All Along the Watchtower" and a tune that specifically comments on the riots, urban violence, and literal "burning" of many inner city neighborhoods following Dr. King's assassination. Whereas Dylan's version meshes with an album addressing serious moral and ethical issues, Hendrix's version intervenes in a more apocalyptic scenario, filled with voodoo, urban unrest, and otherworldly visions. Moreover, it was Hendrix's version that presents a multi-racial musical ensemble, perhaps one capable of projecting some "some way out of" the racially polarized world of 1968.

John Malkovich's directorial debut, *The Dancer Upstairs* (2002) examines the intricate emotional and political environment of a "Latin American" country in the midst of a guerilla revolution. Similar to "the Shining Path" in Peru, the "Ezequiel" movement is lead by a former college professor who has dedicated his life to furthering a Maoist revolutionary agenda. Nina Simone's breathtaking cover rendition of Sandy Denny's "Who Knows Where the Time Goes" frames *The Dancer Upstairs*, heard on car stereo of Ezequiel (Abel Folk) and his small band of revolutionaries as they cross into what appears to be Mexico and, in the film's final moments, as the accompaniment for Captain Augustin Rejas's (Javier Bardem) daughter's interpretive dance. But with only one major exception, Simone's singing is the only actual "song" in the film. Indeed, Malkovich allows ambient, real world sounds to dominate the aural dimension of his film. Therefore, in a soundtrack that includes subtle, austere, and unobtrusive occasional music by Alberto Iglesias, Jul Anderson's interpretation of "All Along the Watchtower" almost sneaks into the film, beginning as a low-volume piano accompaniment to Yolanda's (Laura Morante) interpretive dance in progress. We see her moving slowly and sensuously in time with the piano playing, which features surging and mountainous piano chords reminiscent of Keith Jarrett's improvisations of the early 1970s before eventually settling into a subtle quoting of Dylan's guitar introduction and a harbinger of what is to come. Anderson's piano and vocal "All Along the Watchtower" erupts almost as the film's only musical interlude, thus heightening the significance of the Dylan/Hendrix fusion cover: "There must be some kind of way out of here / Said the Joker to the thief" followed by three jumbled lines that improvise on Dylan's original, and concluding with "all along the watchtower" repeated, and the observation of princes keeping view of the two riders and barefoot servants approaching.

After elaborate surveillance, Rejas and his associates capture the notorious and elusive Ezequiel, who, apparently Yolanda's lover, has been living above her studio. In honoring Rejas for his diligence, the capture and trial is credited to "the effort of one honest man," i.e., a man who knew that the hour was much too late for talking falsely.

Michael D. Almereyda's 2000 contemporized film version of Shakespeare's *Hamlet* includes what must surely be the most detailed, enigmatic, and evocative soundtrack usage of "All Along the Watchtower" ever. Dylan's lyrics fit perfectly in a play and film that traffics constantly on the difference between what *is* and what *seems to be* truth and reality. Throughout *Hamlet*, characters feign truth, sincerity, seriousness, insanity, concern, friendship, and regret. As Hamlet, played by Ethan Hawke, returns from London, Horatio picks him up at the airport, and the two proceed on motorcycle to the cemetery where Ophelia is being buried. Almereyda's filmic translation omits the gravedigger scene in which Hamlet extemporizes over Yorick's skull (a joker, as it were), but as Hamlet (a Prince who tries to keep the view) and Horatio walk towards Ophelia's burial plot, they do pass a man digging a grave while singing the joker/thief conversation about a "way out of here", "too much confusion" and "no relief."

This version of Hamlet recasts Denmark as a modern corporation, giving Dylan's reference to "business men" deeper resonance. Moreover, since murderous Claudius poisons a glass of wine in an attempt to kill Hamlet, even this detail of Dylan's lyrics meshes with Almereyda's vision. Of course, the "business man" drinking Hamlet's wine is his step-father/uncle Claudius, who, by murdering his brother and marrying Gertrude has usurped Hamlet's hereditary claims to the throne and Denmark's riches. "All Along the Watchtower" fades in and out at barely audible volume, but the drift is clear. No longer able to soliloquize and meditate on his course of action, Hamlet, now outraged by the corruption and duplicity pervading his world in a manner fully consistent with the ethos of Dylan's lyrics and Hendrix's instrumentation and interpretation, confronts his adversaries and faces his moment of truth. Indeed, from that moment on, the pace, the intensity, and the carnage in the film increase until Hamlet utters his famous last line, "the rest is silence."

In the two episode finale of *Battlestar Galactica* third season, the popular sci-fi series incorporated it own superb version of "All Along the Watchtower" in what might well be the ultimate thematic embedding of the song into a narrative scheme, utilizing it both in diegetic and non-diegetic ways. For those not familar with the series, *Battlestar Galactica* is a drama of the final humans surviving a cosmic holocaust and their struggle with the robotic Cylons as they try to find their way to their ultimate haven, Earth. Mysteries abound, identities fluctuate and loyalties are tested and revealed throughout the series, with the final two episodes of the third season representing a tension fraught conclusion, "to be continued" in Season Four. Throughout the two-hour finale, various characters (but not all characters) hum and/or hear mysterious, vaguely Asiatic-sounding music; noone recognizes it or know where it is coming from, but many ask questions like "what is that music?" or "That song. Don't you hear that song?". At one point Captain Tigh believes the Cylons have sabotaged their craft by infecting it with the music, and, when asked how that could be, responds: "I can't quite understand it myself. There's too much confusion." The sounds permeate both episodes without ever reaching a recognizable melody until the final moments of the season, with one character noting "I don't even know (the song). I can't get it out of my head." Also throughout the entire episode, characters incorporate quotes from Hendrix's version of "All Along the Watchtower" into their dialogues and internal musings. Consistently, over the course of the final two hours, we hear lines like "Some way out of here," "two riders were approaching," "there's too much confusion," "there must be some kind of way out of here" (Hendrix's addition), "said the joker to the thief," and "I can't get no relief," all in response to crises and confusion aboard the human's craft as they carry on two dramas, the prosecution of an alleged traitor among them and the immanent threat of a Cylon attack. At one critical moment, Anders communicates his feelings about the mysterious music: "Yeah. It's freaking me out. I hear it everywhere, I mean, but I can't ... but I can't really hear it, you know what I mean?" The Chief answers "Yeah, it's like you can grab just a part of the melody and then it goes away. Like it's something from," and then both say "Childhood." Not until a final, climactic power failure aboard the human fleet leading up to a Cylon attack does the mystery music resolve itself into a stunning rendition of "All Along the Watchtower" arranged and performed by Bear McCreary, incorporating electric sitar, harmonium, duduk, yayli tanbur, electric violin and zurna.[15] Whereas every earlier quote from or reference to "that music" played a diegetic function, this swelling into a recognizable melody with complete lyrics exists outside of the dramatic action but, quite interestingly, recapitulates every previous diegetic borrowing. Throughout the episodes it does mark moments of personal resolution, the looming threat to the few hundred surviving human beings, and a widespread conviction that life is not a joke and that "the hour is getting late."[16]

In a remarkable moment of luck, Battlestar Galactica also reprised its "All Along the Watchtower" theme in an episode broadcast the week I was scheduled to finish this essay, in its fifth season. We hadn't heard the song since the Season Three finale. The episode explores Starbuck's identity crisis (nor do the viewers understand her origins), and she's playing a duet with another, unknown character, at first both of them merely exploring up and down a piano keyboard, without giving any indication as to where the theme is heading. The man she's playing with has seemed, up to this point, to be just a piano player in a bar, but then we realize he's an apparition of her father. He leads, and urges Starbuck to "just come in when [she] thinks she's ready." What we hear is a repetition of the first chords of Dylan's original, building and building into a thunderous block of sound, an intensification worthy of Hendrix's electrification of the song, with some of the instrumentation from Season Three in the background. The fact that she plays the song suggests she's a Cylon, because the song seems to be an unofficial Cylon theme, one which both signals and enables their understanding of their identity *as* Cylons rather than humans (if, indeed, there can any longer be a clear-cut distinction). The more Starbuck merges with and plays fully with the theme, the happier she seems. As soon as the song finishes, Captain Tigh, the character who

---

[15] http://en.wikipedia.org/wiki/Music_of_Battlestar_Galactica_(re-imagining)# Season_3_soundtrack. Accessed 24-2-2009

[16] I would like to thank my friend and colleague Christina Fitzgerald for helping me understand the context of *Battlestar Gallactica* in which "All Along the Watchtower" is played. Thanks also for loaning me the DVD!

was obsessed with the song in Season Three, rushes over and asks, "where did you learn to play that song?", to which Starbuck answers, in an important reference to the third season, "I played it as a child." While we don't yet fully understand the significance of the song or of so many characters once thought human to be revealed as Cylons, I venture a guess that *Battlestar Galactica* has adopted "All Along the Watchtower" as the theme for the entire series. In its gradual incorporation of the song to accompany crucial revelations of its characters' identities, characters that viewers had thought were human, the series itself decides to "not talk falsely now" and finally to divulge a crucial undercurrent of its entire narrative architecture. No longer merely a "cover" of the Hendrix version; indeed, no longer a cover at all thematically, "All Along the Watchtower" emerges as the dominant touchstone to the series's pervasive, even definitive, ontological mysteries. Captain Tigh imagined that it was the spaceship actually playing the song at the conclusion of Season Three; he might not have been so far off. None of the characters actually "knows" the song; they merely remember it as some vague remnant of childhood (maybe as it actually is for many baby boomers). Whereas Wim Wenders asserts that his film *Alabama: 2000 Light Years from Home* is literally "about the difference between the Dylan version of "All Along the Watchtower," and the Jimi Hendrix Version," *Battlestar Galactica* might actually be an entire multi-year series "about" the Hendrix version.

Indeed, if the song marked transformational moments for Hamlet, Mother Simpson, various Ax Men, Lester Burnham (*American Beauty*), Coach Pete Bell (*Blue Chips*), Tupac Shakur, Withnail and I, Ali, and all the others, in *Battlestar Galactica* the song reinforces the possibility of the complete annihilation of the human race by the Cylons, or, more hopefully, the possibility of human life evolving into a new, perhaps more enduring, form. Jimi Hendrix's "cover" of "All Along the Watchtower" is probably the key to evolution and remarkable endurance of Bob Dylan's song; Cylons might play a similar role for the human race, evolved into a new form capable of surviving into an unseen future.

Thus both film directors and television producers have drawn on "All Along the Watchtower" to represent and enhance the philosophical, psychological, and existential sense of danger and foreboding in historical dramas from medieval Denmark to contemporary suburbia, in personal crises from Grandma Simpson's decision to dedicate herself to thwarting the evil Mr. Burns's plans for environmental destruction to "Withnail and I" leaving their flat for a drive in the country. The ancient to the sci-fi future, from the profound and the frivolous, from the personal to the communal. Taking inspiration from nearly every line of Dylan's song, every intense riff from Hendrix's interpretation of it, and, increasingly, stunning new realizations of the words and potential sounds of "All Along the Watchtower," films and television programs propel their characters' idle chatter, false talk, and confusing exchanges, sometimes into transformative bursts of understanding, but also sometimes into decisive, if speechless, action. For Hamlet, Grandma Simpson, Lester Burnham, virtually all talk is compromised by the corruption and cliché of their respective social environments filled with political sycophantism, husbandly grouching, and advertising slogans. As their own existential circumstances "begin to howl," each character braces him or herself for some ultimate confrontation, beyond confusion and joking, but also beyond words. Their final embrace of personal transcendence often does result in their deaths, but each character meets their fate with something approaching resolution and dignity. In Hamlet's case, the rest is silence, for the others who realize the hour is getting late, the rest blends political engagement with personal redemption, a far cry indeed from apathy and despair.

Chapter 9

The Same Yet Different/
Different Yet the Same:
Bob Dylan Under the Cover of Covers

Greg Metcalf

Who's the guy at the beginning?"

—guest comment on "Ads of the World" web posting
of "Pepsi Refresh Anthem" video[1]

The 2009 Super Bowl "Pepsi Refresh Anthem" commercial[2] begins with audio of Bob Dylan singing an electric countrified cover of his own "Forever Young" over images of Dylan from the mid-1960s Don't Look Back period, then makes a transition into Will.i.am's hip-hop covering of the song. While Will.i.am raps we hear Dylan's harmonica creep back in. Then Dylan's voice returns for the last line of the song as we see a split screen of an onstage Will.i.am on the right side apparently acknowledging the onstage Dylan on the left. The voiceover informs us that "Every Generation Refreshes the World."

The commercial continues with paralleled footage of the youth and pop culture of "Dylan's" and "Will.i.am's" generations (Gumby and Shrek, John Belushi and Jack Black, concert-goers holding up lighters and concert-goers holding up cell phones, concluding with a split screen image of young women of the Sixties and the Oughts enjoying their Pepsi.) The generations are the same and yet different. Early on Dylan is seen in mid-Sixties attire checking out a pair of RayBan sunglasses that he holds up to the camera to examine then, through the magic of editing, Will.i.am—about forty years later—seems to take the sunglasses and put them on, leading to a split screen where both Dylan and Will.i.am appear to be wearing the same pair of sunglasses. Though the rest of their fashion sense is quite different, the parallel shots show how alike the two sunglassed musicians are.

Twice we see a graphic variation of the recycle logo "rotating arrows" revolving between splitscreened Dylan and Will.i.am and back, suggesting, not just Dylan's influence on Will.i.am but the influence of each on the other. Each shapes the other.

---

[1]   http://adsoftheworld.com/media/tv/pepsi_refresh_anthem
[2]   http://www.youtube.com/watch?v=XCDNaP11hwM&feature

Covering is plagiarism, taking someone else's song and "making it your own." But generally it is an acknowledged plagiarism, which creates a comparison that simple theft would not. We hear the new voice singing but the original voice hangs in the air, though generally not as literally as Dylan's voice and harmonica in the "Pepsi Refresh Anthem" commercial.

The Same, Yet Different. Different, Yet the Same

> There's so many sides to Bob, he's round.
>
> —Bono, 09/12/06 Rolling Stone[3]

As with most things, Bob Dylan forces us to reconsider our definitions of "covering." Dylan has had his songs covered, his style covered, his personae covered. Dylan has covered traditional songs, standards, the hits of others, developed a method of songwriting that grows out of covering and has even come up with a new way of "covering" songs as a radio host. Bob Dylan constantly covers his own songs. Bob Dylan has covered the personae of others. And, of course, Dylan has often covered himself.

The Bob Dylan we know is a cover. Or a series of covers.

In his *Chronicle: Volume One* (2004), Dylan explains his impulse to write songs as the need to "convert something—something that exists into something that didn't yet" (Maslin, 2004). What follows is a consideration of Dylan's use of covers in a broad sense of the term—the way Dylan has reinterpreted existing artwork, style or image, originally as a way of connecting himself to a tradition but then as a (largely unsuccessful) attempt to separate himself from his unwanted cultural role.

> I knew Bobby Dylan back in the days when he lived in the Village. He used to come and see me and sing songs for me, saying they ought to go into my next collected book on American folk music.
>
> —Alan Lomax, Oral History, *American Roots Music Project*[4]

Bob Dylan recorded the folk/blues standard "House of the Rising Sun" for his first album in 1961. As Van Ronk tells the story, the version Dylan recorded was Van Ronk's own well-known arrangement (Scorsese, 2005). Once Dylan's record came out, Van Ronk couldn't record his own arrangement and even had to stop performing it because of audiences insisted that he was copying Dylan's song.

---

[3]   http://www.rollingstone.com/rockdaily/index.php/2006/09/12/on-the-set-of-the-new-bob-dylan-movie-blanchett-rocks-stephen-malkmus-covers-maggies-farm/

[4]   http://www.pbs.org/americanrootsmusic/pbs_arm_oralh_alanlomax.html

There's one more twist, according to Van Ronk. When Eric Burdon and The Animals recorded their version of the song in 1964, Dylan had to stop playing the song because he was accused of plagiarizing them.

"House of the Rising Sun" has been traced back to the eighteenth century and had been recorded by many musicians including Roy Acuff, Woody Guthrie, Leadbelly, Frankie Laine and Joan Baez, but Dylan's version becomes the "authentic" version that other people "covered." Van Ronk is covering Dylan's recording when he plays his own arrangement of the song. And when The Animals create a new arrangement, Dylan and Van Ronk are covering them.

> (Blowin' In The Wind) ... I wrote in 10 minutes, just put words to an old spiritual, probably something I learned from Carter Family records. That's the folk music tradition. You use what's been handed down. "The Times They Are A-Changin'" is probably from an old Scottish folk song ... (Subterranean Homesick Blues) ... it's from Chuck Berry, a bit of, and some of the scat songs of the '40s.
> —Bob Dylan (Hilburn, 2004).

Dylan starts from a folk music tradition where songs are shared property, raw material handed down for any singer who wants to perform it or rewrite it. The assumption is a general one, that a singer is incorporating, and in dialogue with, the songs and the singers of the historical community.

A song in today's environment is a piece of intellectual property. The dominant view in the music industry is of the song as a saleable commodity, not a conversation. Here a cover is a repurposing of someone else's specifically-owned property. Sampling, shout-outs and postmodern quotation all reinvent the folk tradition "wheel" in the vocabulary of contemporary pop culture. When Jay-Z covers the Annie song in "Knockdown Life (Ghetto Anthem)," it's an obvious reference for the audience and his people pay their people for the rights to use their property. When Dylan uses a Carter family song or Henry Timrod's or even Ovid's poetry, the audience generally doesn't have the knowledge to recognize the "cover" and the quotation stands outside the system for paying for rights.[5]

In his interview with Robert Hilburn of the *Los Angeles Times* in 2004, Dylan, accused of plagiarizing parts of his *Modern Times* album, explained that when he writes a song he starts with an existing song and plays it in his head, constantly rolling it around and meditating on it for days on end. "At a certain point some words will change and I'll start writing a song" (Hilburn, 2004). As Dylan describes it, the act of songwriting grows out of the act of covering. He rearranges the "authentic" version to a point that he has "made something new" from it. Dylan enjoys the commercial rewards of the idea of a song as intellectual property, but the process he describes is an anachronistic view of relationship of artists and pre-existing art given the business models that determine our view of music.

---

[5]   Issues of sources and credits are extensively covered in http://en.wikipedia.org/wiki/Modern_Times_ (Bob_Dylan_album)

Dylan has also done easily recognizable covers of a wide range of songs, 500 are listed and annotated in Derek Barker's *The Songs He Didn't Write: Bob Dylan Under the Influence* (2009). He's covered The Marines' *Hymn*, Bruce Springsteen, the Clash, Warren Zevon, Mart Robbins, "Old MacDonald," and "Froggie Went A Courtin,"' to name but a few. His dialogue with existing songs (and their creators) is a long-running process of offering new context for his own songs and the songs he covers. He also appears to cover songs for the fun of it.

Since 2006 Dylan has extended his "covering" in his Sirius satellite radio program *Theme Time Radio Hour.* Here Dylan doesn't perform the songs, he simply backforms the role of the hip hop DJ to its radio host roots and creates a mosaic of the songs of other juxtaposed and interpolated with his word riffs and readings of the words of others. Dylan "covers' the idea of the radio show and turns it into a personal artwork. The "Dylan" persona is an illusive—and elusive—figure who is primarily revealed through the work of others that he re-presents in a new context. A sign of how seriously Dylan takes this work can be seen in the fact that with his *Together Through Life* (2009) album, he also released a disc of the August 23, 2000 episode of the radio show titled "Friends & Neighbors" featuring sixteen songs by others and his spoken word.

Dylan's songs get covered. The web page "It Ain't Me, Babe" lists 5870 cover recordings of 350 different Dylan songs by 2791 artists.[6] The "Dylan Cover Albums" web page lists at least 69 albums of collections of cover recordings of Dylan in English (many with multiple discs), 170 albums of Dylan songs performed by a single artist, about 50 EPs, another 50-odd albums with multiple Dylan songs in non-English languages and at least twenty albums of Dylan instrumentals.[7] That doesn't include albums that are only partly composed of Dylan covers. Perhaps the overwhelming nature of this mini-genre of popular music explains the title of a 2004 three disc collection titled *Oh Shit! Not Another Dylan Cover Album.*

Joan Baez covering a Dylan song in the early 1960s when she was "the Queen of Folk" was an endorsement of Dylan (the equivalent of her inviting him on stage to perform with her at the Newport Festival). Joan Baez covering "Simple Twist of Fate" on *Diamonds and Rust* (1975), even before she does a gently mocking Dylan impression for the third verse of the song, makes it unavoidable that this is a Bob Dylan song possibly written about her, and leads the audience to read the lyrics of the song—and her decision to sing it—as comment on their shared past.

Most covers don't carry so much personal baggage, but the meaning of a cover changes depends on who sings it and when it's being sung. Early in his career, Dylan was a songwriter-singer—in part because, as he puts it, he was not a "melodic singer." The more famous Peter, Paul and Mary covered "Blowin' in the Wind" and became the authoritative version. "Mr. Tambourine Man" was the first of many Dylan songs that the Byrds transformed into hits. The early versions gave credibility to Dylan.

---

6   See http://www.bjorner.com/covers.htm
7   See http://dylancoveralbums.com/various.htm#varioustop

As taste's adjusted, Dylan's versions of his songs became authoritative. Once he was the authority himself, the act of covering Dylan changed. To sing the songs of the "Voice of a Generation" was to claim kinship with that symbol. The counterculture cool of Dylan could be invoked by recording his songs. "Maggie's Farm" raises the complexity of a simple cover. Dylan's original Newport electric performance in 1965 made the song an attack on the limits of the folk movement and a declaration of electric independence. But, over time that specific context dropped away and the song became a more general statement against "The Man" in cover recording like those by Grateful Dead and Rage Against the Machine. In the UK of the 1980s with a conservative Prime Minister named Maggie, a new meaning attached in cover. The Blues Band in 1980 changed Dylan's reference to "The National Guard" to "the Special Patrol Group," the special London police squad to stop protests. But many bands, including U2 and the Specials, recorded covers which blended a new context with the general values associated with Bob Dylan's persona as "Voice of a Generation." Even performers who didn't perform the whole song "name-checked" it in references worked into their protest songs against the PM.[8] Covering Dylan in this context attaches Dylan's authority of historical political protest to a contemporary singer—even though the original song was not a political song. Dylan's persona transcends the specific song.

> Don't you see, Alice, they took it all away. It's not about me anymore, it's all about him (gestures to Jack Rollins billboard). Your "guaranteed, double-your-money-back Voice-of-the-People" ... They took away the meaning Alice. I was a pawn in their game.
> —Robbie playing Jack Rollins (one of the Dylans) in *I'm Not There*
> (Haynes, 2007)

One approach to covers is to attempt to mainstream the songs and take away their unique significance. Interestingly, Dylan has been very much part of this approach to covering the Dylan songs. Dylan's autobiography *Chronicles: Volume One*, confirms that Dylan has spent the most of his career attempting to escape the label of "Voice of a Generation." By the 1970s he was well into covering his classics—intentionally rearranging his songs to take them out of the realm of iconic protest music and re-turn them to popular entertainment or to change them from symbols back into songs. While Dylan's changing public personae—his "covering" rearrangement of the Voice of a Generation Dylan in different styles—are acknowledged as an attempt to free himself from his legendary status, less attention has been paid to Dylan's covering of his own music.

Bob Dylan at Budokon (1978) is a double-disc concert cover album. Twenty-two previously recorded songs are performed by Dylan with his Street Legal backing band (and some of his Rolling Thunder facepaint still in place). The album was widely considered a failure because it wasn't respectful to his own songs. Dylan

---

8   See http://www.absoluteastronomy.com/topics/Maggie%27s_Farm

was not respecting "Dylan." *Rolling Stone* called Dylan's new arrangements his "Vegas Period."

A more sympathetic review of the Budokan album agreed that not all of the songs worked but recognized the purpose these cover recordings served:

> However much they may offend purists, these latest live versions of his old songs have the effect of liberating Bob Dylan from the originals. And the originals—however lasting, however beautiful—constitute a terrible burden. ... (Maslin, 1979)

Dylan doing a "Vegas style" cover of "Blowin' in the Wind" is fundamentally different from Elvis Presley doing a Vegas style cover of one of Dylan's songs. When Elvis records the song he is acknowledging the mainstream success of Dylan's work, suggesting similarity as he adds a bit of Dylan to the world of Elvis. When Dylan does the *Budokan* album, he is moving *himself* away from Voice of a Generation, trying to establish difference. Covering for Dylan becomes an act of creative destruction, a way of separating himself from the legend he did not want to be. He moves from one version of his catalog to another, just as he moves from one persona to another. Changing his songs becomes changing his persona.

Dylan continues to rearrange his standards so completely that he might seem to be moving from simply covering them to attempting to transform them into something enitirely new. I have personally heard Dylan perform his classic sixties anthems as folk songs, punk songs, jazz-blues songs, country swing band songs, Grateful Dead space jams, and various forms of pop rock. A tradition at Dylan concerts of the last few decades has been the clusters of audience members conferring amongst themselves as they try to decide what song it is that Dylan is performing.

Dylan's most exemplary, and self-effacing, self-cover is "All Along the Watchtower." He has performed the song more than any other in his career, an estimated 1393 times by the end of 2003. The significance is that Dylan doesn't perform his own version, he covers Jimi Hendrix's 1968 cover of Dylan's song. Dylan has said ".''I liked Jimi Hendrix's record of this and ever since he died I've been doing it that way ... Strange how when I sing it, I always feel it's a tribute to him in some kind of way" (Crowe, 1985). The action provides an intriguing closure to his use of the Dave Van Ronk arrangement of "House of the Rising Sun."

Theoretically, as Dylan overtly distanced himself from his own version of his song he also distanced himself from the legendary Dylan who wrote it. However, time has shown that it doesn't quite work that way and Dylan's cover of Hendrix has succeeded only in adding a dose of Hendrix into the legendary Dylan persona.

While Dylan's self-covers have been intended to expand the difference between him and the iconic Dylan, the end result seems to be to stress how similar he remains.

Dylan's desire to break away from the Voice of a Generation persona may explain his otherwise inexplicable fondness for U2's Bono and his covers of Dylan's songs. While U2 have performed Dylan songs throughout their career, Bono has made a point of not learning the lyrics or improvising new ones in performance.

In the 1980s, Dylan repeatedly invited Bono up on stage to sing with him. The first time was at a concert outside Dublin where, as Bono describes it

> He took me to the side of the stage and said, "You know the words to 'Leopardskin Pill-Box Hat'?" And I said yes. I was lying. So I came onstage and just sang …. He howled with laughter for a moment. "(Am) I done?" And then Dylan's son came over and said, "Listen, Bob would like you to close the show. He'd like you to sing 'Blowin' in the Wind.'" He obviously figured I knew the words to "Blowin' in the Wind". I went out there, and Dylan sang all the verses I knew, so it was (either) go back and begin the song again or go forward—and I decided to forget it, and I just wrote this other verse. In the middle of this, Dylan turned round and said to his bass player, "What key are we in?" 'Cause I'd changed the tune as well as the words. (Connelly, 1985)

Since Dylan has continued to invite Bono to perform with him, he clearly enjoyed the Irish singer's lack of piety for the legendary songs of the Voice of a Generation Dylan.

> If you could be any Bob Dylan you wanted to, which Bob Dylan would you be?
> —Mick Stevens cartoon caption (2007)[9]

Dylan became the classic example of the way that an artist—not just his songs—can be covered. In fact the failure of Dylan to erase the Voice of a Generation persona is probably best seen in the now waning phenomenon of "The New Dylan." The label of New Dylan has been applied to folkies, to protest singers, and to singer-songwriters for the last few decades, leading to lists of "New Dylans" including Bruce Springsteen, Tracy Chapman, Steve Goodman, John Prine, Beck, Donovan and Billy Bragg.[10] It even led to the inevitable band named The New Dylans. Similarly, a quick Google search of "Bob Dylan" and the name of a nation or region will reveal that every area of the planet seems to have its own Dylan. Scott Seward suggests that "New Dylan" refers to style not substance. His reading stresses the Voice of a Generation Dylan to stress that NWA, Public Enemy and Bob Marley were the true New Dylans, not Wilco, Loudon Wainwright III, Steve Forbert and the Bodeans (Seward, 2001).

Parody is the cover where persona plays out most completely. A parody works not just on style or lyrics but also perceived meaning of its subject. Dylan's unique voice and style of songwriting makes it easy to cover the persona. The classic Dylan parody is still the Voice of a Generation folk protest song sung in a broad nasal voice with idiosyncratic phrasing.

---

[9]   ID: 124694, Published in *The New Yorker* December 10, 2007.

[10] See http://www.mesh5.com/tension/febmarch/dylan.htm

The most complicated parodic cover of Dylan is probably the 2007 anonymously web-released album *Dylan Hears a Who*, a tone perfect rendition of seven Dr. Seuss poems and books sung by a" Like a Rolling Stone" era Dylan (Brekke, 2007). The artistic success of the album as a collection of covers comes from the skill in imitating Dylan's singing and phrasing but also the successful fitting of existing music and the creation of new music and arrangements that sound like they are outtakes from Dylan's recordings of the mid-1960s. This work shares much with Dylan's folk processes except it is intended to be funny. The simple joke is that the "unimportant" children's stories are sung in the "important" Dylan voice. But, as with any good cover, the recordings force us into a comparison of the Voice of a Generation and the Voice of a Different Sort of Youth Culture. Unexpected similarities between Dylan's and Seuss's voices emerge and the deadpan treatment of the material makes for some surprisingly affecting songs.

The success of the parody points out Dylan's failure to separate himself from his earlier personae. Just as the Pepsi "Refresh Anthem" seamlessly blends mid-Sixties visuals with a cover of a mid-Seventies song, *Dylan Hears a Who* works because we blend the Voice of Generation persona with the Electric Dylan persona. Regardless of Dylan's effort to be seen as "different" we continue to read "the same."

> Chief Tyril: There must be some way out of here …
> Colonal Tigh: … said the Joker to the Thief …
> Anders: … there's too much confusion …
> Tory: … I can't get no relief.
>
> *—Battlestar Galactica* (Verheiden 2007)

Dylan's music has also become a staple of film and television soundtracks. The Internet film data base lists 258 movies and television shows using at least one Dylan song.[11] The songs, whether interpretations or originals, function as covers in the way they invoke the meaning and context of the original recordings but also add a sense of meaning through juxtaposition to the original. *Brokeback Mountain* (2006) used as part of its soundtrack a Willie Nelson cover of "He Was a Friend of Mine" to underscore the story of two men. *North Country* (2005) used a combination of ten covers and Dylan originals to establish both a Northern Minnesota setting and reinforce the film's political message.

Watchmen (2009), based on a set of comics by Alan Moore, who self-consciously used Dylan lyrics like a cover, sets up new meaning for the lyrics as they are juxtaposed with events in the story. As with the Pepsi Anthem mentioned earlier, this process works in both directions—it attaches Dylan authority to Moore's story but it also attaches something of Moore's narrative to the song.

That process is transferred to the film where three songs are used. Dylan's "The Times They are a Changin'" is used doubly, to establish a late 1960s setting

---

[11]　http://www.imdb.com/name/nm0001168/

of unrest but also as a literal—and ironic –warning that the we are looking at an alternate version of history. My Chemical Romance's cover of "Desolation Row" and Hendrix's "All Along the Watchtower" are used to enhance and comment on the seedy reality and characters in one case, and an approaching apocalypse in the other.

"All Along the Watchtower" is not just performed in the last two seasons of the SciFi Channel series *Battlestar Galactica*, it is central to the plot. The song is the trigger that awakens awareness in the secret Cylons who had thought they were human and it is the series' last word as we see that the inescapable cycle of history is going to repeat itself yet again. The Bear McCreary cover is pleasantly dislocating as it takes a "South-Asian Metal" approach to the Hendrix arrangement, but the more extreme covering takes place in the show's script. Taking the Voice of a Generation persona to the Eric Clapton extreme, the song doesn't just awakens characters to their destiny, the show's ending implies that Dylan's song, which we find precedes Dylan by several millennia, might be the voice of God.

> All I can do is be me, whoever that is.
>
> —Bob Dylan[12]

Since the 1970s, Dylan has played covers of himself in film. As Alias in Sam Peckinpah's *Pat Garret and Billy the Kid* (1973), Dylan plays the obscure witness to history, a variation on his role in the *John Wesley Harding* album, enhanced by a series of period songs for the film's soundtrack.

In *Renaldo and Clara* (1978), Dylan built an art film around the Rolling Thunder Revue concert tour with self-covering performances by himself (Renaldo), his wife Sara (Clara) and Joan Baez (Woman in White) and Ronnie Hawkins playing a character called "Bob Dylan." The key players blended life and image as they re-enacted a cover version of the romantic triangle of their real lives.

Dylan plays a Dylan cover as Jack Fate, the Voice of a Generation gone to seed, who is released from prison to perform a benefit concert in an unspecified time and country in *Masked and Anonymous* (2003), a film he co-wrote with director Larry Charles. The cover on his persona is reinforced by a soundtrack of dozens of covers of Dylan songs recorded by Dylan and other artists, many singing in languages other than English. The non-English covers dislocate us further than a standard cover of a classic, even one sung by Dylan, because they make the familiar words and language that define Dylan unfamiliar, reinforcing the film's version of Dylan. The same, yet different.

Christian Bale
Cate Blanchett
Marcus Carl Franklin

---

[12] See http://thinkexist.com/quotation/all_i_can_do_is_be_me-whoever_that_is/200186.html.

Richard Gere
Heath Ledger
Ben Wishaw
are all Bob Dylan.

—I'm Not There movie poster

In his 2007 film *I'm Not There*, Todd Haynes creates a form of biographical film that embraces the reality of Dylan as a continuing set of "cover" version of Bob Dylan. Haynes never uses Dylan's name in the film. Instead, building on a soundtrack of Dylan covers, Haynes covers seven of Dylan's personae with six actors. Marcus Carl Franklin plays the 11-year-old African-American "Dylan" who calls himself Woody Guthrie. Arthur Rimaud (Ben Wishaw) plays the deflecting obscure wordplayer being interviewed—or interrogated—about his politics, Jack Rollins, the "Voice of a Generation Dylan" is played by Christian Bale, later to return as Pastor John, a born-again preacher. Jude Quinn (Cate Blanchett) is the electric "Dylan" of the *Don't Look Back* period and Richard Gere plays the old West "Dylan" as Billy (the Kid) McCarty, having survived his recorded death moving toward another showdown with Pat Garrett. Of special interest is Robbie Clark (Heath Ledger), an actor who became a star playing Jack Rollins in a bio-pic. The most painful moments of Dylan's private life are doubly distanced as they occur in the version of Dylan that results from an actor covering another cover of Dylan's Voice of a Generation persona.

It's worth noting that each actor's presence—not just the character they play—becomes another version of a Dylan cover. While Arthur and Jack play variations on traditional images of Dylan, Marcus Carl Franklin looks so much like a young Dylan that his cover forces us to consider race in Dylan's identity. Cate Blanchett's cover of Dylan visually confronts us with the androgyny in the authentic Dylan.

In an interview about the film, Haynes describes the script's creation and got to the heart of the relationship of Dylan's music and personae:

> It always started with the music. Everything sort of came from the music but the music and his life were so closely kind of constructing the other. They were each in this constant mirroring of the other I thought, and I decided that the film should be made up of the places where that was most true, where the music and his creative imagination and the genres he was getting into were reflected in some way with his life and his activities … . Bob Dylan has taken many names. Every song he sings he's assuming a different identity.
>
> —Todd Haynes (Roberts 2007)

But the film manipulates the idea of covers beyond the specifics of Dylan's identity, continually reshuffling the pieces and the focus. So in the Electric Dylan era, Haynes tightly covers the documentary *Don't Look Back*—restaging the feel and scenes from that film but also adding new scenes that never made it into the film. Later Haynes creates a much looser "cover-medley" on the idea of the late Sixties

Dylan-in-hiding as a wanted man, blending Dylan's songs from *Pat Garrett and Billy the Kid* with the outlaw Americana of Dylan's *John Wesley Harding* album bled out across two centuries in a threatened escape called Riddle that is populated by characters from Dylan's *Basement Tapes*.

And, of course, *I'm Not There* is saturated with the, by comparison, conventional blend of cover recordings of Dylan's songs by others with Dylan's own versions of his songs. Just as Dylan creates a personal statement by re-presenting the songs of others for his radio show, Haynes assembles thirty-three covers of Dylan by distinctive musicians ranging from Ramblin' Jack Elliott to Sonic Youth and one unreleased song from Dylan's *Basement Tapes* days. The resulting collection of songs doesn't fracture into thirty-four points of view, instead they blend together as facets of a single aural portrait of Dylan himself.

Haynes juxtaposes the music with the personae in a way that shows the link between the sameness runs through the differences in the same way Dylan is covered by manifestations of his different personae. Echoing Dylan's discussion of his writing process, Haynes' film ponders the way that Dylan takes pieces of others—Billy the Kid and Woody Guthrie—and blends them into something new that is the same yet different from his sources. At the same time he points to the way that Dylan's style and persona shifts like Dylan's protest and gospel periods seem very different, yet the underlying song of Dylan remains the same. With its wide range of covers on the soundtrack and the different personae on the screen, the film repeats Dylan's attempt to escape the Voice of a Generation label. In the end, though, while Dylan generates a wide range of covers of himself, the result hasn't been to establish his distance from that role but, paradoxically, Dylan's covers just reinforce the authenticity of his own original.

As *I'm Not There* ends, we see the real Bob Dylan from the mid-1960s performing a harmonica solo. After two hours of covers that seemed to say so much about the man, the songwriter, the artist, Dylan plays a song we don't know and, even in extreme closeup, tells us less than the covers did.

DON'T FORGET TO DANCE: TECHNIQUE AND TECHNO TRANSFORMATIONS

Chapter 10

"Hide and Seek": A Case of Collegiate A Cappella "Microcovering"

Joshua S. Duchan

In the fall of 2006, something remarkable happened on the campus of the University of Michigan. British singer Imogen Heap's pop ballad "Hide and Seek" was everywhere, covered by a cappella singing groups. With thirteen such groups, Michigan's campus was (and remains) one of the Midwest's hotspots of collegiate a cappella—a musical genre and practice in which self-directed student groups take popular songs and arrange, perform, and record them without instrumental accompaniment. To varying degrees, a cappella groups mimic their recorded models, from the sounds of the drums to distinctive guitar riffs to minute details of the original vocalist's recorded performance. Although American college singing groups date back at least to the colonial era, and the oldest remaining collegiate a cappella group (the Yale Whiffenpoofs) has been around for about a century, the 1980s and 90s saw an explosion of collegiate a cappella, with new groups popping up from Maine to California as well as a few places in the United Kingdom.[1] A distinctive subculture emerged, complete with its own unwritten rules of conduct and performance. One of these stipulated that if one group on a campus includes a particular song in its repertory, the others should not. So it is remarkable that, by autumn 2006, *three* groups at Michigan were singing "Hide and Seek."

Equally remarkable is the fact that, unlike most of the collegiate a cappella repertory, the original recording of "Hide and Seek" is, in a way, *a cappella*. Heap's recording is based on a single vocal track, from which harmonizing vocal lines were constructed using pitch-shifting studio technologies, and then additional effects were applied, including filters and EQ. The song thus poses an unusual challenge to a cappella arrangers. As I have explained elsewhere, collegiate a cappella is stylistically based on the idea of emulation, of trying to sound as close to an original studio recording as possible, but without the instruments used in that recording.[2] A cappella groups use a variety of techniques to achieve this goal, including particular vocables—which the singers simply call syllables—and voicings conceived in terms of instruments and instrumental functions rather than

---

[1]   See Joshua S. Duchan, "Powerful Voices: Performance and Interaction in Contemporary Collegiate A Cappella" (Ph.D. Diss., University of Michigan, 2007), pp. 29–42, 61–94.

[2]   Joshua S. Duchan, "Collegiate A Cappella: Emulation and Originality," *American Music* 25/4 (2007), pp. 477–506.

voice parts or vocal ranges. What made "Hide and Seek" challenging was not instrumental imitation, since there were no instruments to imitate, but the sonic and timbral qualities of Heap's effect-laden vocals.

Yet it was clearly worth the challenge, since the Michigan groups were willing to "break" the unwritten rule of repertory exclusivity in order to perform the song in their concerts and record it on their albums.[3] Moreover, "Hide and Seek" became the song-of-the-moment in the wider a cappella world, with both collegiate/ amateur and professional a cappella groups from around the nation singing it.[4] My goal here is less to discern the motivations for covering this particular song than to explore the techniques the three Michigan groups used to do so—to emulate the original "Hide and Seek" recording, with all its electronically enhanced timbral aspects, in live performance and then in the studio. This case study is all the more interesting because of the subtle differences between the arrangements (one of which was mine), which result in varying representations of the same source.

Aside from the valuable contributions to this volume, the topic of covering has received limited attention from music scholars. I have previously used Deena Weinstein's distinction between "cover" and "version" as a point of departure, where a "cover" refers to a previously recorded performance and a "version" refers to an extant song, independent of any particular performance of it.[5] Weinstein's definitions lay the groundwork for her effort to recast the history of twentieth-century popular music in terms of covers, versions, and the changing ways that they refer to their past. More recently, Michael Coyle's work focused on popular music's pasts and varying deployments of the idea of authenticity, but he distinguishes between "covering" and "hijacking hits" while tracing the racial implications of both.[6] Missing from the discourse has been closer investigation of the musical aspects of the practice of covering, however defined.

---

[3]   The track appeared on the following albums by University of Michigan a cappella groups: *Shades of Blue* by Amazin' Blue (2006), *Harmonettes: Hold the Elevator! Songs from the Seventh Floor* by the Harmonettes (2008), and *Single Greatest Threat* by Gimble (2008).

[4]   A selected list of collegiate a cappella groups whose albums feature "Hide and Seek" includes the all-male University of North Carolina Achordants (*High Stakes Old Maid*, 2007), the co-ed University of Pennsylvania Off the Beat (*Kenophobia*, 2006), and the all-female University of Oregon Divisi (*Roots*, 2008). A brief description of Divisi's live performance of the song, focusing on its choreography, appears in Mickey Rapkin, *Pitch Perfect: The Quest for Collegiate A Cappella Glory* (New York: Gotham, 2008), p. 121.

[5]   Deena Weinstein, "The History of Rock's Past Through Rock Covers," in Thomas Swiss, John Sloop, and Andrew Herman (eds.), *Mapping the Beat: Popular Music and Contemporary Theory* (Malden, MA: Blackwell, 1997), p. 138.

[6]   Michael Coyle, "Hijacked Hits and Antic Authenticity: Cover Songs, Race, and Postwar Marketing," in Roger Beebe, Denise Fulbrook, and Ben Saunders (eds.), *Rock Over the Edge: Transformations in Popular Music Culture* (Durham: Duke University Press, 2002), pp. 133–57.

Whether covering, versioning, or hijacking hits, such musical recontextualizations constitute the representation of preexisting musical material, which, depending on the new context, may or may not be recognizable. In collegiate a cappella, recognizability is paramount; the focus is not so much difference, as Coyle suggests, as it is similarity.[7] Songs are regularly versioned in broad strokes: harmonic progressions are maintained, lyrics are unchanged, and melodies are faithfully reproduced. But in some cases a cappella groups focus not only on large-scale musical features but also on more limited and specific ones, which are just as important in establishing a song's distinctiveness. The techniques the Michigan groups used to represent Heap's recording include those I call "microcovering" because they reference a particular recording, thus fitting Weinstein's definition of "cover," but do so on an extremely local level. "Microcovering" techniques display an attention not only to musical features that may come first to mind— melody, harmony, rhythm—but also to those that may be more difficult to represent discursively or notationally—timbre, inflection, distortion, and the interplay of overdubbed and layered vocal tracks.

Imogen Heap's *Hide and Seek*

As an early twenty-first-century pop song, Imogen Heap's original recording of "Hide and Seek" is both typical and atypical. Formally, it comprises seven and a half eight-bar phrases. The song spends its first two minutes and fifty-two seconds alternating verses and chorus, but then, just as Heap's voice seems angriest, it departs in new melodic and harmonic directions.

Texturally, "Hide and Seek" is homophonic (like most pop songs), but it is distinctive for its degree of homorhythm. Heap sings the melody, but all of the other voices were created by a harmonizer, a sophisticated electronic device that, given parameters such as key and mode, will input an instrumental or vocal line and output one or more lines in (mostly parallel) harmony. In an article in the magazine *Remix* Heap described the song's composition and recording. After a malfunction disabled her computer (one of her crucial instruments), she turned to the equipment she could find in the studio:

---

[7]   Ibid., 134. Collegiate a cappella's valuation of similarity and the reproduction of many commercial recordings' musical features also contrasts with Christine R. Yano's observation that "cover songs and other forms of repetition in a Euro-American context face derision over the issue of ... singular authenticity. Covers which do not significantly depart from the original, then, carry little cultural capital. Instead, they become inauthentic versions of the real by virtue of their redundancy" ("Covering Disclosures: Practices of Intimacy, Hierarchy, and Authenticity in a Japanese Popular Music Genre," *Popular Music and Society*, 28/2 [2005], p. 203).

I didn't want to leave the studio without having done anything that day. I saw the [DigiTech Vocalist Workstation] on a shelf and just plugged it into my little 4-track MiniDisc with my mic and my keyboard and pressed record. The first thing that I sang was those first few lines, "Where are we? What the hell is going on?" I set the vocalist to a four-note polyphony, so even if I play 10 notes on the keyboard, it will only choose four of them. It's quite nicely surprising when it comes back with a strange combination. When it gets really high in the second chorus, that's a result of it choosing higher rather than low notes, so I ended up going even higher to compensate, above the chord. I recorded it in, like, four-and-a-half minutes, and it ended up on the album in exactly the structure of how it came out of me then.[8]

The lyrics may strike listeners as unusually obscure. I interpret them as depicting a sort of post-apocalyptic, post-modern, cosmopolitan scene in broad strokes— "When busy streets, a mess with people, would stop to hold their heads heavy," "Hide and seek, trains and sewing machines / all those years, they were here first"—before zooming in on the emotional impact of abandonment, loneliness, and desperation—"Oily marks appear on walls where pleasure moments hung before," "Speak, no feeling, no, I don't believe you / You don't care a bit, you don't care a bit." On the discussion forum associated with Heap's website, fans suggest the song is about the dissolution of a romantic relationship, citing as an example the lyric "crop circles in the carpets" as a metaphor for imprints of furniture recently removed.[9]

An important feature of Heap's "Hide and Seek" is the rhythmic tension between the lyrics and the harmony: chords often change not at the beginning of a lyric, but partway through. This delay creates a sort of harmonic melisma or suspension, where the chords change and harmonies resolve around an unchanging melody pitch.[10] During the verses, this harmonic melisma occurs regularly on most downbeats and sometimes on a measure's third beat. Chord changes thus become noticeable harmonic events and several include extended harmonies such as ninths, elevenths, and thirteenths. What results are closely clustered chords whose prominent placement renders them a crucial musical feature in collegiate a cappella covers, as I will show.

---

[8]   Genevieve Powers, "Imogen Heap," *Remix Magazine*, 8/1 (January 2006), p. 20.

[9]   For example, one Oklahoma City-based contributor to the on-line discussion forum (writing under the alias "Danger for Dollars") wrote of *Hide and Seek*: "To me, it's about the end of a relationship ... Looking around a starkly empty room that you used to share with someone. The crop circles in the carpet are the impressions the furniture made before it was moved out" (posted to www.imogenheap.com / "'Speak for Yourself' Discussion" / "analyse of Hide and seek" [sic] on December 18, 2006).

[10]   Alternatively, one may interpret these events as anticipations, in which the melody arrives at an important pitch in advance of the accompanying harmony.

Heap's vowel sounds and diphthongs seem carefully selected to take advantage of the studio effects that underline the recording's significant emotional impact. To bring out these sounds, "Hide and Seek" features not only the studio technologies of panning, reverb, and filtering, which have become standards in the rock recordist's arsenal,[11] but changes in their parameters. For example, at the end of the second verse, Heap moves from the lyrics "people would stop to hold" into those that follow, "their heads … heavy" (between approximately 1:00 and 1:12 on the commercial release). During this transition, the duration of reverb on her voice(s) increases and a delay is added to "their heads" and "heavy." The vowel at the end of "heavy" further exaggerates the effect, as its forward placement and nasality render the timbre of the voice(s) harsher and more piercing than those of the softer, British English-inflected vowels Heap has so far provided. The delay, in particular, is striking because it allows the listener to hear two harmonic melismas during the lyrics "heads" and "heavy," which echo several times and disappear into the sonic distance. The original instance of "heavy" in fact does not reverberate or fade out, but instead stops abruptly and artificially just before the first echo occurs. Moreover, each instance of an echo of "heavy" is panned to a different location in the stereo spectrum; I hear three distinct echoes, with the first panned far left, the second far right, and the third in the center. These echoes add an additional two beats to the end of the verse, disrupting the song's harmonic rhythm, before Heap's voice reenters with the chorus ("hide and seek …") and the reverb, delay, and panning return to their previous parameters.

Of course, it would be unreasonable to expect collegiate a cappella groups to reproduce all of Heap's effects in a live performance, especially those that depend on carefully manipulated studio technology, such as reverb, delay, and panning. Instead, the three Michigan a cappella groups emulated the *overall effect*, a gestalt of Heap's effects-laden recording. They did so by attending to specific and selected musical features and thereby engaged in "microcovering."

Amazin' Blue

I arranged "Hide and Seek" for Amazin' Blue, a mixed group, in April 2006. My goal was to reproduce the dense cluster-chords and eerie dissonances of Heap's recording and, in a later recording session, to use some effects that differed from Heap's yet achieve a similarly artificial—and perhaps spooky—mood. I was inspired by a recording of the song by the professional a cappella group, Transit, which convinced me that the effect and affect of Heap's recording could be reproduced satisfactorily, though not completely, without all of Heap's electronic mediation. My arrangement was scored for four parts (SATB) plus a soloist and several additional harmony parts in certain passages.

[11]   See Albin Zak, *The Poetic of Rock: Cutting Tracks, Making Records* (Berkeley: University of California Press, 2001).

Achieving the effect and affect of Heap's dense voicings didn't require mimicking them exactly. For example, at the start of the second verse ("Spin me round again and rub my eyes") I included the harmonic melismas on the downbeat (under "again" and "eyes"), but whereas the chords in Heap's recording included both sevenths and ninths, I voiced them as triads with only an added ninth (this had the added benefit of avoiding doubling in the background parts). The harmonic melismas then arose from suspensions or anticipations in either the soloist's melody or the alto part, each time resulting in an emphasis on the dissonance provided by the ninth (see Example 10.1). Thus, while I did not recreate the exact pitch collections found in Heap's original recording, I achieved a similar overall result by including selected dissonances that would be recognizable to those familiar with the original recording.

Whereas the timbre of Heap's vowels was one contributing factor—along with EQ and changing filters—in her evocation of "a kind of lovesick cyborg alienation,"[12] Amazin' Blue's performance of "Hide and Seek" sought to achieve a similar effect through the use of diphthongs and unconventional vocal sounds. On the second verse's "Spin me round" I directed the singers to emphasize the "n" of "spin." This was contrary to their instincts, which suggested they instead sustain the lyric's vowel. However, the sequence of a sibilant "s," a brief plosive "p," an unusually short vowel "i," an extended closed and nasal "n," and then slowly changing diphthongs—"ah" to "ooo" on "round" and later "ah" to "ee" on "eyes"—made for a passage that attended as much (or perhaps even more) to the *sound* of the words as to their meaning or their musical setting. I later learned that Heap uses a similar compositional approach, which emphasizes the acoustical properties of sound. In other works, she focuses on the manipulation of (sometimes extremely brief or esoteric) samples of recorded sound rather than the sequencing of musical instructions via MIDI.[13]

When collegiate a cappella is recorded, groups sometimes apply a doubling or pitch-shifting effect to the bass part, creating a line an octave beneath that of the human singer(s). The result—a much deeper, stronger bass—gives a cappella recordings more energy or presence, perhaps enabling them to compete with pop songs whose recordings include electric bass. We took such an approach on Amazin' Blue's recording, but did so selectively. The "octavizer," as some a cappella groups call the effect, depended on the register of the bass part, reinforcing its lower-pitched portions but disappearing from the higher ones. These higher-pitched portions tended to situate the basses relatively close to (and in a few spots, higher

---

[12]   Laura Sinagra, "With Her Synthesizer, She Mesmerizes," *The New York Times*, January 13, 2006, p. E3.

[13]   "'I get seriously irritated by MIDI timing,' admits Imogen. 'It's always shifting ever so slightly. But in the computer, working with audio, I can make everything exact. [...] It's so much more fun to create and mangle audio manually, to mold it like Play-Doh. I'd much rather do that than spend hours changing parameters on my JV-1080 [MIDI workstation]" ("Imoen Speaks," *Keyboard Magazine*, 32/2 [2006], p. 33).

Example 10.1   "Hide and Seek." Words and music by Imogen Heap, Rondor Music (London, 2005), arranged for the University of Michigan Amazin' Blue, second verse (mm. 9–16)

Example 10.1 continued

than) the tenors, contributing to the dissonance of closely clustered voicings. In those passages, the addition of a second bass line an octave lower might have resulted in a perceptual "spreading out" of the voicing, lessening the cluster effect. When it was applied, each instance of the octavizing effect became a musical event, giving the song a noticeable sense of urgency before its disappearance left a seemingly unmoored middle-register ensemble swirling in its absence.

The Harmonettes

The Harmonettes, a women's a cappella group formerly associated with the Women's Glee Club (but since 2001 an independent student organization), also began singing "Hide and Seek" in the spring of 2006. Their arrangement is voiced for two soprano and two alto parts (SSAA), although at various times each part divides into two parallel lines (with thirteen members, four on the second alto and three on each of the other parts, such *divisi* passages were not difficult to accommodate). The Harmonettes' arrangement differs from Amazin' Blue's in several ways, including rhythmic treatment and voicing, and lack of a solo singer on the melody. Some differences can be attributed to the gender differences between the two groups, while others reveal varying methods of achieving the same emulative goals.

The harmonic melismas, which Amazin' Blue emphasized by having three, four, or even five parts changing pitch on strong beats and under single lyrics, are approached more subtly in the Harmonettes' arrangement. Examining the same passage discussed above (the second verse), we can see that the melismas are executed by only one or two parts at a time, usually with a delay of a sixteenth note between the initial pitch and the one to which the part changes (see Example 10.2). Moreover, the Harmonettes delay the second syllable of certain lyrics, shifting them to the next beat instead of making them sixteenth-note pickups. For example, in the line "Spin me round again," both Heap and Amazin' Blue begin the second syllable of "again" on the last sixteenth-note of a measure, and then execute the harmonic melisma on the subsequent downbeat. On their studio recording, however, the Harmonettes begin the first syllable of "again" on the last *eighth*-note of the measure (in contrast to the sixteenth-note figure notated on their arrangement) and place the lyric's second syllable on the next downbeat. The harmonic melisma then follows later within the measure's first beat rather than upon its arrival. In live performance and on the group's recording, one can still hear these effects, but their emulative impact is weaker due to the rhythmic treatment and the voicing.

Example 10.2   "Hide and Seek." Words and music by Imogen Heap, Rondor Music (London, 2005), arranged for the University of Michigan Harmonettes, second verse (mm. 9–12)

In Heap's recording, one can usually distinguish her voice, singing the melody, from the copies of her voice that serve as its accompaniment, despite their similar timbres. Unlike most pop songs, however, "Hide and Seek" is entirely homorhythmic, a quality that diminishes the distinction between melody and accompaniment. Collegiate a cappella often highlights this distinction in its arrangements through rhythmic and syllabic differences, where the soloists sing words and the background voices sing more percussive or "instrumental" syllables. But "Hide and Seek" offers a cappella groups the rare opportunity to have all members singing in a more integrated manner. In other words, the homorhythmic quality of Heap's version makes it rather easy to imagine an a cappella version of the song as an *ensemble* piece, without a soloist. This setting would have certain social advantages[14] while likely altering only slightly the musical impact and recognizability of the piece.

Amazin' Blue's arrangement retained the solo quality of the lead melody, effectively adding a fifth vocal line to the arrangement, but the Harmonettes' did not, instead presenting an ensemble piece with the melody mostly in the soprano 1 part. However, the melody is mostly pitched lower than a typical soprano part— or even, in some passages, the arrangement's alto parts. Kira Lesser, the group's music director during the 2006–2007 academic year, described the choral setting as the group's strongest musical style and one that yielded the most effective social bonding. She also linked such "group songs" directly to the fact that the Harmonettes are a women's group:

> I think being an all female group, choral arrangements create a certain group bond. It really increases our feeling of female empowerment and love for each other. When we have soloists, there is sort of this feeling that the girls singing the supporting parts are bonding with each other, separately from and in support of the girl up front. [...] Through "group songs," as we usually called them, we all felt happy and able to shine, and we remembered why we loved singing and why we loved the Harmonettes. And we felt proud.[15]

Staying firmly within the choral milieu, the Harmonettes utilize traditional choral arranging and performing techniques to provide variation and interest. For example, during the second verse they insert a complete stop after the lyric "stop" in the line, "when busy streets, a mess with people would stop ... to hold their heads heavy." This word painting creates a dramatic effect in both live performance and the group's studio recording, but departs from the original, where Heap connects "stop" to "to hold" without any discernible break. Like Amazin' Blue, the Harmonettes emphasize the "n" of "spin" in the second verse, but they do not dwell on the diphthong of "round" and otherwise generally do not bring out the song's diphthongs.

---

14   See Duchan, "Collegiate A Cappella: Emulation and Originality."

15   Kira Lesser, personal communication with the author, 2008.

Although it is not unheard of for women's a cappella groups to use the "octavizer" technique described above, the Harmonettes choose not to do so. Their arrangement, performance, and recording thus lacks the low end of a co-ed or male arrangement. In certain passages they use a technique, which I have observed in other women's groups as well: to adapt songs to suit the female vocal range, they re-voice chords by inverting them, putting the third or fifth in the bass. For example, the first chorus's "sewing machines" is transformed from a vi chord (F#-minor) to vi⁶. A few bars later, under the half-cadence that ends the chorus (IV–V under "they were here first"), the lower alto part, functioning as the bass voice, sings the third of each chord. But the impact of these changes is diminished by the delicate articulation and *piano* dynamic. Overall, the Harmonettes manage to avoid the compromise of re-voicing Heap's harmonies too often and thus maintain much of their striking quality.

Gimble

The third version of "Hide and Seek" to appear at Michigan came from Gimble, a mixed a cappella group. Their arrangement shared certain similarities with those of Amazin' Blue and the Harmonettes, most notably in its efforts to reproduce Heap's harmonic melismas and maintain an ensemble (rather than lead-and-accompaniment) texture. But it departed from the other two by taking the choral approach further, altering Heap's articulation in more pronounced ways and by adding new parts to obscure the 8-bar phrase structure and create a more fluid presentation. The arrangement is scored for six parts (three men's, three women's), though a few split in certain passages.[16]

The harmonic melismas are reproduced in Gimble's recording of "Hide and Seek," but in a manner emphasizing the beat as much as the anticipatory syncopation. In the second verse ("spin me round again and rub my eyes"), all three women's parts plus the baritone part begin the lyrics "round," "(a-)gain," "rub," and "eyes" on the last eighth note of successive measures, but the tenor and bass parts begin the same lyric at the start of the following beat. These delayed entrances create a sort of echo effect unique to Gimble's arrangement while also emphasizing the beat more explicitly than in the others I have examined. Moreover, to my ears they create a more deliberate mood, as if some voices were figuratively leading others through the song.

Gimble maintains a more traditional, Western choral presentation than Amazin' Blue or the Harmonettes. They do not use diphthongs to mimic Heap's vocal timbre nearly as much; "spin" is delivered with an emphasis on the vowel,

---

[16]   Like those of Amazin' Blue and the Harmonettes, Gimble's arrangement maintains the same key as the original recording (A major). Unlike the other arrangements, it is metrically faster—although scored in 4/4 time, each measure lasts half as long as in the previously discussed arrangements.

not the consonant, "n." They also do not feature a soloist, but set the melody within the arrangement's parts. Whereas the Harmonettes simply had one of the voice parts sing the song's melody, however, Gimble's arrangement weaves the melody through nearly all its parts. In the second verse, for instance, all three of the women's parts and two of the three men's parts carry the melodic line for at least part of a measure. This has the effect, in performance, of burying the melody somewhat and presenting the audience with a sequence of harmonious chords rather than a distinct tune. As collegiate a cappella is largely a genre of cover songs chosen for a predominantly college student audience, it may be presumed that at least some listeners were already familiar with the melody and could either pick it out of the choral texture or imagine it during Gimble's performance.

As I have mentioned and Lesser explained, ensemble settings have social advantages. Each individual may feel more important to the overall success of the song than if there were one soloist and several background singers. Gimble's efforts to pass the melody around among the parts furthers this social effect by allowing the singers on each part a few moments to carry the song's tune, but not long enough to truly emerge from the sound of the larger ensemble.

Gimble's choral approach extends to their recording practice as well. Their recording does not include an octavizer, nor are there any other noticeable studio effects. The seemingly unaffected presentation matches Gimble's recording practice, wherein most of the group's singers record their parts simultaneously in manner that differs minimally from a live performance.[17] On songs that involve a soloist or vocal percussion, those parts would be overdubbed later, but "Hide and Seek" includes neither. When I spent time with the group in the studio, the music director explained that they usually recorded every song in this manner, doing only two or three takes of the background parts before choosing the one with the fewest errors and moving on to other tracking tasks. Some errors could be mitigated with digital editing or while mixing, but the recording process was more about documenting the group's repertory and singers than creating a flawless musical work.

Conclusion

By examining these a cappella covers, I hope to have accomplished three things: First, to make explicit what is sometimes left implicit in discussions of covering—that the same original recording can inspire varied cover versions, even in a genre whose focus is squarely on the faithful reproduction of an original and even in a case where such reproduction should be unusually straightforward, since a

---

[17] Other groups make their recordings differently, having individual singers or voice parts record separately. This method yields better sonic isolation and accuracy, which can be advantageous for digital editing and mixing, but sacrifices interaction between singers as they perform the song in the studio.

cappella groups are covering an a cappella song. Second, while some scholarly discussions of "covers," "versions," "covering," and "hijacking hits" use such concepts to reframe histories of music, I offer renewed attention to musical detail. My term, "microcovering," highlights aspects of composition and arrangement that sometimes lie at the margins of analysis. And finally, I hint at the social dimensions of collegiate a cappella covering. While the present essay does not tackle the social aspects of the musical practice head-on, I aim to inspire future research that will demonstrate just how rich, musically and socially, the genre and practice of collegiate a cappella truly is.

Acknowledgments

I must acknowledge the members of Amazin' Blue, the Harmonettes, and Gimble for sharing their time and music with me: Fiona Linn of Amazin' Blue, Kira Lesser and Christina Macholan of the Harmonettes, and Sunny Park, Andrew Johnson, and Stuart and Veronica Robinson of Gimble, for sharing their arrangements, recordings, and insight. I also thank Fiona Linn, Katherine Meizel, and Colin Roust for their contributions to and feedback on this chapter.

Chapter 11

The Mashup Mindset: Will Pop Eat Itself?

David Tough

The "mashup" represents a relatively new subgenre of the cover song. A largely undocumented, underground, and dynamic movement, the mashup is a form that continues to raise intriguing questions about creativity, technology and legal dimensions of popular music.

Mashup music, in its simplest definition, is a song or composition created from the master track and instrumental music of one song and the a cappella vocal master track from another. This process is seen by DJs as a furthering of the jazz instrumentalist's mentality of covering a standard popular song and interpreting it as the artist's own. The mashup prototype was first found in the sampling craze embodied by early hip-hop in the 1980s. Simply type in the search word "mashup" on YouTube and you will enter another world of musical compositions and composites such as "Destiny's Child vs. Nirvana," "ABBA vs. 50 Cent," "Snow Patrol vs. The Police" and "The Beatles vs. Nine Inch Nails."

Every popular song has a shelf life. Cover artists have always tried to capitalize on the public's familiarity with prerecorded songs by altering the original composition and therefore extending the appeal of the song several decades later. During the summer of 2008, Warren Zevon's "Werewolves in London" and Lynyrd Skynyrd's "Sweet Home Alabama" received a mainstream chart boost when Kid Rock's mashup of the two songs appeared in "All Summer Long," which became a top ten hit in the US, a crossover hit on the country music charts and a number one hit in several other countries.

The mashup movement has created several interesting cultural interactions. For example, older fans are now able to be exposed to newer songs, trends and technologies of music making. Younger fans get exposure to older classic song catalogs they may have never otherwise heard. The nightclub hipster of today is exposed to songs and albums such as "Sweet Home Country Grammar," where Nelly's "Country Grammar" vocal is mashed with the classic Skynyrd track; or the Kleptone's underground album, "A Night At The Hip-Hopera" where vintage Queen is mixed with hip-hop; or even a ragtime mashup of Eminem on Mei Lwun's bootleg, "Marshall's Been Snookered." This type of cross fertilization is bringing up new definitions and uses of music composition and technology and is questioning the fundamentals of music law and copyright (Cushman, 2007).

The term "mashup" can apply to any art form, not just music. The methodology itself is an extension of our current society and the digital DIY culture. Mashups can be seen as content aggregation; they combine existing data from two or more sources in innovative ways. Mashups are not revolutionary, they are evolutionary. Mashup by scholarly definition is "the modification of existing digital works to create a derivative work." Like any other derivative work, it can either be viewed as a tribute to the original artist or an otherwise blatant theft from the original creator. Many pop critics simply call mashup music a "dance remix" or "audio collage." However, today's DJs point to mashup as the newest form of cover song ("Mashup," 2004).

Another distinguishing feature of mashup music is its underground, do-it-yourself nature that usually falls below the commercial radar. Mashup music is both unique in music composition and distribution. The mashup artist does not need a distributor or record label since most mashup music (or "bastard pop" as it is called in the UK) is released as a bootleg on the internet via peer-to-peer (P2P) sites. The mashup artist does not need a traditional recording studio since they can create the composition on their own home computer. Mashup singles almost never have traditional distribution and many times cannot even be found on iTunes or other commercial internet sites (Anders, 2008).

Mashup borrows from the strains of early hip-hop where a rapper would take an existing music track and put their own new original vocals on it. The artistic process harkens back to the year 1979 when the Sugar Hill Gang created new lyrics over the existing track of Chic's "Good Times." Like any other cover or sampled song, mashup music also obscures the identity of the original creator. Issues of authenticity and ownership are nothing new in the world of cover songs. How many average listeners still think Sinead O'Connor's "Nothing Compares to You," Tone-Loc's "Funky Cold Medina," or Guns N' Roses' "Knocking on Heaven's Door" were original compositions penned by the artists themselves?

With the current number of popular instrumental and a cappella vocal versions of popular songs available to the mashup artist on P2P sites, vinyl and CD releases; mashup music is an art form that appears to have staying power in the music marketplace. Digital audio workstations (DAWs) have made the combining of the two songs quick, easy and affordable, making the contemporary sound of mashups more appealing to a significant audience (Wolf)

The Technology of Mashup Music

"Borrowing" an existing chord progression and layering a different melody "on top" has been a norm for classical composers, jazz and blues musicians alike. For example, "Anthropology" (Charlie Parker/Dizzy Gillespie) and "Meet the Flintstones" (Hoyt Curtain) both borrow the same chord progression from George Gershwin's "I Got Rhythm." However, what distinguishes mashup is the digital technology involved. Since mashup music is all processed and reproduced from other music, the genre of mashup music could not exist without the continued lowering cost of the personal computer and the advent of the internet and related software that supplies music and music production tools so easily and inexpensively.

The computer DAW is the instrument the mashup artist employs to produce their music. Since the mid 1990's, audio software companies have been producing recording tools that have served as both the paintbrush and easel for the mashup artist. These tools include music sequencers, audio recorders, pre-made loops, digital effects and virtual instruments. With all the quick and accessible technology available to the mashup artists, one notable mashup artist, Osymyso, is able to complete a "blended" song in less than five hours (Wolf).

Mashup also ties in directly with the interactive DIY culture of YouTube, Guitar Hero and Rock Band. With mashup, music fans not only play the music of their favorite artist, they can play with them and alter the song. This interactive gaming emboldens the musical amateur and the bedroom hobbyist to become the artist. Hennion (Gomart, 1999) points out that there is now no brick wall between musician and listener; they are part of the same whole. The remix or mash-up DJ also occupies a part of that space, as does the participant on a P2P system that makes files available for sharing.

Here is a quick primer on how mashup music is made in a bedroom studio: The DJ or music creator must first come up with an *idea* of two songs to merge. This decision can be based on similar thematic material, i.e. "For The Love of Money" and "Mo Money, Mo Problems" or a humorous or unlikely combination such as "Bootylicious" and "Smells Like Teen Spirit" = "Smells like Booty." The objective of the mashup artist is to combine two well-known songs and make them sound like a totally original piece of music. The two songs should remain recognizable to anyone who has heard the original versions. Most DJs agree that mashup is not randomly throwing two songs together; the art is more complex. The professional masher will be able to create an entirely new message from two messages that are otherwise unrelated.

The desktop DJ uses an industry standard computer digital audio workstation (DAW) to perform the digital editing of the music files. This is simply a personal desktop or laptop, PC or MAC, installed with audio software. Simple DAWs such as GarageBand, Sony Acid, Ableton Live, Wavelab, Cool Edit Pro, Mix Pad, Acid Pro and Soundforge are all simple audio editing programs that can serve as cheap ways to edit and apply digital processing to pre-existing music. Advanced software choices include Cubase, Logic, Digital Performer, Samplitude and Protools.

Next, an unprocessed a cappella vocal of the original artist must be obtained. This is the most difficult element to locate since most famous artists tend to protect their egos and do not release their naked vocal by itself. Hip-hop vocals can sometimes be found on vinyl releases or as bonus tracks. Some artists such as Jay Z and Radiohead purposely release their vocal takes (vocal stems) and instrumental tracks in order for them to be remixed, therefore providing the artist more exposure. This, however, is not the norm. For the more advanced engineer, vocals can be extracted using equalization (equalizing all of the music out except for the midrange where the vocal line is typically found) or through phase inversion (using phase inversion to cancel out any instrument or vocal that appears in the center of the stereo field). Another more recent trick is to "steal" the original artist's vocal from the center channel of a surround sound mix. This technique was used on some of the first Beatles 5.1 channel mixes.

As with the a cappella vocal, an instrumental mix of the opposing song must be located. These types of mixes can usually be found on P2P networks and/or on B-sides of the single release of the song. Recently, a technical-minded Rock Band fan cracked the video game and managed to separate the stems/tracks (the instruments and vocals) of several of the songs and released them on P2P sites for mashup.

The mashup producer must then set a tempo-grid in the DAW program and beat map the programmatic material. In this process, each element (the vocal and the music tracks) are assigned a metronome tempo corresponding with the original tempo of each piece of music. At this point, the mashup artist can see how each tempo relates to each other and choose to time stretch (speed up or slow down the element without affecting the pitch) one or both of the elements to match up rhythmically. The time stretching process is much easier in the digital world than it was with analog tape before the advent of the DAW. Other elements can then be added, if necessary, with the use of virtual instruments or loops. After the technical and musical elements are added, the song is then mixed down on the home computer and distributed over the internet in mp3 format, usually via a P2P site such as Kazaa or Limewire.

One of the newest trends in mashup is for the desktop producer to take royalty free sample libraries released from famous musicians and combine them into a musical product. Even though none of the famous musicians have ever played with each other, they can now be an internet virtual supergroup. The best example of this is the "sample band" CD by the virtual band Fleetwood Mashup. Produced by DJ Mashine-Gun Kelly, the CD features songs using sample tracks from four famous artists (Mick Fleetwood: Drums and Percussion; Bill Laswell: Processed Beats, Samples, Percussion; ILONA!: Vocals; Rudy Sarzo: Bass Guitar) that Kelly combines into songs. This trend will likely continue among DIY desktop DJs as more and more famous artists release their signature sounds in the form of sample libraries.

It's Just a Copy, Right?

Most mashup songs and albums have continued to exist and thrive without mainstream CD distribution. Peer to peer sites offer mashed albums such as "The Grey Album" by Danger Mouse (taking Jay Z's rap vocal and placing it over the The Beatles "White Album") and Dean Gray's "American Edit" hip-hop remixes of Green Day's "American Idiot"). These compilations exist solely as fly-by-night bootleg internet uploads, mainly for fear of legal repercussions from publishers and record labels.

Mashup traditionally is not a money maker, however, and is used to highlight the artist's mashing talents. If there is revenue made, it usually goes to someone other than the original artist, songwriter and publisher. In the past, mashup artists have followed a rebellious trend not to follow the compulsory provisions of the copyright act. Many mashup artists felt it an artistic right to sample other artists' work and profit from it without sharing their rewards with the original artists. Most mashup songs are created from songs where the publisher has not licensed the sample. Even if the mashup artist wanted to come clean, it is hard to know which publisher(s) to pay their 9.1 cents.

There are legal actions by record labels related to mashups on record, but the two most famous are those revolving around *The Grey Album* by Danger Mouse and The Beachles *Sgt Petsounds* album by Clayton Counts. In 2004, EMI tried to stop online distribution of *The Grey Album* by Gnarls Barkley's producer, Brian Burton (i.e. DJ Danger Mouse). However, because of all the media attention, the album became the most widely downloaded mashup album to date. The action also triggered an online revolt, known as Grey Tuesday (Healey, 2004).

In the case of Counts, he originally approached EMI to negotiate licensing terms for his original and dissonant mashup of The Beatles album *Sgt Pepper's Lonely Hearts Club Band* and The Beach Boys album *Pet Sounds*. According to Count's blog (http://claytoncounts.com/blog/the-beachles/), the label sent numerous cease and desist letters and demanded that he "provide Capitol with information regarding downloading and/or streaming of the Beachles Mash-Up Recordings and the Other Mash-Up Recordings to date, including but not limited to: (1) the dates on which those recordings were streamed and/or downloaded; (2) the number of times those recordings were streamed and/or downloaded; and (3) any and all available information regarding persons who streamed and/or downloaded those recordings."

In both of these cases, the record labels' actions are reminiscent of the Napster-era game book, where instead of embracing and negotiating copyright issues, they either ignore them or heavily prosecute a few cases. Regarding mashups, labels have tried to quickly shut down any creative reinterpretation of their catalogs citing the original intent of copyright law, "to encourage people to take the time and energy to make creative works." However, most DJs feel that there needs to be a practical and reasonable sampling right offered by more major labels (Healy, 2004).

It is an interesting phenomenon that the few legally licensed mashup mixes by the record labels are now producing revenue for the original owners of the songs. Cover bands are now beginning to perform the mashup music in clubs. Thus, it appears that mashup is taking pirating full circle pointing directly back to legitimacy.

In May 2002 Island Records released a legal mash-up that combined songs from Adina Howard, Gary Numan and the Sugababes. In 2004, David Bowie offered a mashup contest challenging DJs to mashup two of his songs. The prize was a sports car from Bowie himself. Since Bowie owns his publishing, this was a legal form of mashup promoted by Bowie's record label.

Some mashup artists view their role as one of providing a new artistic conduit of exposure for the original artist. Eric Kleptone, the leader of the mashup group the Kleptones, states in his blog at www.kleptones.com:

> As all downloaders are aware, this stuff does not belong to us. We have virtually no right under current copyright law to redistribute the sources we use in the manner we do. It's a debatable situation, and one we'd rather not be arguing in a law court, thanks. We've been very lucky so far that no-one has seen fit to make a determined effort to stop us. (Waxy's Cease & Desist, we think, was an unfortunate shot across the bows. So it goes.) However, the time that we have to do this is limited, as we have to convert a large chunk of that time into cash, so we can pay the rent, eat, and get the beers in from time to time, just like most other people. We'd like more time to do more stuff, but hey, wouldn't everyone? So, the conclusions we've come to are these: If you want to donate some money in payment for any of the albums you've downloaded, we're sorry, we can't accept it. We don't own the rights to the sounds we use, and therefore are risking infringing on people's copyright in a far more personally damaging way if we accepted payment for it. We believe that people should have the right to make not-for-profit derivative works, remixes, parodies, social commentaries, whatever, of music that they own, therefore accepting money in that way is virtually impossible, sorry. One day, things will improve (we're optimistic), but till then ….

The Monster Mash: A Brief History of the Mashup

In *Cassette Culture*, Peter Manuel (1993) says the concept of mashup goes back centuries to traditional Indian music where familiar "texts" are laid over borrowed tunes and melodies, mixing folk and popular styles. In Western classical music, quodlibets have been used in the finales of musicals, film music and classical compositions to "mashup" several different melodies that either were popular at the time or appeared earlier in the composition. Contemporary examples of the quodlibet include The Grateful Dead's medley "The Other One", pianist Glenn Gould's in-concert improvisation of a quodlibet including "The Star-Spangled Banner" and "God Save the King" and John Williams' medley of character's themes at the end of Star Wars Episode III. Early mashup evolved from the work of the 1950s duo of Bill Buchanan and Dickie Goodman. Their break out song entitled "The Flying Saucer" used uncleared samples of Orson Welles' faux radio broadcast, *War of the Worlds*, intermingled with musical bits and pieces. This broadcast used the technology of tape splicing, where snippets of tape were marked with chalk and cut up with a razor blade. The tape sections were then reconstructed to give the desired effect. This tied in directly with the new recording philosophy of "creating a recording" (rather than the old method of "capturing an acoustic event") that appeared with the new technology in the 1950s which was brought back directly from the defeated Germans after WWII.

In the 1970s, the BBC radio show, *I'm Sorry I Haven't A Clue*, began featuring a segment known as "One Song to the Tune of Another," where the participants sing the words of one popular song to the melody of another. During the same decade, Frank Zappa introduced his "xenochrony technique" where he extracted a guitar solo from its original context and placed into a completely different song. This technique appeared on his 1979 albums, *Joe's Garage: Act I* and *Acts II & III* (notably in the guitar solos for "On the Bus" and "Keep It Greasey"). In 1975, John Oswold put snippets of a Southern US evangelist to the background of Led Zeppelin in his tune "Power." He called his technique "plunderphonics." Oswold also continued this tradition on his 1990 track "Vane," which mashed "You're So Vain" by Carly Simon and the cover of the same song by Faster Pussycat.

During the 1980s, the group Kon Kan released the underground mix "Puss in Boots" in 1989 which mashed "Boots" with "Immigrant Song." One of the first licensed mashes also appeared in the 1980s which was the mix of John Truelove/ Candi Staton's "You Got the Love" with Frankie Knuckles/Jamie Principle's "Your Love" (Manriki, 2003).

The composition and sound of mashups, like any other musical genre, are tied to the era of recording technology they occur in. It was in the mid 1990s that the desktop computer DAW (or ADATs) became affordable enough for most DJs to purchase. This provided them not only a method of mixing and editing various sounds for their home studios, but also more signal processing options, such as compression and reverb, and higher sound quality.

True mashup fans cite the first modern mashup as appearing on Evolution Control Committee's bootleg cassette album *Gunderphonic* in 1994. The track combined a Public Enemy rap over a Herb Albert instrumental. The song was released and played briefly on US college radio (Manriki, 2003). The underground nature of mashup was accelerated by the peer to peer networks and mp3 culture of the early millennium. In 2001, DJ Freelance Hellraiser mashed Christina Aguilera's "Genie In A Bottle," and The Strokes "Hard To Explain" in his track "A Stroke of Genie-us." Distributed on sites like Napster and Bearshare, this track became one of the most talked about underground hits of the year. In 2002, mashup received its first worldwide press with the mainstream release by the *The Flying Dewaele Brothers* (Soulwax) when they mashed up 45 songs on the compilation *As Heard on Radio Soulwax*. In 2004, DJ Danger Mouse created *The Grey Album* where every sound sample used in the mashup album came from The Beatles *White Album*, with the vocals taken from the a cappella release of Jay-Z's *The Black Album*. This album helped inspire the official release of "Collision Course," a mashup of Jay-Z and Linkin Park ("Mashup," 2004). More recently, mashup has evolved into the mainstream. Madonna's 2005 hit "Hung Up" used portions of the track from ABBA's hit "Gimmie, Gimmie,

Gimmie" with an original vocal, resulting in Madonna's biggest selling single to date. In 2006, Sir George Martin and son Giles were given permission to mashup vocals and instruments from different songs taken from The Beatles master tapes to create the album *Love*, commissioned for the Cirque du Soleil show by the same name. In 2008, FM2 Radio and DJ Muggs created a nationally syndicated radio show; "Mash-Up Radio" featuring mashups of notable artists.

In 2009, "songsmith mashers" came into the spotlight. Microsoft's Soundsmith can take a song sung into a computer microphone and automatically add a MIDI-based backing track to it. Mashers have separated the vocals from well known classics and have fed them into the program to create new backing tracks automatically. The results, ironically synched up by the mashers to the original music videos, can be found on YouTube.

During this modern era, anyone with a computer can create a mashup. Recording software now comes *de facto* on most computers (i.e. Garageband on Mac computers). Sound files are more prevalent than ever through P2P networks and legal download sites such as itunes. Tutorials on how to create a mashup abound on the internet. Distribution sites such as youtube.com, make it easy for many to hear your composition and further accelerate user defined content.

Coda: Mashing up the Future

Mashup is an example of one more trend that the music industry and music technology helped create and, once again, is slow to understand and embrace. As a cover subgenre, mashup generates discussion about many assumptions about creativity, originality, repetition and borrowing. It also forces us to embrace the democratization of creativity, media creation and distribution. We no longer have a special higher class of musical creator (the king's court musician or the 1970s rockstar) that is unique and detached from the consumer. Mashup fits the postmodern ethos in its blending of styles and collaborative nature with P2P networks and social networking sites serving as the conduits. It has also spurred a new form of political activism, symbolized by Grey Tuesday and expanded by groups such as Music for America.

Of course, the negative aspect of mashup is that it can provide an easy path towards copyright infringement, especially for those oblivious to the rights of copyright law. However, labels and music publishers should see the value in stimulating interest in the original works by modifying or adapting them and being able to re-circulate the music again. Perhaps the record labels of the future will follow the lead of Radiohead and Beck and begin to release or sell instrumental and vocal stems to the world of mashup artists and desktop producers. It is undeniable that the youth culture downloading from P2P sites and experimenting with Garageband today will have the opportunity to become the pop music composers of the future.

Chapter 12

Camp Transitions: Genre Adaptation and the HI-NRG/Dance Cover Version

Lee Barron

The cover version has a long-standing place within popular music, and (as suggested by Middleton's example), it is a recording practice that frequently crosses musical styles, boundaries and genres, often to radical effect. The practice of appropriation casts covering in a distinctly postmodernist light, and this is the direction that I will take within this chapter. Habitually, musical forms such as rap and hip-hop are those most potently argued to manifestly display postmodern characteristics in terms of the penchant for the use of "collage, pastiche and quotation [and the] selective pasting together of different musics and styles" (Strinati, 1994: 435). Indeed, Lemert goes so far as to endorse rap and its routine reliance on sampling as a "near perfect illustration of the postmodern form" (1997: 23).

But rap and hip hop are not alone as a musical mode that routinely employing pastiche. Such a sensibility is similarly evident within contemporary western popular Dance music. Although Dance is not so much a genre but rather a myriad of sub-genres, from 1970s Disco, through to Acid House, House, Euro-house, Techno, Jungle/Drum 'n' Bass, Happy Hardcore, Garage, Grime and Dubstep in the 1980s, 1990s and 2000s, like Rap and Hip Hop, it is characterized by cultural "borrowing and hybridization" (Thornton, 1995: 76). For instance, David Shire's 1976 "Night on Disco Mountain" is a disco track that utilizes Mussorgsky's classical music, and in a similar fashion, Walter Murphy's "A Fifth of Beethoven" fused a disco sound with Beethoven's Fifth Symphony. More contemporary examples include Roger Sanchez's "Another Chance" which sampled Toto's 1982 song, "I Won't Hold You Back," and Eric Prydz's "Call On Me," built upon the chorus of Steve Winwood's 1982 recording, "Valerie" and Lovefreekz's "Shine" which extensively samples the 1979 Electric Light Orchestra song, "Shine a Little Love." However, the linking of dance music with musical borrowing can be extended to dance tracks which do not utilize samples, but rather, consist of cover versions that equally evoke a postmodernist practice of appropriation and pastiche. Within HI-NRG, and latterly NRG expressions of Dance music, the cover is not a diffused presence, but serves to define this particular sub-genre.

HI-NRG, as Osborne (1999) states, emerged principally from the UK gay scene in the late 1970s and early 1980s and became particularly popular in Europe. While UK certain pop music and musicians within this period were visibly establishing visible gay sensibilities, frequently with a political edge, from

Boy George, Bronski Beat/Jimmy Somerville to Frankie Goes To Hollywood (Reynolds, 2006), HI-NRG Dance alternatively emphasized a more hedonistic and apolitical expression. In terms of style and form, HI-NRG is typified by speeded up bass lines and drum tracks and songs which are invariably "cheesy disco anthems" (1999: 137). However, although there would be striking examples of HI-NRG tracks which were original recordings, such as Dead or Alive's "You Spin Me Round" (which reached #1 in the UK charts in 1985), many of the "disco anthems" which typified the HI-NRG sound would be cover versions of often classic, and frequently iconic, songs drawn from a multitude of musical genres. Notable examples from the 1980s and 1990s include Bona-Riah's "House Of The Rising Sun," a song popularized by The Animals in 1964, and Quantize's versions of "You've Lost That Loving Feeling," "Stop In The Name of Love," "The Sun Ain't Going To Shine (Anymore)" and "Yesterday Once More" by The Righteous Brothers (1965), The Supremes (1965), The Walker Brothers (1965) and The Carpenters (1973) respectively. Taking Bona-Riah's "House Of The Rising Sun" as an example, the opening iconic chord guitar progression is initially absent in favour of insistent swirling keyboard, then the progression appears, but in a "synthentic" machinic form of driving bass/keyboards. Moreover, the vocals consist of a fusion of male and female voices. So, the cover version remains highly recognizable, but it is highly modified in its strident, up-tempo format.

Hence, Quantize's array of cover versions follows a distinctive dance-oriented format, with higher-pitched male vocals, drum machines and synth/keyboards replacing original "traditional" instrumentation. And although songs such as "The Sun Ain't Going To Shine (Anymore)" have themselves been extensively covered (from Frankie Valli, The Walker Brothers, Neil Diamond and David Essex, to Cher and Keane), Quantize place it firmly within a Dance setting. But it is not merely classic tracks of the 1960s and 1970s that have been re-interpreted by HI-NRG acts. Notable examples of tracks from the 1980s abound, with recordings such as Boy's HI-NRG version of Mr. Mister's 1985 AOR rock/pop track "Broken Wings" and Nicki French's rendering of Bonnie Tyler's 1983 song "Total Eclipse of the Heart." French's version retains a close vocal connection with that of Tyler's original (soaring female singing), but the difference again lies in the musical arrangement, which replaces the "organic" instrumentation and ballad cadence with a vibrant drum-machine/keyboard arrangement and rapid tempo.

In terms of general effect with regard to the cover process, for Osborne, HI-NRG is a dance sub-genre that "glorifies in campness" (1999: 137) and the various cover versions discussed manifestly exhibit this quality. For Susan Sontag, camp chiefly involves "a relish for the exaggeration of sexual characteristics ... a vision of the world in terms of style" (1994: 279). It is a concept and practice which is especially centered upon "actions and gestures of exaggerated emphasis" and "apolitical frivolity" (Robertson, 1996: 3). Furthermore, for Sontag, the camp sensibility seeks the theatricalization of experience, so much so that "the whole point of camp is to dethrone the serious. Camp is playful, anti-serious" (1994: 288). Consequently, returning to the popular gay club culture in which HI-NRG flourished, it is perhaps little surprise that the soundtrack albums for the Russell T. Davies television drama *Queer As Folk*, concerning the lives of three young gay men in and around the Manchester club scene, contain a rich array of vibrant HI-NRG-style cover versions drawn from a wide spectrum of musical genres including: Madonna's "Holiday," Fleetwood Mac's "Everywhere," Aerosmith's "I Don''t Want To Miss A Thing," Kylie Minogue's "What Do I Have To Do" and "Better The Devil You Know," No Doubt's "Don't Speak," Deep Blue Something's "Breakfast At Tiffany's," Robbie William's "Angels," Shania Twain's "That Don't Don't Impress Me Much," Lighting Seed's "Marvellous," and New Order's "True Faith." While some of the original songs fall within the realm of camp (Madonna and Kylie Minogue), others assuredly do not, and therefore represent adaptations that serve to transform the experience of such songs. For example, Aerosmith and Fleetwood Mac are bands traditionally located within conventional rock musical settings, and both are firmly indicative of "authentic" musical expression in terms of instruments (guitars, keyboards, drums and bass). This is all the more pertinent in relation to Aerosmith, who, in the form of lead "guitar hero" Joe Perry, represent a classic hard rock band (although they themselves, via their collaboration with Run DMC, helped to efface generic boundaries between rock and rap with "Walk This Way" in 1986).

Yet, it is within such a context that HI-NRG, or HI-NRG-style dance resonates with postmodernist "surface" borrowings. Because, in many cases, in terms of structure and integrity, the cover versions can be precise and true in form to the original versions. In many of the examples cited so far, there are no explicit changes to the verse/chorus structures of the songs, rather, the radical changes are with regard to tempo, technology and vocals. It is within this dimension that the cover versions become separated from their originals, particularly when the originals are drawn from very different genres. I cited the example of Aerosmith being a dance-reconfiguration, but there are some notable and striking further contemporary examples. For instance, the Spanish dance performer and producer, DJ Sammy has produced a series of successful cover versions drawn from the rock genres. Beginning his career in the mid-1980s, DJ Sammy's output constitutes an updated form of the HI-NRG sound, with similar technologically-driven, upbeat and "pop" formats. Although recording a number of non-covers ("You're My Angel," "Prince of Love" and "In 2 Eternity") DJ Sammy's significant hits have been cover versions. The first, which reached #1 in the UK charts and #8 in America, was a cover of Bryan Adams' 1984 song, "Heaven." The most striking difference is the replacing of Adams' distinctively gruff voice with a female vocalist, and this is a common dimension within dance music, as Dickinson states with reference to the technological nature of the music, because the "(usually female) voice often serves as an emblem for pure human physicality within dance genres" (2001: 339). Again, this track discards guitars (bar a brief acoustic interlude) for strident keyboards and a bouncy beat. Of course, the tempo issue is related to the genre in which the song has been appropriated into, dance, so it is little wonder that the leitmotif of the cover versions I have discussed thus far is that upbeat addition, which is central to the effect and intention of the music: to enable people to dance.

As Frith states, "dance is an activity defined by its capacity to produce pleasure. The pleasure may be inward-directed or outward-directed; in either case it has frequently been seen to be "redolent with sexual tensions and possibilities" (1978: 180). While DJ Sammy's version retains the romance and sense of longing that is present within Adams' original, and serves to enhance its "life-affirming" qualities, it was DJ Sammy's next hit, "The Boys of Summer," again a cover version, which explicitly linked dance with pleasure and which displayed a distinctive postmodern sheen.

The original recording of "The Boys of Summer" was released by Don Henley, of Eagles fame, in 1984, drawn from his *Building the Perfect Beast* solo album. Although synth/keyboard laden and possessing an insistent drum machine percussive backbeat, Henley's song begins with a striking guitar riff and is characterized by sweeping guitar chords and slide bass throughout. However, although all lyrics are arguably open to polysemic readings and contain a number of possible meanings and avenues for understanding (Fiske, 1978), Henley's "The Boys of Summer" suggests a sense of loss and feelings about the past. As Puterbaugh (1985), in his *Rolling Stone* review of *Building the Perfect Beast* stated, it is a song that constitutes "a wistful look over the shoulder at a faded summer romance." DJ Sammy's version, released in 2002 and reaching #2 in the UK charts, like "Heaven," replaces Henley's vocal with that of a guest female singer, Loona, and although retaining a sound like the opening guitar riff of the original, the song soon develops into anthemic keyboard chords for the chorus. Moreover, within the context of the accompanying video for the song, any overt "ideological" and discursive meanings are effectively discarded or overwritten in terms of pleasure relating to dance and dancing. The video, although framed by DJ Sammy's search for a "dream girl" (who he finds) is dominated by bodies in motion and brightness, with the central action being set beside the sea, with a number of attractive males and females engaged in leisure and joyful abandonment.

This process of overwriting lyrical intent is most manifest with the line, "I saw a Deadhead sticker on a Cadillac." In the context of Henley's version, this line can be read as a rumination on lost visions of 1960s radicalism, or countercultural stances, the "drop out" sensibilities of the hippy epoch giving way to the materialism of the 1980s. In this sense, there is a keen political aspect to the song (Gilmore, 1987). DJ Sammy's version however, although not changing the lyrics or the structure of the song at all, effaces any such reading. Maintaining the strong melody, the song becomes joyous, a quality actively and deliberately enhanced by the video. Indeed, eschewing the moody black-and-white visuals of Henley's 1984 video, DJ Sammy's version is awash with vibrant colour and attractive, young bikini-clad females and bare-chested and shorts-wearing male figures; and the discarding of political discourse is keenly underscored by the lyrical/visual matching between the "Deadhead" line, which, in DJ Sammy's video, coincides with a young man hurling a cupped handful of seawater over a sun-bathing women in a moment of carefree, hedonistic fun, rendering the lyric meaningless. Ultimately, the video culminates in a beach party and dancing, emphasizing the generic nature of the song, which is intended to be played within clubs for clubbers to dance to.

What the cover version achieves is a strategy of "flattening out" the lyrical and discursive content into a musical text in which rhythm, tempo and vocal melody become the central tenets. Interestingly, "The Boys of Summer" was covered again in 2003 by the American rock act, The Ataris, who slightly modified the Grateful Dead reference to a "Black Flag sticker on a Cadillac," to update the sentiment from 1980s American punk to the 2000s but still retain the air of cynicism. However, DJ Sammy, by changing nothing except the sound and gender of the vocalist, changes the trajectory and nature of the song radically by reducing it a receptive status that favours sound over lyrical content. Thus, the rhythm and sound/vocal adaptation, in addition to a decontextualizing video, neutralizes encoded reception and places the revised version within that strand of camp that has an emphasis upon "apolitical frivolity" and hedonistic, carefree pleasure.

A further notable contemporary example of classic song being translated into the Dance style is the Scissor Sisters' cover of the Pink Floyd track "Comfortably Numb." Drawn from Floyd's famed 1979 concept album, *The Wall*, and dealing with the dark themes of isolation and drug use, the Scissor Sisters' version transforms the song into a disco extravaganza. With a sound that varies from disco and glam (most notable on the gloriously camp song/video "Filthy/Gorgeous"), and displaying a distinctive Elton John influence, "Comfortably Numb," their debut UK single, stands out within the Scissor Sisters sound as a HI-NRG-inspired track. Although the Scissor Sisters' version begins with a muted repeated guitar chord, the sound rapidly gives way to an idiosyncratic HI-NRG/disco sound. With the falsetto vocals of Jake Shears and female backing vocals supplied by Ana Matronic, the song is swathed in keyboards and is variously punctuated with electronic "disco" bleeps and it omits "Gilmour's pleasantly melodic solo" (Rose, 1998: 121). Consequently, although the feel of the song is transformed, the lyrics remain intact, as does the song's essential structure, but the effect is that a classic song of the "prog rock" era is re-invented for a twenty-first-century audience within an entirely different musical milieu. And further iconic rock songs have been similarly transformed into upbeat dance anthems, Pink Floyd's "Another Brick in the Wall" was covered by Eric Prydz in 2007, and, delving into the world of heavy metal, Guns 'n' Roses' "Sweet Child O' Mine" was covered by The Lazy Boyz as "Sweet Child Of Mine" in 2004, with drum machine, sequenced music and a female vocal replacing the tones of Axl Rose. Moreover, the now-classic chiming guitar intro riff by Slash is retained and maintained as a leitmotif throughout the song, albeit in an electronic form.

Appraising the appeal of cover versions of classic songs, Plasketes suggests that they can:

> Create consumer curiosity and incentive for fans and collectors, in particular completists attracted to a cut that is unavailable elsewhere … The presence of a cover song on a record contains the intrigue of hearing a familiar song

being performed by another artist, which can often sway a borderline purchase decision (2005: 148).

However, with regard to Dance cover versions, this is perhaps not so clear cut. It is one thing for Bruce Springsteen to record the songs of Pete Seeger, Bryan Ferry to release an album of Bob Dylan classics, Rod Stewart to revisit classic American standards, Annie Lennox to translate Procol Harum and The Clash, or even Tori Amos to re-interpret a divergent array of artists such as Eminem, The Stranglers, Joe Jackson, The Beatles, Neil Young, Nirvana, and Slayer; but, the vogue for covers within that sub-section of Dance is arguably of a different order. Certainly, with regard to covers of classic rock and metal songs, it is unlikely that aficionados of such music (other than the most obsessive collector) would seek out Dance music cover versions of songs originally recorded by beloved artists and bands. Indeed, to illustrate qualitatively such negative reception, a brief survey of Youtube commentary for the Scissor Sisters' version of "Comfortably Numb" reveals a distinctive sense of "sacrilege" that is frequently elicited and expressed by Pink Floyd fans, with comments such as:

- "They destroyed Pink Floyd's awesome 'Comfortably Numb'"
- "How dare you ruin Pink Floyd for me"
- "Those who actually enjoy this song have never heard the original, or have no comprehension at all of the pure beauty of Pink Floyd's music. Beauty that was destroyed in this excuse for a cover"
- "This doesn't have a chance against the original"
- "Disco Pink Floyd is right up there with Hip Hop Iron Maiden on the list of things I never want to hear as long as I live."

Therefore, the Dance cover version is potentially limited to Dance music circles or to general listeners who may simply causally "like the tune," and to a receptive audience who are not concerned with the provenance of the songs, but merely their quality in terms of inspiring dance. In terms of the covering process, Weinstein has recognized an array of specific roles which cover versions have fulfilled: commercial and aesthetic modification, validation of artistic authenticity, demonstrations of musical virtuosity, parody, homage, generic transformation, or the resolution to a lack of creativity. Consequently, she argues that regardless of the era and regardless of the motivation, "musicians … plunder the past with abandon" (Weinstein, in Inglis, 2005: 168).

With regard to Dance music, and especially HI-NRG Dance, the onus is firmly upon a plundering strategy and generic transformation with the creation of frequently camp musical pastiches in the Jameson-sense of pastiche as neutral practices of mimicry (1991: 17). As stated, many of the cover versions are "pure" in the sense that they do not change lyrics, chorus, verse or structure, but what such covers do change is the "feel" of the songs. Typically, this comes in the form of replacing male vocals with female vocals, but a primary element is the changing of tempo and the removal or "organic" instrumentation in favour of technology, be it keyboards, synthesizers, sequencers, DJ decks, or drum machines. In terms of critical appraisal, the "profane" aspects of transforming iconic rock tracks into driving dance forms evokes the longstanding charge that Dance music and dance culture is a form of inferior "mass music," a symptom of mass culture. As Thornton states:

> Dance culture has long been seen to epitomize mass culture at its worst. Dance music has been considered to be standardized, mindless and banal, while dancers have been regarded as narcotized, conformist and easily manipulated (1995: 1).

Dance music, Thornton maintains, differs from rock music and rock performances because they elicit a different set of bodily movements and bodily stances that is not "dancing" as the focus is upon something specific, such as the performer(s) and their musical prowess and stage dynamism. In this sense, rock music is about listening not dancing, hence, "dancing is still frequently stigmatized as being uncritical and mindless to the extent that is can debase the music with which it is associated" (1995: 71).

Certainly, the Dance cover versions of "The Boys of Summer" and "Comfortably Numb," the lyrics are fully intact and are thus still there to be interpreted and preferred readings accepted. However, the "disco" quality and the feel of Dance covers arguably serves to negate such an interpretive process and the most direct mode of reception is geared towards a "sensual" rather than an interpretative one. Dance music is primarily designed and crafted to be danced to, and this indicates what such cover versions qualitatively add in their covering techniques. Although examining television adaptations of classic novels, Cardwell (2002) states that the adaptation process from one text to another inevitably constitutes the modifying of a thing so as to suit new conditions, of adapting one original "standard whole" into another medium. In essence, the adaptation is a text in itself and should not be judged on how faithful it is to the original text. Therefore, HI-NRG and Dance cover versions accord with Cusic's defence of the covering process, that cover songs can act as "a history lesson for a new, young audience who never heard the original" and "allows new interpretations, new voices, and new audiences to discover it" (2005: 174 and 176). With reference to "The Boys of Summer," "Comfortably Numb" and "Sweet Child of Mine," it is highly likely that Dance/ pop listeners have no knowledge of the Eagles/Don Henley, Pink Floyd or Guns 'n' Roses, and subsequently hear and respond to these songs in different ways than fans of the originals would. The partial or total removal of the guitar would attest to this. Moreover, the reception of such songs are diffused across and within a range of different transmission and media contexts, from commercial radio, specialist Dance radio/music TV channels, to dance clubs/events, and Dance-oriented leisure locales, such as Ibiza. It is with these reception aspects that the Dance adaptation and covering process does demonstrably add a further dimension to the songs. As John Gill states:

> Dance music as it is perceived now—Soul, disco, funk, techno, and the many
> mansions of House—is, I believe, the one form of music which, even in its
> most degraded form, is bound up in something that closely resembles Roland
> Barthes' notion of *jouissance*, that is, rapture, bliss or transcendence (in Gilbert
> and Pearson, 1999: 64).

This assessment can be readily extended to HI-NRG and the HI-NRG cover
versions, and if it is not, as Gilbert and Pearson suggest, always a pure sense of
jouissance that Dance music produces, then it is arguably a source of the more
everyday *plaisir*, or a sensation that is someway between the two states of pleasure.
Consequently, as one commentator states of their affection and connection with DJ
Sammy's "The Boys of Summer" on Youtube: "I love this song it reminds me
of the great summers in Spain when they are playing at the beach and dancing."
And so, irrespective of the song's origins, Dance cover versions are received and
interpreted in their own singular ways, producing affections and connections
that are explicitly tied to the cover version and the pleasures that it produces and
continues to produce.

Even if the "HI" aspect has seemingly vanished from the scene, this sub-generic
form of Dance music is alive and well and still expressing itself through the cover
version. For instance, the *NRG-X* 2008 album collection consists exclusively of
Dance cover versions that plunder songs from the last three decades of British
and American popular music, ranging from a number of 1980s tracks such as Talk
Talk's "Such A Shame," Survivor's "Eye Of The Tiger," Cutting Crew's "I Just
Died In Your Arms Tonight," T'Pau's "China In Your Hands," and Bonnie Tyler's
"Holding Out For A Hero," with more contemporary songs in the form of Blur's
"Boys And Girls," Blondie's "Maria," Snow Patrol's "Chasing Cars" and The
Fray's "How To Save A Life." Classic rock is not ignored in the form of Blonde
Ambition's rendering of Journey's 1981 track, "Don"t Stop Believing," excising
guitars and pushed by a metronomic drum machine, and replacing Steve Perry
with the almost obligatory presence of a female vocal.

Consequently, while rock purists may recoil at the apparent "blasphemy"
of Dance cover versions; and while the songs may be neutralized and political
dimensions effaced by camp "postmodernist" pleasures and genre-swapping
adaptive ploys, they are nevertheless positively transformed. Thus, the chorus
of DJ Sammy's "The Boys of Summer" replaces Henley's strained lament for
the past with an anthemic and euphoric chant designed to move the body if not
necessarily the mind, but which succeeds in instilling a sense of affirmation into
a text that is suffused with a sense of loss. Whether the ease with which meanings
and political sentiments can be jettisoned within the covering process is a positive
or negative quality is a debate that has dogged postmodernism since its cultural
ascension (Von Gunden, 1991); but, with reference to the cover version and
the songs discussed within this chapter, in structurally changing very little with
regards to the arrangement of original songs, the Dance cover version can change
everything.

CONTEMPLATING COVERS

Chapter 13

In Defense of Cover Songs: Commerce and Credibility

Don Cusic

There is a dilemma that recording labels—both major and independent—face in Nashville: they insist that singers write their own songs.[1] This is a dilemma because not all singers are writers. Still, they must try because critics and fans as well as the business of music demands it. And this has come to the point where it is hurting the music industry.

What happens if an artist seeks a major label deal and doesn't write? Well, the first thing they must do is try to write some songs. If they can't do it, or can't do it very well, then the next step is to get with established songwriters to co-write. Only if they have their name listed as a writer or co-writer will most labels show an interest.

And what happens if a major label signs an artist who doesn't write? Well, they soon get them with established songwriters who will "help" them write a song. This is the way many songwriters make a living these days. Their only hope of getting a cut with a major label is to find a recording artist and co-write with them so their songs can end up on a major label release for a "single" or at least an album cut.

Why is this bad? Because the "real" songwriters don't like it. They are often put into the position of having to write a song with an artist in the room—perhaps giving some ideas of what they want the song to say or maybe vetoing a line or two—and then getting only half credit and half the income for what is, essentially, their own creation. It is bad for the recording labels because the artists, their managers and publishers will insist some of these songs be included on the album. It makes good financial sense for the artists, managers and publishers.

If an artist has no songwriting credit on an album, they have lost a revenue stream. If a songwriter writes one song on an album that goes "Gold" (sells 500,000 units) they will earn $22,750. This is computed by taking the mechanical rate (currently at 9.1 cents) and multiplying by the number sold and then dividing that figure by half—because the publisher receives half the song income (.091 x 500,000 = 45,500 x .5 = $22,700). If that song is written by two people, then the figure must be divided again, so each co-writer earns $11,375.

---

[1]   This essay appeared in a special issue on cover songs, *Popular Music and Society* Volume 28, Number 2, May 2005: 171–7.

If the artist has co-written ten songs on a Gold album, the calculations are .091 (mechanical rate) x 10 (the number of songs) = .91 x 500,000 (units sold) = 455,000 x .5 (songwriters share) = \$227,500 x .5 (co-writer's share) = \$113,750.

If there is a "controlled composition clause" whereby the labels pay 75 percent of the mechanical rate, then the co-writer would receive \$85,312.50. And that's a lot of money.

If the songwriter also controls his/her publishing, then that figure would double, or be \$227,500 or \$170,625, depending on whether or not there is a controlled composition clause. That only applies to an album cut, not a single.

If the song is a single and reaches the top five on the pop charts, the song could earn \$400,000 to \$1,000,000; the songwriter's share would be half of that and a co-writer half of that or between \$100,000 and \$250,000.

So, for business reasons, an artist wants to write or co-write songs on his/her/ their albums. The label also views this as good business because it assures them that the artist has a steady stream of material. Otherwise, they have to "find" songs to record.

Critics and fans tend to feel an artist is more "legitimate" if they write or co-write their own material. And so if a label releases an album where the singer does not write any of the songs, a critic will often dismiss the effort. They're not a "real" artist if they only sing! This critical premise is rampant with *American Idol* contestants.

So why is this "bad"? Because it ignores the great singers and musicians who can "interpret" a song. Back in 2002, I interviewed Elana Fremerman and Whit Smith from the group Hot Club of Cowtown, a jazzy trio with roots in western swing who are no longer together, and they told me of the frustrations they faced as musicians giving new interpretations of old songs rather than only doing songs they wrote. Fremerman explained:

> We didn't start this band as songwriters but now people ask "did you guys write these songs"? And we say, "No, we're arranging it and soloing over it and 90 percent of what you're hearing in this is our original spontaneous playing." But they want to hear a song that we wrote, that we named, that we sing. I can understand that. There's a kind of artistic development that's absolutely valuable and we're trying to do that. We get that pressure a lot because we're classified as country and pop-ish. But if you're like Diana Krall, she doesn't have to write her own songs. She just sings standards and it touches everybody. For some reason they don't call her songs "covers"—they're standards. Stuff from Frank Sinatra and Tony Bennett and Bing Crosby aren't dismissed. But nowadays there's this kind of thing that's like confessional—if you're singing somebody else's song, how can it be truly evoking what you are because it's somehow disingenuous. And we don't really like that. (2002)

Whit Smith, another member of the group, added, "It's hard for the press and people to talk about things. Improvisations are so abstract. To say something is original and talk about the person's angst—well, there's a lot more to talk about" (Smith, 2002).

Fremerman added, "Plus you'd have to go back and do your homework when you're hearing a new interpretation of an old song. They'll always misinterpret. There's a certain level of historical understanding that is required to really look into it" (2002).

For example, "Blueberry Hill" by Gene Autry in the 1940s is quite different from that song by Fats Domino in the 1950s; the same is true of "Blue Christmas" by Ernest Tubb compared to the version by Elvis Presley; and the versions of the Hoagy Carmichael song "Georgia On My Mind" by Ray Charles, the Righteous Brothers, Wes Montgomery, Michael Bolton and Willie Nelson are all quite different. In each of these cases, the cover version of the song reached a new audience who never heard the "original version." The "new" audience was separated by a generation or by musical taste—a hit in country music was probably not heard by the pop audience or the rhythm and blues audience did not know the country version. Ray Charles did an album of "country" songs (*Modern Sounds in Country and Western Music*) in the early 1960s that reached the R & B and pop audiences and Willie Nelson did an album of pop standards (*Stardust*) in the mid-1970s that introduced a new generation of country and pop fans to these songs.

Reaching back further, the version of "How High the Moon" by Les Paul and Mary Ford in the early 1950s showed how an old jazz song could benefit from using advanced recording technology to "update" it.

"Hound Dog" by Elvis was a cover of Big Mama Thornton's R & B hit—but the young rock and roll crowd heard it for the first time from Elvis. The same is true with the early 1950s hit "If" by Perry Como that was re-done by Bread in 1971. Wes Montgomery's instrumental version of the Beatles' "A Day in the Life" added a new interpretation of that song; the same is true of John Coltrane's instrumental of "My Favorite Things," which originally came from *The Sound of Music* soundtrack.

Sometimes a cover recording shows the influences of a particular act; examples here include the Beatles' versions of the Carl Perkins songs "Honey Don't" and "Everybody's Trying to Be My Baby," the Beatles versions of the Motown hits "Please Mr. Postman" (done originally by the Marvellettes) and "You've Really Got a Hold On Me" (done originally by Smoky Robinson and the Miracles); the Rolling Stones' version of Chuck Berry's "Oh, Carol," or the Merle Haggard albums of Jimmie Rodgers' songs (*Same Train, Different Time*) and Bob Wills (*A Tribute to the Best Damn Fiddle Player*).

"Crying in the Chapel" was a hit song in country (Rex Allen), R & B (the Orioles) and rock (Elvis Presley); "Blowin' in the Wind" was a hit in pop (Peter, Paul and Mary) and R & B (Stevie Wonder).

New interpretations of a song are illustrated by looking at the versions of "Try a Little Tenderness" by Frank Sinatra and Otis Redding; or Hank Williams' version of "Lovesick Blues" and comparing it with earlier versions by Emmett Miller and Rex Griffin.

Many times a "cover" is a history lesson for a new, young audience who never heard the original. Other times it may reflect the fact that fans of one type of music don't listen to another type of music—e.g. an R & B version of a country song or vice versa. From a business perspective, this makes good sense: a "hit" song that transcends genres if it is recorded by an artist within a genre. This is what happened during the covers of the early R & B hits by pop acts in the early 1950s. Each new "hit" of an old song generates new revenue from the publisher and provides labels and artists with a new market.

From an artist's perspective, covers are important because they (1) provide a song proven to be a hit to the repertoire, (2) show an important influence on the artist and (3) give the audience something familiar when introducing a new act. Audiences in general like to hear something they are familiar with when seeing a "new" artist perform live and an old standard makes them a little more comfortable, especially when most of the material presented is unknown to the audience. The Beatles' classic "Yesterday" has proven a timeless cover for all of these reasons.

The reason that the singer/songwriter is "good" for fans and critics is that no historical knowledge is needed to review or appreciate an album—it's a contemporary opinion. It's great for the lazy or uninformed critic. But there's another reason that it's bad for fans.

Fans will often complain that they've purchased an album and liked the hit single, or perhaps one or two cuts—but the rest of the album "sucks" (to use the popular term of critical evaluation today). And so you ask, "Who wrote the songs that 'suck?'" The fan will look at the credits and with mild surprise say, "the artist!" In other words, just because the artist has put his/her songs on the album doesn't mean those songs are the strongest—and so the buyer is "cheated." Thus the value of albums in general goes down, which partially explains a trend in the music industry for compilation albums of hit singles. Those who download music tend to download singles (or single songs from an album) often use this same argument: "I only want a cut or two—not the whole album."

This is not a plea to rewind to the days when there was a fairly strict division of labor: songwriters wrote songs and singers sang them. However, it must be pointed out that this was the case of songwriters like Irving Berlin, the Gershwins, Cole Porter, Gerry Goffin and Carole King, the Holland-Dozier-Holland team from Motown, and Jerry Leiber and Mike Stoller, who all wrote some incredible songs. And it must also be pointed out that some of the great interpreters of songs, such as Bing Crosby, Frank Sinatra, Elvis Presley and Ella Fitzgerald made some great recordings of songs they didn't write. These singers accepted their talent as a "singers" and did not feel compelled to fill up albums with songs that had them listed as a co-writer.

The definition of a "cover" song is one that has been recorded before. This has been confused with a cover record, which has come to mean a recording exactly like the original, or first, recording except sung by a different singer and played by different musicians.

A great song should be "covered." And countless have been. Even cover records have their place, although that is not a popular argument when talking about early rock and roll. It has long been convenient and trendy to malign Pat Boone for his covers of Little Richard songs. But Pat Boone came from a long tradition of singers covering other recordings; he happened to be caught in the time warp when "pop" music was shifting to rock and roll. He did the same thing that Fats Domino, Elvis Presley and, later, The Beatles and numerous others did during that time—he found some great recordings and "covered" them.

It is nice to rewrite history and say that this shouldn't have happened, that the "original" artists (most of whom were black) should have gotten the radio hits and the credits for these songs—but that ignores the very real historical fact that the United States was a segregated country during the mid-1950s and those songs done by African-American artists would not have gotten the exposure they eventually received if an artist like Pat Boone had not covered them at that time. You may make the aesthetic judgment that Pat Boone's covers were "inferior" to the versions by Little Richard ("Tutti Frutti" and "Long Tall Sally"), but the undeniable fact is that during that time, Pat Boone's recordings outsold Little Richard's. It was the market forces at work in popular music.

While fans, critics and academics make aesthetic judgments of music and musical recordings, the music business judges recordings by commercial criteria: If it sells it's "good" and if it doesn't, it's not. "Good" means the artist can make more recordings while "bad" means the artist is dropped from the label because they are not deemed commercially viable. It may not be the way some think it should be, but it is pure and simply the way things are: Numbers don't lie and money talks louder than the music playing. In the music business, it doesn't matter who likes it, what matters is who buys it!

A singer wants a successful long-term career; if the career is successful, the singer will develop fans and buyers of their recordings. The fan loves (1) the singer's voice and (2) the songs they record. In the past, successful singers sought out "hit" songs because there was a proven market for that song. If you look at some of the great pop singers in the past—people like Bing Crosby, Frank Sinatra, Ella Fitzgerald—or even rock singers like Elvis or country singers like Eddy Arnold—they consistently sought to record "their" version of songs that were hits for others.

Somehow, through the years, this has come to be considered illegitimate. Granted, in those eras there were a number of singers who "covered" songs and the results were neither aesthetically pleasing nor commercially successful. But that's the product of a capitalist, open market system of pop music. Indeed, it's the very heart of "popular culture." It's also part of the music business—there's always lots of "junk" out there. Every recording is not a masterpiece. A whole lot of recordings are released and some connect with audiences, become "hits," are considered "great"—and a whole lot don't. Trouble is, nobody knows what's going to work and what ain't. The claims of musical prophets aside, the history of the recording industry is filled with stories of songs, recordings and artists that weren't supposed to become "hits" but did as well as the "can't miss" stuff that missed by a mile.

There is a difference between cover records and cover songs, although that distinction often gets buried by the fact that the recording industry—not sheet music—dominates the music business. During the first half of the twentieth century it was sheet music that sold more than recordings so the song was "bigger" than the record. A cover song allowed new interpretations, new voices, and new audiences to rediscover it. A great musician could add to this song, enhance it, and give it a new life. So could a great singer. This same can be true today, although a song today tends to be measured by the recording from the first artist to record it rather than on its own as a piece of sheet music.

On the business side, music publishers love covers because they prolong the life of a great song, perhaps creating a "classic" that will earn money for years and years. The greatest compliment a songwriter can receive is for a variety of artists to cover his/her song—it says the song transcends genres and time. It is what every songwriter aspires to with his/her songs.

So why the disdain for covers? Fans and critics may say that the song expresses the songwriter's soul and not the artist's. This is true today because most songwriters are "confessional" and tend to write songs about their feelings and thoughts. This wasn't always the case; many of those songwriters who wrote The Great American Songbook—those classic songs from the period roughly 1920–50—were poor immigrants, mostly from Eastern Europe and mostly Jewish. They did not want to write about themselves—they wanted to write a song that embraced culture, sophistication and something beyond themselves. Granted, many of these songs were written for musicals where the song had to fit a character or story line, but those songwriters tended to write outside of themselves rather than pull songs from within themselves.

A disdain for cover songs often denies the timelessness of great works. It also denies everyday human experience. There are songs you have heard that seemed to "fit" you, that articulated your thoughts and feelings, that connected you with your own heart. Everyone has had this experience—with a song they did not write!

A commercially successful singer needs to sing songs that connect them to an audience. A great singer communicates to a mass audience and they communicate for numerous individuals in that audience. People don't buy somebody else's feelings, they buy their own, but sometimes our feelings are expressed by a singer through a song he did not write, regardless of whether the singer's personal experience mirrors that or not.

In today's world, cover songs and cover recordings are a lost art. By demanding that singers write their own songs, the public is "cheated" of hearing great singers and musicians interpret a great song. And by denying that a recording is only "authentic" (a favorite term these days) if the singer wrote it, the creative genius of the non-singing songwriter is denied. Songwriting is a talent all its own. Sometimes the songwriter can sing well and sometimes not; sometimes the songwriter can sing well but chooses to write instead of perform.

This is not to dismiss the efforts of singer/songwriters. There is a place and tradition for them. But they should not be regarded as the end-all and be-all in popular music. Especially when you see that new talent must be young and good looking above all. Those are the attributes that "sell" to a young audience. That same audience wants to hear great songs but often these singers lack the experiences and emotional maturity to pull it all together.

Being a "star" is a full-time job that requires lots of time in the public eye. Songwriting is an art that requires quiet reflection away from the public eye. It's hard to find a great depth in songwriting when the singer/songwriter is a young person busy being a star.

The singer/songwriter should be the exception and not the rule. Songwriting should be an honored profession all its own. And cover recordings should be a way for singers and musicians to express their creativity that is as honest and authentic as music can be.

Listen to some of the great artists of the past century. Listen to Ella Fitzgerald, Louis Armstrong, Bing Crosby, Frank Sinatra, Tony Bennett, Elvis Presley, Jerry Lee Lewis, Eddy Arnold, Roy Acuff, John Coltrane or numerous others. And ask yourself: Would it have been wise or worth it to demand that each of these artists write everything—or nearly everything—that they recorded? Would it have dimmed their greatness? Does it make their contribution to American popular music any less? I don't think so.

Chapter 14

Artist Intentions: A Case for Quality Covers

Remy Miller

My daughter's interest in popular music began in earnest five or six years ago. One thing I vividly remember from that time was that a large number of songs she listened to were remakes of pop and rock hits from the 1960s, 1970s and 1980s. One was a cover of Earth Wind and Fire's "Shining Star." Another was a version of The Monkees' "I'm a Believer" from the soundtrack for the film *Shrek*, which also included a cover of Joan Jett's "Bad Reputation." Teen idols Aly and AJ remade The Lovin' Spoonful's "Do You Believe in Magic" and Katrina and the Waves' 1980s hit, "Walking on Sunshine" on their 2005 album. The teen group Play covered Elvis's "I Can't Help Falling in Love With You." The list could go on. This trend coincided with my awareness of Disney Radio, which seemed to be my daughter's primary source for her music rotation. Clearly, the sounds emerging from my daughter's room were an echo of an earlier era.

The song recycling seemed rather odd to me on some levels, particularly since it appeared that record companies and radio stations had worked hard to establish a market for relatively serious teen pop singers and musicians such as like Avril Lavigne and Vanessa Carlton who aimed at the burgeoning adolescent music scene. This attempt to capitalize on a newly moneyed audience required songs tailored to that audience rather than re-recordings of older songs. Unlike previous manufactured teen idols like Debbie Gibson in the 1980s, Lavigne admirably wrote her own material and led her own band. Perhaps Lavigne and the others could only have so many hits so programmers resorted to cover songs to fill the space between. Whatever the case, for a while I faced the nightmarish situation of hearing songs I did not like thirty years ago re-invading the airwaves in my home squealed with teen enthusiasm and energy by miniature divas and maestros. Pretty vacant, indeed.

While I found this curious and unsettling it was also nothing new. Sanitized cover versions of pop songs recorded with cold-blooded calculation for the teen marketplace are as old as rock and roll. There is certainly nothing in recent pop history more egregious than Pat Boone's recordings of Little Richard's hits, which carried a disturbing racial aspect in addition to the objectionable aesthetic limitations.

Presumably, the prevalence of re-recorded hits may serve as an indicator of a kind of quality recognized by a younger generation, but I don't really believe that. Teen pop stars being manipulated by producers and record labels is a cliché because it has been true since the beginning of rock 'n' roll, if not longer. What ever the case may be it did start me on the path to this essay because I found myself mulling over the question of what makes a great cover song.

During the period of growth and development of my taste in music, roughly the late 1960s through the early 1980s, the long-playing album was the dominant format for pop and rock recordings. During the 1960s, the focus of pop recordings had shifted from the single 45 rpm to the LP or album. Before that time, a performer's popularity was tied to their ability to have hit singles. Albums were often just collections of previous single hits or sketchy affairs including a hit or two amongst hastily recorded fillers. With the advent of artists such as Bob Dylan and the Beatles, many bands and songwriters began to see an album as a more or less unified set of songs that carried a particular point of view. 45's were still important for many bands, but mostly to promote albums. Often singles were plucked from albums by record companies (with or without input or agreement from the artist) in order to promote them.

The Beatles' *Sergeant Pepper's Lonely Hearts Club Band* and The Beach Boys *Pet Sounds* are only the most obvious and famous examples of the apotheosis of this trend. For any serious band worth their satin shirts and leather pants the album was a serious artistic matter. This trend was taken to the extreme in so-called "concept albums" like The Who's *Tommy* or the Kinks' *Preservation Acts I and II* among many others. Whatever the relative merits of such albums the idea behind them was that serious artists considered carefully the inclusion and the running order of songs so that each album existed as an artistic statement that took its place in the context of the musician's oeuvre.

In the context of the album, the use of cover songs is extremely important and interesting because the self-conscious artist didn't waste space on an album just recording any old song, popular or otherwise. Fans and critics paid attention. If a cover song was to be included on an album, choosing the appropriate one was a matter of great importance. Certainly artists chose covers with the idea in mind of having a hit. But those songs also needed to fit within the context of the artist's own songs on an album. For an artist who operated within the mainstream during the time of album-oriented rock it wasn't enough to just look for a potential hit to cover. Any cover version had to contribute to the overall concept and spirit of an album.

It occurred to me that there must be some common qualities that distinguish great cover versions from those that are less so. Arguments about quality are frowned upon in art criticism circles these days, but I hold to the belief that everything is not as relative as we may like to think. Admittedly, absolutes are hard to come by in art. For one thing, most great art embodies contradiction and paradox. Great artists embrace and revel in these ideas. Nonetheless, I still hold on to the basic idea that in the pursuit of the cover version as art, the majority of successful ones share some common qualities that explain their impact. I propose the three following broad qualifications, though subjective, might be useful in understanding what makes a great cover song. One may be more important than another in a given song, but I think they all apply all the time.

Love and Understanding

An artist who has no commitment to the original material cannot create a great cover version. A great cover requires that the coverer have a deep appreciation of the song and an understanding of its meaning to the degree that they can express its idea in a different and personal way. It may be unfair and too easy to pick on Pat Boone, but it is abundantly clear that he had no idea what in the world "Tutti Frutti" was about and it is hard to believe he had any particular reverence for the song. The basic fact is that a cover song is someone else's idea. In order to interpret the words and music, and make it personal, the cover artist has to empathize and sense a potential in the song that is implied but not fulfilled in the original recording. This isn't possible if the artist doesn't care about the song.

The Intention of Art

At the most basic level, intention is the most important element necessary for art of any kind. In essence: the true artist has to *mean* it. Like any great work in any field of the arts there must be a conscious intent to create a work of art. This may be reflected in many ways and in rock and roll it almost never entails the artist stating baldly, "I meant to create art." Such a statement would be anathema to most rock and rollers. Only a few, such as Patti Smith, Bono, or Bruce Springsteen would have the gall to say such a thing. Most of the time I believe it can be understood by the level of ambition involved in taking on a song generally accepted to be untouchably great or perhaps in the recognition of qualities not apparent in an original or perhaps the will to record a song that tests the skills of the cover artist. No matter what, the intention to create art must be present to achieve greatness.

Interpretation

Without the ability to bring a personal point of view to a cover there is only a re-recording of a song, not a new statement. This is where so many covers fail to move us. This is where the phrase "Something to say" becomes of the utmost importance. Without something to say, without a coherent worldview expressed in the context of their chosen field of art, the artist simply is not. With nothing to say, the term "artist" becomes a generic description for somebody that put a brush to canvas, picked up an instrument or wrote a sentence or a line of poetry. It may be true that "everybody's a star," as Ray Davies said in "Celluloid Heroes", but not everybody is an artist.

Four Cover Cases

There are four examples of cover versions of songs that I think illustrate one or more of these categories. Only one of the songs I have chosen to examine was a hit in either the original incarnation or the cover. Popularity has no bearing on quality. It is also not necessary for the cover version to have surpassed the original in quality. My arguments in this situation are about what differences exist between the versions and how the cover version succeeds in comparison to the original.

Graham Parker and the Rumour's version of The Jackson Five's "I Want You Back" may seem a strange place to start because it was not included on any of their original albums. It was released only as a B-side to one of many of Parker's failed attempts to have a hit record. Therein lies the value of this song for my argument. Parker, a songwriter of tremendous intelligence, skill, and depth, has always treated his albums as statements in themselves and has always seen his entire body of work, from start to finish, as a more or less complete artistic statement. Parker rarely records cover songs. He certainly plays them live, but the inclusion of covers on albums or as singles is rare. Therefore, the recording of "I Want You Back" (Alive) is notable and his treatment is instructive right down to the parenthetical attachment of the title. Parker's vision of the song within the context of his oeuvre required that the song bend to his will rather than provide the opportunity to sell records. One reviewer described Parker's treatment as singing the song "as if he was repossessing a car" (Guterman, 1993). This is a humorous remark and anyone who has heard the song would understand the point and humor, but it isn't really accurate. Parker sings the song like an adult and it is in his interpretation of the song in an adult context that it gains a power and believability that actually does surpass the original.

The original "I Want You Back" is certainly a great pop song and my appreciation of Parker's interpretation in no way diminishes the original. However, all the emotional power of the lyric is lost in Michael Jackson's squeaky, adolescent voice. The melody, arrangement, and the novelty of a song being sung by a little kid in the original, something much more uncommon then than now, belie a lyric that is very adult. The gist of the song has nothing to do with the teen love that initially appears to be the message. The singer of the song is a bit of a jerk. He only wants his girlfriend back because he realizes that other men find her attractive. Michael Jackson simply did not have the real experience to put the lyric across in a believable way. This may explain Parker's recounting of his one time meeting Jackson whose reaction to Parker informing him he had just recorded the song resulted in the following: "He looked like I had just spoken to him in an alien language" (Guterman, 1993).

Parker's version brings the full meaning of the lyric out with a growling, drawling, and even soulful performance that makes it clear what the lyric is really saying. He drags out the ending syllables of various lines in an exaggerated Dylanesque fashion and it is clear that the song has nothing to do with teen love. The songs form really doesn't change much. True, the horns and strings are gone along with some of the more complex backing vocal parts, but The Rumour are faithful to the original to the point of singing the backing vocals in falsetto. It is a muscular, driving version as the Rumour was a superior rock band and they play with a unity and commitment born of years of touring and recording together.

Parker is exemplary for my purpose here in that he sees his entire body of work as being "of a piece". The implication for cover versions included in any album by such an artist was that the cover was as important as the artist's own songs and its meaning had to mesh with the overall thematic or conceptual intention of the album. It had to function within the album as an enforcement or even a contrast to the overall vision of the album.

Nils Lofgren's version of Carole King's "Goin' Back" fulfills just such a function on his initial solo album released in 1975. Lofgren, only 24 at the time, was already a veteran rocker having released four critically well-received albums with his band Grin and played on albums with Neil Young and his backing band's Crazy Horse's albums as well as touring extensively. "Nils Lofgren" is not a concept album, but it is a particularly strong and consistent set of songs that followed Lofgren's tendency to balance tough but melodic rock songs featuring virtuosic lead guitar with overtly sensitive, sometimes innocently sentimental, ballads featuring piano. This was a tremendously attractive aspect of Lofgren's music and persona for those that followed his career. He was a guitar slinger with the heart of Christopher Robin.

This persona is part of what makes Lofgren's version of "Goin' Back" so strong. The inclusion of this song of retrospection and introspection is at odds with the majority of the content of his other songs and in marked contrast to his image in general. Nowhere is this contrast more obvious than the album cover photograph. Leaning against a circus sideshow painting of a fat boy Lofgren appears as a prototypical rocker clad in a black leather jacket, bedecked with flowing scarves, his halo of messy curls surrounding his head. He tips a bottle of brandy up to his lips and appears to be winking at the viewer. The choice of "Goin' Back" for inclusion on this album added a depth and balance to the song list which ultimately helps make the album more powerful and cohesive. It also demonstrates an intelligence and subtlety of thought that separated Lofgren from more run of the mill musicians of the period.

Carole King's original version of the song is a restrained, understated performance seemingly appropriate for the subject as she reexamines her life, and considers what relevance childhood has on her future. Based on the jaunty, upbeat nature of Lofgren's version, he has already accepted and embraced the child-like qualities that King describes and adopted them as a key aspect of his approach to life. This is reflected in the content of many of Lofgren's songs, in his high-energy performances, and even in his voice, which has a high-pitched child-like quality. Subsequent live versions of the song often included a jazzy piano snippet of "Mary Had a Little Lamb" as an introduction.

I would hazard a guess that the most famous cover in the pop/rock field is Jimi Hendrix's version of Bob Dylan's "All Along The Watchtower." Hendrix's massive reworking of Dylan's modest acoustic poem is a glorious (if obvious) example of a cover in which everything goes right. His sonic landscape perfectly complements Dylan's existential lyrics. There are, of course, many, many covers of Dylan's songs, but few others have obscured the original recordings by Dylan.

Interestingly, there are relatively few notable covers of Hendrix's songs and none that have achieved acclaim to the degree that "Watchtower" has. In my mind, one of the best, and one that succeeds in much the same way that Hendrix did with "Watchtower" is Derek and the Dominos' version of "Little Wing." The Dominos parallel Hendrix's treatment of the Dylan song in that they took a rather subdued, restrained performance of a poetic lyric and turned it into a swirling, impassioned barrage of sound.

Layla and Other Assorted Love Songs is widely regarded as one of the premier rock guitar albums ever recorded. The interplay between Eric Clapton and Duane Allman is a high point in the recorded output of them both. However, another aspect of The Dominos' treatment that differs dramatically from the original perfectly illustrates one of the key ideas for the band according to keyboard player and singer Bobby Whitlock. It is the vocal interplay between Clapton and himself. Whitlock commented in the notes for the twentieth anniversary re-release of "Layla" that one of his initial ideas for the band was vocal interplay along the lines of a soul duo like Sam and Dave. In many of the songs from "Layla", Whitlock's deep, husky voice doubles or backs up Clapton's lead vocal pushing him to a level of intensity he rarely achieved before or since. Their impassioned interplay is as much a part of the success of the album as the more celebrated guitar work of Clapton and Allman. On "Little Wing" they transform Hendrix's low-key, psychedelic love poem into a wall of sound out of which the garbled, passionate vocals emerge and recede. What is restrained and lyrical in Hendrix's original becomes, like much of "Layla", so overcome with unrequited passion that the words and music seem to coalesce into one long tragic, but beautiful, wail. Lyrically you may not know exactly what is going on, but emotionally you know *exactly* what is going on.

"Layla" was recorded in 1970, just after Hendrix's death. Because "Layla" is a double album and is a particularly cohesive album and because the song "Layla" was the only hit from the album it is rarely noted that this song was, for many years, the only Hendrix song Clapton recorded. Of course, Hendrix and Clapton were friends, bound by their celebrity as two of the greatest guitarists of their generation. "Little Wing" was chosen from the whole of Hendrix's catalog to be recorded and is certainly a tribute to him.

"No Fun" by The Stooges is a two-chord rant about loneliness and anger. It is a two minutes and thirty seconds of garage band angst driven by raucous guitars just barely on the edge of control. The band is barely competent and Iggy Pop's deep droning vocals aren't beautiful, but their commitment and their truthfulness about the banality of life give the song real power. There are no dynamics, no subtlety, just a slice of teenage boredom and lust for something better. There are no answers in this song. It's just a short reality show from 1968 that starts in one place and ends in that same spot a few minutes later.

The Sex Pistols version of "No Fun" replaces the Stooges droogy aimlessness with speeded-up sledgehammer efficiency and the extended yowl of Johnny Rotten's voice. Propelled by Paul Cook's drums and Steve Jones' buzz saw guitar the Pistols version is five minutes longer than the original. One marvels at their ability to sustain intensity in such a simple song over the course of seven-plus minutes. This is probably the first time the Sex Pistols have been accused of subtlety, but the way Rotten's voice ebbs and flows over the bed of sound laid down by the band is truly dynamic. While it may be generous to describe Rotten's vocal as nuanced, what he does with his voice is frighteningly expressive. It's like a catalog of negative emotion ranging all the way from threatening to cowering and changing almost from line to line. He moves from complaining to cajoling to caterwauling to screeching as the band pounds away behind him. It is a performance that is amazingly powerful. He equals the truthfulness of Iggy's original vocal, but he surpasses him in his ability to suggest different emotions with his voice. From righteous anger to pathetic helplessness. As the songs lurches to the end, Rotten hoarsely screams, "I'm alive." It's a self-realization, a threat, and a statement of fact all in one phrase. When he bluntly rasps, "It's no fun, it's not funny" it is the awful truth. "No Fun" is not a song one enjoys unless you like the sound of things going terribly wrong, but it is a powerfully human song and the emotion generated in this performance is tremendously affecting.

Johnny Rotten would, I'm sure, just as soon spit in your face as admit that he was attempting to make great art at the time "No Fun" was recorded. His later career makes it perfectly obvious that art was always on his mind, but the level of ambition and intelligence at work in "No Fun" is just as plain despite the limitations of the recording and the band's anarchic pronouncements. If nowhere else it is betrayed in the short introduction to the song before the band kicks in behind him. "Here we go now," Rotten sneers, "A sociology lecture … with a bit of psychology, a little neurology … a bit of fuckology … No funnnn … ." He's being ironic and sarcastic, but it's clear he understands that this song is a direct, unselfconscious reaction to Iggy Pop's life at the time of its writing. With distance in time and geography, Rotten was making a connection between the lyric by a bored Michigan teenager and the life of Britain's lower class youth a decade later. Rotten connects to the feelings of anxiety and helplessness expressed in the original and his interpretation made it a clear reflection of the socio-political situation in England in 1977 and directly relevant to his life and the lives of his audience.

The recording of "No Fun" also confirms one of the principle critical points made about influences on the Sex Pistols and punk rock, in general. Bands like the New York Dolls, The MC Five and, indeed, The Stooges are often cited as precursors that anticipate the stripped down, high energy, low fidelity nature of punk. In Rotten's choice of "No Fun" (and in his own song "New York) he makes explicit this historical connection. Another demonstration of his advanced sense of history and irony is the Sex Pistols recording of "(I'm Not Your) Stepping Stone" a hit song for The Monkees. The Sex Pistols, through their relationship with manager/huckster Malcolm McLaren (who also managed the New York Dolls for a short time) have often been compared to the "Pre-Fab Four."

Johnny Rotten and the Sex Pistols are a particularly fitting example of the rich intertwining of many levels of history, irony, self-promotion, and criticism that is often at the heart of great rock 'n' roll. Rotten's pronouncements about the advanced state of decay he saw in rock in the late seventies is born of a sharp critical ear and eye and of a love for the passion and rebellion that he thought was lost.

Covers and Criticism

In many ways I see the decadence that, in Rotten's view of rock at the time made the music lame, paralleled in a broader art world and cultural context now. This essay is an attempt to show a way to look at music and all art that I love with a fair critical eye. My arguments reflect a long-standing personal engagement with art of all kinds and a need to analyze its qualities. The point is not to denigrate it, but to understand it and articulate a way to use it to change my life in some great or small way.

As a kid, I had no background in art making or art criticism through the first fifteen years of my life. Until I became interested in music, as a teen, I had no experience with art, much less art criticism, of any kind. Nonetheless, I craved some understanding that allowed me to distinguish what I thought were good and poor songs. That discrimination is the essence of criticism. Making judgments about the differences in quality between songs and albums was the beginning of my experience with aesthetics and a greater enjoyment of musical, written, and visual art.

Rock criticism was, for a period of years, the whole of my experience with written criticism. Luckily, the good rock journalists of the time maintained a healthy skepticism about the significance of their profession. I certainly hold a similar view of my efforts here.

However, after spending all of my professional life involved in the visual arts, I believe a higher level of critical thinking in all of the arts is more necessary than ever. During the postmodern period, from roughly 1960 to the present, the idea of quality has been under attack from well-meaning but misguided people who frown on judgments about the relative quality and importance of art. What has, in many instances, replaced critical judgment is description, which often verges on nothing more than reportage. How one criticizes without making judgments is beyond me, but a vast array of art writers do this. Some of these writers claim that the notion of quality is an outmoded, elitist, self-deception. Most, I believe, are simply following the trend that they see in the criticism they have read.

This trend in criticism finds a parallel in our everyday lives in the sort of pop psychology that has contributed to the destruction of quality in public education. It is based on an unwillingness to recognize the basic differences in us. This type of "I'm O.K., You're O.K." attitude that says everyone and everything is "special" is ultimately destructive as it eliminates the necessity to analyze, criticize, understand, and improve.

We need to understand why one thing is different than another so we can decide if it is better and if we should use that understanding to make what we do better. Will everyone agree that the same things are better? Of course not, but the conversation and ultimately the argument is important. Appreciating why something is different is of no use when it is not employed to make us do what we do better.

In this view intention is crucial. In this essay, for instance, I have indirectly noted the difference in skill level and musicianship between Derek and the Dominos, musicians of the top rank in their field, and the Sex Pistols who were comparatively crude. The Dominos were better musicians. They were more skillful, more versatile, and just as passionate. I make no distinction, however in the quality of their achievement in the context of each of the songs mentioned. Both bands were successful based on the fulfillment of the songwriter's intentions and their interpretation of it. This is crucial. It is the fulfillment of intention on which we must judge quality and it is our job to discern intention.

As an example, I wonder if anybody would be willing to argue that Bob Dylan's intentions in writing "Like a Rolling Stone" were on the same level as Chuck Berry in writing "Johnny B. Goode," one of the greatest and most influential rock and roll songs ever written? I wouldn't be surprised if Dylan, out of respect, would be loathe to admit that "Like a Rolling Stone" is a song of greater depth and intellectual scope, but it is. That doesn't mean "Johnny B. Goode" isn't a great song. I would be hard-pressed to say which I liked better, but what I like is not at issue here. "Johnny B. Goode" is great and important and if I had to decide which song to launch into space to contact other life forms I would probably choose it as well. But, I still think the content and the form of Dylan's song makes it more important.

This is not an "apples and oranges" argument, either. The "apples and oranges" claim is, in my mind, a cop out, a lazy, cheap excuse not to analyze and engage the material in question. These songs share common sources and instrumentation, both employed virtuosic bands, and similar recording technology. The real difference is in the level of thinking about the subject matter. This is not to denigrate Chuck Berry or his song. Chuck Berry is as great a figure in rock as Dylan is, but Dylan works at a different and higher level. There is just no getting around it.

I realize that these arguments are nothing new. Cover songs inherently invite critical comparisons and contrasts. Part of what I think makes them important is that they worked so well in the past. Great art has often been created in a hail of negative criticism, some of it good and relevant, some of it mean-spirited and reactionary. If the extremes, particularly the negative edges, weren't really necessary we can look back and see what to avoid in our judgments of contemporary art, whether visual or music. We can provide a thoughtful critical comparative context for artists to judge their efforts against.

Now, if I could only convince my daughter that Lil Wayne is the nadir of contemporary culture and that she should be listening to Little Richard!

BACK COVER: EPILOGUE

Chapter 15

Appreciating Cover Songs: Stereophony

Deena Weinstein

Rock, and rock criticism, emerged under the sign of high modernism, wildly waving a revivalist Romantic flag that valorizes creative artists expressing their unique selves in innovative ways. Romanticism dismisses cover songs as inauthentic ugly ducklings. Appreciating cover songs and recognizing that they are not foul—that they belong to a different and rather lovely species of fowl—requires a non-romantic aesthetic discourse that jettisons the obsession with authenticity and accepts that the raw material of rock is not life, but culture, albeit infused with "experience."

Musicians have long since grasped this point. For decades now, they have been plundering the past, recycling culture in a variety of ways—hip-hop sampling, dance remixes, mash-ups (like Danger Mouse's *The Grey Album* which combines Jay Z's *The Black Album* and the Beatles' *White Album*); or Beatallica's hybridization of Beatles' songs done in the performance style and with words resonating Metallica;[1] and, of course, cover songs.

But what is it that we seek here to appreciate—what is a cover song? It is not some performer's version of a song—the way that styles as diverse as folk, classical, blues, pop and jazz, understand iterations. For them, the song, whether copy-righted or written by that most prolific songwriter, Anonymous, exists in some abstract state. Rock, in contrast, having come into being in the Benjaminian age of mechanical reproduction, takes as the song the recorded performance. Those subsequently recording their own takes on that original recording create covers. But only in part. There is a second criterion crucial to covers: that the listener also knows the original. Otherwise, they are only hearing a recording, not a cover. For example, Elvis' early hit, "Hound Dog," was not a cover song to nearly all who heard it when it topped the charts in 1956, since they were innocent of Willie Mae Thornton's original 1953 release.

In recent decades, covers that meet both of these criteria have burgeoned for two reasons. One is that the number of recordings that remake some older

---

[1] Beatallica's *Sgt. Hetfield's Motorbreath Pub Band* (Oglio, 2007) songs include "Blackened the U.S.S.R.," an amalgam of the Beatles' "Back in the U.S.S.R." with Metallica's "Blackened," "... "And Justice for All My Loving" a marriage of "All My Loving" to "... And Justice for All," and "Helvester of Skelter" which lashes "Helter Skelter" to "Harvester of Sorrows."

recording have mushroomed in the last two decades.[2] They are created for a variety of reasons (including writer's block, some commercial advantage, because cover musicians find that originals express their own dispositions, a desire to show one's influences or to pay homage, or to kill one's idol by besting their best) that are irrelevant to their appreciation.

Secondly, in the same period, audiences have become inundated with rock's past. They are bombarded by reissues of old and older releases, and tours by dinosaurs or merely acts long past their peak, and are drawn to classic-rock radio formats. Then there is the proliferation of tribute albums that began in the late 1980s. A marketing director, Tim Johnstone, says that the practice "started on little teeny labels with bands that could barely pay the rent. But as soon as they started selling, big labels saw a cash cow" (Proctor, 1995). The major labels, however, had a freezer full of butchered cash cow, their back catalogues, which made tribute albums less than a tasty morsel for them. People now take advantage of the ease of obtaining music from all eras and styles—made possible by the record industry's conversion to digital distribution and then the mass use of the internet. Video games like Guitar Hero and Rock Band get listeners to focus in on golden oldies. Music fans have become gourmandizing musical omnivores, conversant with many different styles and eras; leading some of these uncertified musical archeologists to claim: "I like everything." These two trends, one on the musicians' side and one on the audience's, add up to a perfect storm of covers.

Any cover is an instance of what Umberto Eco (1985: 166) calls seriality, a type of repetition. And repetition is what has generally been seen, until the advent of the postmodern aesthetic, as inimical to art. Repetition is the antithesis of novelty, of some new creation. However, Romanticism does approve of one kind of cover—the "steal"—which seems to abolish the original, erase the past, and is "a negation of the already said," in Eco's words (Eco, 1992: 225). Steals appear to be innovations.

Of course, recordings covered by others are not as fully original as the term "original" would have us believe. No recorded performance is fully original; each is a bricolage of various intertextualities, including the artist's/band's own signature sound and genre, and a wide spectrum of borrowed musical, lyrical, performative, and production tropes. "The absolutely original artist is an extremely rare and possibly imaginary creature, living in some isolated habitat where no previous works or traditions have left any impression" (Pareles, 2003).

In contrast to Romanticism's focus on the creative individual, poststructuralism's key term, its central idea, is difference, which creates a play within intertextuality. We are creatures of difference, poststructuralists insist: meaning is differential, not referential. Texts, including works of art, signify by their difference from

---

[2]   For a discussion of the changes in rock cover songs over time see Deena Weinstein, "The History of Rock's Pasts through Rock Covers," pp. 137–51 in Thomas Swiss, John Sloop and Andrew Herman (eds.), *Mapping the Beat: Popular Music and Contemporary Theory*, Malden, MA: Blackwell, 1998.

other works. Derrida concludes that meaning, paradoxically, is the effect of the trace of what it is not in what is—contrast effects. Cover songs, then, are for poststructuralism, nothing unexpected. All songs, not only covers, are bricolages, cobbled together from existing materials. Rock musicians do not invent anew drums, bass and guitar, and do not originate a 4/4 beat. Nor do they invent the form of the pop song—intros and outros, number of minutes, verse-chorus-verse pattern, etc. The signature sound of a band evokes their other recordings and genre elements in a given recording evoke a whole genre, e.g., guitar solos, and lyrical and musical phrases.

Covers exist along a continuum from those that are drastically different from, to those nearly identical to the original. The "is it real or is it memorex?" imitative cover is especially prevalent in the ubiquitous tribute albums by bands influenced by the tributee. Tribute bands attempt, often more successfully than the original band playing in concert, to match the recording in their live performances, but they hardly ever make recordings.

Some of the most indistinguishable covers are found on Todd Rundgren's 1976 release *Faithful,* which includes his mimicry of recordings including the Beach Boys' "Good Vibrations." "By turning technology upon itself," Steve Bailey notes (from a Romanticist perspective), "Rundgren takes the Benjaminian aura-smashing potential of mechanical reproduction one step further. Not only is art reproducible, it no longer requires an original. "Good Vibrations" by Rundgren becomes indistinguishable from "Good Vibrations" by the Beach Boys, and thus the technology that allowed Brian Wilson to create his pop masterpiece renders the achievement meaningless" (Bailey, 2003: 153).

On the other extreme are those covers that are so unlike the original, in performance, arrangement, production and/or modifications to the composition itself, that it is difficult to know that they are covers at all. Is Nirvana's "Smells Like Teen Spirit" a cover of Boston's "More than a Feeling?" Is Coldplay's "Viva La Vida" taken from Joe Satriani's "If I Could Fly"? Indeed, some of these covers are only discovered in court, as various musicians have learned. George Harrison's "My Sweet Lord," a single from his 1970 release *All Things Must Pass*, was taken, the clueless Harrison learned, from the Chiffon's 1963 hit (composed by Ronald Mack) "He's So Fine." Some of Led Zeppelin's most famous creations were judicially determined to be not exactly their own. For example, their "The Lemon Song" was found to be a cover of Howlin' Wolf's (b. Chester Burnett) "Killing Floor."[3]

---

[3] For analyses of this case see Joseph C. Self, "The 'My Sweet Lord'/'He's So Fine' Plagiarism Suit," *910 Magazine*, 1993; reprinted at http://abbeyrd.best.vwh.net/stweet. htm and Dave Headlam "Does the Song Remain the Same? Questions of Authorship and Identification in the Music of Led Zeppelin," pp. 313–63 in Marvin, Elizabeth West and Richard Hermann (eds). *Concert Music, Rock and Jazz Since 1945: Essays and Analytical Studies*. Rochester: University of Rochester Press, 1995.

Most covers fall between these extremes. The reasons for the greater or lesser similarity to the original, intentional or unintentional, is irrelevant. "What matters who's speaking?" Foucault asks rhetorically, quoting Samuel Beckett (Foucault, 1977). Riffing on Foucault, the author of a cover song is created by that text—the cover song—not some creative artist standing outside the text. Thus, the reason or reasons, actual or stated, for making the cover are of no relevance to its appreciation. The degree of a cover song's artistic innovation, of its novelty, is also irrelevant to the appreciation one can derive from it. Whether it is (to use Romanticist terms) some "genuinely creative reworking" or an "essentially parasitic cover" is inconsequential.

Stereophonic listening is the key to appreciating covers. It is a distinctively postmodern and non-romantic experience constituted by the play of differences between the original and the cover. Both are consciously co-present and co-active, leading to shifting emphases on one or the other, or the (mediated) gap between them.

The experience of stereophony only works with two iterations of a "song." When there are more—and there are many songs with dozens or more covers[4]—the only way this form of listening works is by having all but one iteration in one's head; yet, other iterations may flit in and in and out of one's consciousness. It is also necessary to recall that the term "original" divested of Romanticism refers to the first iteration of a recorded performance that the listener knows, not necessarily the earliest recording in a chronological sense.

In appreciating covers, one feels and recognizes similarities and differences between the original and the cover: the first plays in your mind's ear, while the other comes in through your ears from some playback device. The appreciative act is not aimed at evaluating or getting pleasure from the cover as such and is not dependent on the artistic innovation so privileged by Romanticism; it resides in the appreciation/pleasure brought on by stereophony.

Obviously, interesting covers change the sensibility of the original—its overall mood or its meaning, or both. But covers that are rather similar to the original, or even major attempts at recreating the original in all ways, also provide pleasures.

Metal Church revisited Deep Purple's "Highway Star," transforming the classic metal staple into thrash metal. Faster and heavier than the original, it seemed more appropriate to the lyrics, and for those of us deeply into thrash metal when it was released, it was a welcome updating. But the cover also reinforced the genius of the original's guitarist, Ritchie Blackmore. When you heard Metal Church do the key guitar solo, it was clear that they were playing the same melody line but hitting far fewer notes than Blackmore. And for some listeners, that guitar solo is

---

[4]   There are a host of songs with more than a hundred cover recordings, including Procul Harum's Bachian "A Whiter Shade of Pale," Golden Earrings "Radar Love," and several Beatles' songs. The online database of cover songs, http://SecondHandSongs.com, lists close to 40,000 songs with at least one cover.

the song's centerpiece, the filling in an iced cake, making the preferable new icing and cake irrelevant.

A poor cover from the perspective of the Romantic aesthetic, one that has little or no novelty, a slavish imitation of the original, can still interest the listener. This type of cover is prominent in tribute albums by bands influenced by the tributee, but is increasingly done without such an excuse. Consider the song for song, note for note, replication of the entirety of the Ramones' first album by the Screeching Weasels in 1992 (including releasing the work on vinyl). But there is a slight difference; the cover album is a bit faster. That alteration makes me, at least, realize why after seeing the Ramones live, I found that their recordings were no longer pleasing. They played far faster live—most bands do. And for many styles of music, that increases the excitement—perhaps, in part, because it encourages one to breathe faster. The cover was a kill-your-idol creation, although I seriously doubt that was the band's intention.

Another example of how small differences are revelatory appears in Hammerfall's recent release, *Masterpieces*, which contains a cover of one of Judas Priest's best known works, "Breaking the Law." The Swedish power metal band's version is remarkably similar to the original in tempo, instrumental timbres, note-for-note guitar riffs, and vocal acrobatics that seem to ape Priest's vocalist Rob Halford better than his döppelganger, Tim "Ripper" Owens, who replaced Halford in the band for some years. But hearing this cover in "stereo" revealed that the original was far more exciting. Why? A second listen provided an answer. Hammerfall's cover was done in a precise metronomic, probably protooled, fashion, whereas Priest's recording had a slightly more raw rhythmic feel—and it was that rawness that created the excitement. The precision that mechanically synchronizes all the instruments and vocals, which studio equipment now makes rather simple, removes something that a listener, or at least this listener, rather enjoys. Another cover of "Breaking the Law," Unleashed's death metal version, growlier and faster than Priest's, reveals, better than the latter's recording, a sense of menace. In contrast, a pop-punk iteration by Pansy Division, a San Francisco-based originator of queercore, was void of threat, but, given the band's public image as gay men, underscored the meaning of the song's lyrics. Whether or not any of them actually were gay (not all were) is beside the point here. Gay sex was against the law in many areas, and is seen to be against "god's law" by a vocal minority of the public. (Pansy Division's release, two years before Priest's singer Halford publicly came out of the closet, might also have been in solidarity with him.) We might want to include as covers the videos of songs that MTV once played 24/7. Judas Priest's video for "Breaking the Law" uses the recorded track, so sonically it was not a cover. But the addition of the visual elements, basically an amusing Beatle-esque (à la "Help") bank robbery, removed any of the song's sense of frustrated rebellion against society.

Major differences between a cover and the original often involve a cut'n'paste genre or signature-sound transplant. When the change is from a style that one dislikes to one that one prefers, it allows the listener to enjoy, or to understand, the basic composition—its melody and/or its lyrics—abstracting it from the recordings. This is akin to translating a work from one language to another, where one is not particularly fluent in the first, reading in a halting, stumbling, effortful way. When the work is translated into one's native language, and yes, something is always lost in translation, the fluidity of the reading process allows a greater appreciation of the basic composition itself.

Basic composition can also come into awareness when the change is from a style that one likes to one to which one is indifferent or antipathetic. The original recording's genre or signature sound can be so appealing to the listener that it obscures the composition. Some of us resemble toddlers on Christmas morning, so interested in the wrapping that the present inside is forgotten. The Byrd's "Mr. Tambourine Man" was the "original" for me, and I found their sound so attractive that I scarcely attended to the lyrics. When I finally got to hear Dylan's original, it sounded rather naked to my ears, and I also found his voice somewhat unattractive. Both of these factors allowed the lyrics to stand out. (Years later, as Dylan's voice aged, its graininess was so appealing to my aging ears that by now I must put in effort to attend to his words.)

Genre or signature sound transplants can also provide entry to appreciate a style that was once beyond one's tolerance, since the familiar composition serves as a mediator, gently introducing one to it. The cover serves here as a friend in a foreign place, a Virgil in an Inferno of otherness, allowing one to taste hellish things safely. One can, perhaps, then return there alone. Having missed out on British hard psychedelia the first time around, I was led into it by discovering that one of the bands in that genre—Hawkwind—did a recording of a song I knew and liked very well, Motörhead's "Motörhead." Initially I didn't realize that my original was not chronologically prior, and had no idea that the "Motörhead"'s writer was in Hawkwind at the time it was recorded. I only found out the truth, disconcertedly, when I was happily chatting with the writer some fifteen years after he had recorded my original with a band he had named after that composition. Instead of letting me die of embarrassment then and there, Lemmy Kilmister indulgently remarked that he had written "Motörhead" to be performed as it is in his band, and that it was Hawkwind that "really" did the cover version. (Hawkwind's chronological original is without the umlaut; I didn't ask if the writer had put that in originally.) And the song led me into a genre that I would not have appreciated, even if I had stumbled into it in some other way, without having my original to guide me.

Kilmister was not so indulgent with another band's cover of one of his very best recordings, "Orgasmatron." Sepultura's savage aggro-thrash iteration was released eight years after his recording. "They did it without feeling," he grumbled. "I don't think that they understood what they were singing. I tend to sing it as insidious creeping evil where they just shout at it" (Dasein, 1992: 12). Sepultura's singer, Max Cavalera, provided his interpretation: "That song, it's really a hateful song, in a positive way. We didn't just repeat the original version. When I got the lyrics, I worked on them. I tried to express the feeling, like I was really feeling that. It has pretty heavy lyrics. We play it with a lot of hate. That's why we decided to cover that song. It is the first cover that we ever did" (Dasein, 1991: 10). Motörhead's performance is a straight ahead call to live; get liberated, God is dead. Sepultura's focuses on the hatred of the oppression that incites liberation, particularly the power of the Catholic Church in their homeland. "In Brazil where there's so much suffering already, people don't need to suffer more by having guilt thrown at them," Cavalera said (Dasein, 1991: 10). Each of these is a plausible take; there is no authorial privilege to Kilmister's, and taken together they deepen the work.

The comparison and contrast demonstrates Simon Watney's assertion "that a good song contains a multitude of performative possibilities" (Watney, 1994:16). Or as Eco puts it:

> *Every* work of art, even though it is produced by following an explicit or implicit poetics of necessity, is effectively open to a virtually unlimited range of possible readings, each of which causes the work to acquire new vitality in terms of one particular taste, or perspective, or personal *performance*. ... all performances are definitive in the sense that each one is for the performer, tantamount to the work itself. (Eco, 1989: 21)

Shockingly, Dylan, one of the poster boys of Romantic authenticity, seems to agree with Watney. In concert, he often covers his own originals, performing them in different arrangements from his recordings. In a sense, Dylan doesn't record any originals; his compositions are abstractions, to be arranged, and rearranged, as the mood takes him. Releases of material that Dylan left on the cutting room floor show that he was doing alternative arrangements in the studio too. What listeners hear in the original recording is simply the iteration that Dylan chose at that moment. As a reviewer of Dylan's live performance observes:

> Those who puzzle over why Dylan rarely plays his songs straight miss the point. Even his recordings are snapshots of a moment; he never intended his songs to be preserved as definitive statements, viewing them instead as mutable organisms that shift shape and meaning depending on the year, the mood, the weather (political, social, metaphysical) this afternoon. (Kot, 2002: 1)

Covers are capable of changing the overall sensibility of an original, and can do so by deploying a wide variety of techniques. A cover can provide a different mood, another emotional tone, and can alter the meaning of a composition, inverting it or merely providing a new understanding of the subject. And many covers change both mood and meaning. Heard stereophonically, these changes remind us of all the ways we have experienced something at one time that was felt or grasped in a radically different way at another, yet the second time around we are still haunted by the first.

Genre and signature sound transplants provide an alternative emotional response to that evoked by the original. Goth renditions, for example, tend to infuse a composition with a sense of weakness or misery. Other genre shifts remove weakness; for example, the Scissor Sisters' disco-on-speed "Comfortably Numb" relieves all the melancholy from the Pink Floyd classic.

Punk, a genre that began, in part, as a revolt against Romanticism, does not look askance at covers, and many of its covers provide a distinctively different sensibility from the originals. The most effective take smarmy pop recordings and deflate their "sincerity," rendering them as road-kill. The Sex Pistols' Sid Vicious' "My Way," which sneers at and ironizes the Frank Sinatra original (written by Paul Anka who appropriated the tune from a French song), and the Dead Kennedy's send-up of Elvis' "Viva Las Vegas" are prime examples. Each underscores contempt by starting with an exaggeration of the original's pomp before grinding fast feet in its face. Most punk covers change the sensibility by goosing up the tempo, injecting their performances with a vitality that gladdens a sad original, or rejuvenates a creaky one, creating vibrant irony. Less Than Jake's ska-punk cover of "Every Step You Take" removes the menace of the Police's recording. Likewise, the Dickies' cover of Barry McGuire's "Eve of Destruction" makes us think that the inhumanity of man around the globe isn't all that bad.

But one need not wreak such major changes as genre transplantation. Changing the rhythm or tempo, flattening out or enhancing the melody, adding or subtracting vocal harmony, or changing the key, among other moves, evoke a new hearing. Vocal delivery itself, as so many fans of karaoke will attest, makes for meaningful variation. The actual words comprising the lyrics probably provide less meaning than the way in which the singer delivers them. (Dogs and children demonstrate that this is true of human speech itself.) Listen to Johnny Cash's gravelly grave iteration of the Eagles' "Desperado" to grasp how horribly sad that its basic composition can be made. Or how Elvis Costello's earnest transformation of Nick Lowe's snarky anti-hippie rant "What So Funny About Peace, Love and Understanding?" brings out a pathos absent from the original.

Meaning is also filtered through the differences in the instrumentation of segments of the recording. Many people thought that Bruce Springsteen's "Born in the USA" was a rousing exaltation of America. A cover that had the same arrangement for the verses as the chorus would provide a different meaning.

Covers about that other source of emotional change, drugs, provide perhaps the clearest case of how covers enhance appreciation through contrast. Operation Ivy's faster punk cover of the Ramone's "I Wanna Be Sedated" shows how the punk progenitors were not that fast, and, more importantly, delivers a more meaningful plea for a sedative. The Byrd's harmony-encased "Eight Miles High" is a pleasurable trip, while Husker Dü's iteration seems to see the unfortunate underside, or maybe record the effects of a bad dose, as their wild trip ends in a disconcerting crash. Black Sabbath's "Snow Blind" makes one reconsider whether Sabbath had really messed with cocaine when one hears System of a Down's jumpy in your face iteration which more credibly reflects the impact of the drug. Sacred Reich's thrash reworking of Sabbath's paean to pot—"Sweat Leaf"—underscores at least the writer's (bassist Geezer Butler's) fine grasp of the know-thyself trip, but it also gives you the idea that the boys from Birmingham had been smoking ditchweed while the Arizona thrashers were inhaling sensimilla.

As the many examples of the varied play between "original" and "cover" show, the two are equiprimordial for the act of appreciation, dispelling any priority that has been given to the former. A post-structuralist aesthetic of the act of appreciation liberates the relation between "cover" and "original" by making them relative to the listener's history rather than the temporal precedence of one recording to the other. The binary original-cover, considered in terms of temporal precedence is rooted the Romantic conceit that the "original" is somehow an authentic creation, the measure of any of its future iterations.

The stereophonic act makes no such judgments of privilege—one iteration is playing in the mind's ear, another is received from a piece of machinery, and an act of conscious mediation occurs that brings them both into one or more of the manifold possibilities of play between them.

The act of appreciating covers is also indifferent to any other aesthetic valuations about the quality, evocative powers, meaningfulness, or any other criterion of aesthetic criticism—stereophonic listening is a form, the content of which varies indeterminately. One might or might not like one genre, song, or recording better than another—whatever the case, the listener can still gain value from the stereophonic act.

The many pleasures derived from the stereophonic act are dependent on the listener's history—which iterations came first and the listener's musical tastes (the subjective content that fills the form and propels the play of difference). Personal taste begins the appreciative act, but then the play of differences takes over, bringing the listener to a new position, broadening and deepening appreciative capacity.

The importance of the cover is that it makes possible an enhancement of appreciative capacity by giving the "original" a cultural sibling, setting up contrast effects of rivalry and/or mutuality.

Bibliography

Adinolfi, Francesco. *Mondo Exotica: Sounds, Vision, Obsessions of the Cocktail Generation* (Durham, NC: Duke University Press, 2008): 82.

Adorno, Theodor W. "On the Fetish Character in Music and the Regression of Listening," as printed in *The Culture Industry* (New York: Routledge, 2005): 36–8.

Almereyda, Michael D. (Dir.). *Hamlet* (Double A Films, 2000).

Allen, G. "More subversion than meets the ear." In Denisoff, R.S. and R.A. Peterson (eds.), *The sounds of social change: Studies in popular culture* (Chicago: Rand McNally College Publishing Company, 1972): 151–66. (Reprinted from American Opinion, vol. 12, pp. 49–62, 1969.)

Amurri, Franco. (Dir.). *Flashback* (60/80 Productions, 1989).

Anders, Charlie Jane (Sept 12, 2008). "Mashups: The Future Of Music?" (September 12, 2008) Retrieved October 25, 2008 from http://io9.com/5049120/mashups-the-future-of-music

Anonymous. *Ouen Shitaku Naru Kashu no Jouken to Wa?* (What are the Conditions for A Singer Who Wants to Gain Public Backing?) Konfidensu 26 (1335) (1992): 21–37.

Amagasaki, Akira. "Nazori to Nazorae" (Copying and comparison). in Shoji, Yamada (ed.), *Mohou to souzou no dynamism* (The dynamism between copying and creativity). Tokyo: Bensei Shuppan. (2003): 49–66.

Appel, Richard. (Scriptwriter) "Mother Simpson." *The Simpsons.* David Silmerman (Dir.),. James L. Brooks, Matt Groening, Sam Simon (Prods.). Fox TV (November 19, 1995). (Episode: 136, 3FO6).

Auslander, Philip. *Performing Glam Rock: Gender and Theatricality in Popular Music* (Ann Arbor: University of Michigan Press, 2006).

——. "I Wanna Be Your Man: Suzi Quatro's Musical Androgyny," *Popular Music* 21/1 (2004): 1–16.

Awkward, Michael. *Soul Covers: Rhythm and Blues Remakes and the Struggle for Artistic Identity* (Raleigh, NC: Duke University Press, 2007).

Azerrad, Michael. "Songs From the Heart," *Rolling Stone* (March 19, 1992): 104.

Bailey, Steve. "Faithful of Foolish: The Emergence of the 'Ironic Cover Album' and Rock Culture" *Popular Music and Society.* Vol 26, No. 2 (2003): 141–59.

Barker, Derek. *The Songs He Didn't Write: Bob Dylan Under the Influence* (London: Chrome Dreams, 2009).

Barthes, R. (1977). "Introduction to the structural analysis of messages" in Heath, S. (ed. & trans.). *Image, music, text* (New York: Hill and Wang, 1977): 79–125 (Original work published 1966).

Beers, Thom, and Geoff Miller (Prod.). *Ax Men*. The History Channel (2008).

"Beneath the Covers: Rickie Lee Jones Chats About Her Latest Album of Interpretations—From the Beatles to West Side Story." *Pop Interview* , Barnes & Noble.com Music. (September 12, 2000.)

Benjamin, Walter. "The Work of Art in the Age of Mechanical Reproduction," (1935), reprinted in *Media and Cultural Studies*, Meenakshi Gigi Durham and Douglas Kelner (eds.), (Malden, Massachusetts: Blackwell, 2001): 51–2.

Bennett, Andy. *Cultures of Popular Music* (Philadelphia: Open University Press, 2001): 14–15.

Binkley, Sam. "Kitsch as a Repetitive System. A Problem for the Theory of Taste Hierarchy," *Journal of Material Culture* 5(2) (2000): 131–52.

Bligh, Tom. "A Treatise on Cover Songs: Ooh, Child Let the Soulful People In." *The Oxford American* Issue 54 (2006): 162–8.

Booth, M.W. (1976). "The art of words in songs." *Quarterly Journal of Speech*, 62 (1976): 242–9.

Bowie, David. (Liner notes) *Pin-ups* (Rykodisc Vinyl Reissue, 1990).

Boyarin, Jonathan. *Thinking in Jewish* (Chicago: University of Chicago Press, 1996).

Bragg, Billy. (Liner notes) Billy Bragg and Wilco *Mermaid Avenue* (Elektra Records, 1998).

Brake, M. *The sociology of youth culture and youth subcultures: Sex and drugs and rock 'n' roll?* (London: Routledge & Kegan Paul, 1980).

Breakfast With the Arts. "Cassandra Wilson" Arts & Entertainment (A&E) (January 2003).

——. "Cyndi Lauper" *Arts & Entertainment* (A & E). (September 26, 2004.)

Brekke, Dan. "Tangled up in Seuss," *Salon* (April 13, 2007). Retrieved from http://www.salon.com/news/feature/2007/04/13/dylan_seuss/

Brett, Philip, Elizabeth Wood and Gary C. Thomas (eds.). *Queering the Pitch: The New Gay and Lesbian Musicology* (London: Routledge, 1994).

Bromell, Nick. *Tomorrow Never Knows: Rock and Psychedelics in the 1960s* (Chicago: U of Chicago Press, 2000).

Brooks, Daphne A. *Grace* (New York: Continuum, 2007).

Butler, Judith. *Gender Trouble: Feminism and Subversion of Identity* (London: Routledge, 1999).

——. *Bodies That Matter: On the Discursive Limits of Sex* (London: Routledge, 1993).

——. "Imitation and Gender Insubordination," in Fuss, Diana (ed.), *Inside Out: Lesbian Theories, Gay Theories* (London: Routledge, 1991): 13–31.

Campbell, H. "Drug trafficking stories: Everyday forms of narco-folklore on the U.S.-Mexico border. *International Journal of Drug Policy*, 16 (2005): 326–33.

Cann, Kevin. *David Bowie, A Chronology* (NY: Fireside Books, 1984).

Cardwell, Sarah. *Adaptation Revisited: Television and the Classic Novel* (Manchester New York: Manchester University Press, 2002).

CBS Sunday Morning. "Paying Musical Homage to the Greats". CBS News. September 9, 2007).

——. "Linda Ronstadt" CBS News. (December 5, 2004).

Chesky, K.S., Hipple, J., and Ho, K. "Perceptions of widespread drug use among musicians". *Texas Music Education Research* (1999): 1–9.

Chye, P.S. and Kong, L. "Ideology, social commentary and resistance in popular music: A case study of Singapore". *Journal of Popular Culture*, 30, 1, (1996): 215–31.

Clarence-Smith, Keiko. "Copying in Japanese magazines; unashamed copiers". In Cox, Rupert (ed.), *The Culture of Copying in Japan.* (London: Routledge, 2008): 51–68.

Colapinto, J. "Heroin". *Rolling Stone*, 735, (May 30, 1996): 15–20 and 58–60.

Connelly, Christopher. "Keeping the Faith" (March 14, 1985). Retrieved from http://www.rollingstone.com/news/coverstory/26242277/page/5

Copetas, Craig. "Beat Godfather Meets Glitter Mainman." *Rolling Stone.* (February 28, 1974). In Thomson, Elizabeth and David Gutman (eds.), *The Bowie Companion* (NY: DeCapo Press, 1996).

Cox, Rupert (ed.). *The Culture of Copying in Japan* (London: Routledge, 2008).

——. "Hungry Visions; The Material Life of Japanese Food Samples. In Cox, Rupert (ed.), *The Culture of Copying in Japan* (London: Routledge, 2008): 257–69.

Coyle, Michael. "Hijacked Hits and Antic Authenticity: Cover Songs, Race, and Postwar Marketing." In Beebe, Roger, Denise Fulbrook, and Ben Saunders (eds.), *Rock Over the Edge: Transformations in Popular Music Culture.* (Durham: Duke University Press, 2002): 133–57.

Crowe, Cameron. (Liner notes) *Bob Dylan: Biograph* (Columbia Records, 1985).

Cushman, Jack. "Mashups Bad! Covers Good – Should Copyright Prefer Cover Songs To Remixes?" (Dec 10, 2007). Retrieved from techregulationblogspot.com

Cusic, Don. "In Defense of Cover Songs." *Popular Music and Society*, vol. 28, no. 2 (2005): 171–7.

Dasein, D. "Tribute Albums: Looking Back in Honor." *Illinois Entertainer* (March 5,1995): 52.

——. "Mötorhead Raising Hell, Again." *Chicago Area Metal Magazine* 3 (1992): 11–13.

——. 1991. "Sepultura *Arise* to take the Thrash Crown." *Illinois Entertainer* 17 (August, 1991): 10, 64.

Denisoff, R.S. *Sing a song of social significance* (2nd edn.) (Bowling Green, OH: Bowling Green State University Popular Press, 1983).

Denisoff, R.S. "The evolution of the American protest song." In Denisoff, R.S. and R.A. Peterson (eds.), *The sounds of social change: Studies in popular culture* (Chicago: Rand McNally College Publishing Company, 1972): 15–25.

DeCurtis, Anthony. "Q&A: Bryan Ferry." *Rolling Stone* (8–22 July 1993): 20.

DeNiro, Robert. (Dir.). *A Bronx Tale* (B.T. Films, 1993).

DeRogatis, J. "Shannon Hoon 1967–1995." *Rolling Stone*, 722 (November 30, 1995): 23–4.

Diamond, S., Bermudez, R., and Schensul, J. "What's the rap about ecstasy?: Popular music lyrics and drug trends among American youth." *Journal of Adolescent Research*, 21, 3 (2006): 269–98.

Di Martino, Dave. "Reviews: Flattery Gets You Nowhere." *Musician* (November 1994): 83–5.

Dickinson, Kay. "Believe"? Vocoders, Digitalised Female Identity and Camp." *Popular Music*, vol. 20, no. 3 (2001): 333–47.

Doty, Alexander. *Making Things Perfectly Queer: Interpreting Mass Culture* (Minneapolis: University of Minnesota Press, 1993).

Downey, Pat, George Albert, and Frank Hoffmann. *Cash Box Pop Singles Charts, 1950-1993* (Englewood, Colorado: Libraries Unlimited, 1994).

Duchan, Joshua S. "Powerful Voices: Performance and Interaction in Contemporary Collegiate A Cappella." Ph.D. dissertation, University of Michigan (2007).

———. "Collegiate A Cappella: Emulation and Originality." *American Music*, vol. 25, no. 4 (2007): 477–506.

Duff, C. (2004). "Drug use as a 'practice of the self': Is there any place for an 'ethics of moderation' in contemporary drug policy?" *International Journal of Drug Policy*, 15, 385–93.

Du Noyer, Paul. "Contact." *MOJO, The Music Magazine* (July, 2002): 74–89.

Dyer, Richard, *Heavenly Bodies* (2nd edn.). (London: Routledge, 2004).

Dylan, Bob. *Chronicles, Volume 1* (New York: Simon and Schuster, 2004).

Eco, Umberto. "Postmodernism, Irony, The Enjoyable" in Brooker, Peter (ed.), *Modernism/Postmodernism*. (London: Longman, 1992 [1985]): 225–8.

———. *The Open Work* (translated by Anna Cancogni) (Cambridge, MA: Harvard Univ. Press, 1989).

———. "Innovation and Repetition: Between Modern and Post-Modern Aesthetics." *Daedalus* 114 (September, 1985): 161–84.

Eder, Bruce (Review) David Bowie: *Pin-Ups All Music Guide.* Retrieved 12 January 1998 from http://www.allmusic.com/cg/amg.dll?=amg&sql=10: hifxxqq5ld0e`T1>

Evans, Treveleyan Evans and Pete Sinclair (writers) *All Along the Watchtower.* Dir. Lissa Evans, (six episodes) (BBC, 1999).

Feldstein, R. "'I don't trust you anymore': Nina Simone, culture, and black activism in the 1960s." *The Journal of American History*, 91, 4 (2005): 1349–79.

Ferris, Timothy. "David Bowie in America." *Rolling Stone* (November 9, 1972). In Thomson, Elizabeth and David Gutman (eds.), *The Bowie Companion*. (NY: DeCapo Press, 1996).

Fiske, John. *Reading Television* (London: Methuen, 1978).

Flanagan, Bill. *Written in My Soul* (Chicago: Contemporary, 1986).

Foucault, Michel. "What Is an Author." In Bouchard, D.F. (ed.), *Language, Counter-Memory, Practice: Selected Essays And Interviews By Michel Foucault* (Ithaca: Cornell University Press, 1977): pp. 113–38.

Fremerman, Elana. Personal interview, Nashville, Tennessee (March 7, 2002).

Fresh Air. "Ron Sexsmith" (interview with Terri Gross). National Public Radio (June 5, 2001).

Friedkin, William. (Dir.). *Blue Chips* (Paramount, 1994).

Fricke, David. "Opinion: Tribute LPs Filled With Quirky Covers Are Just No Fun Anymore." *Rolling Stone.* February 4, 1993: 23.

Frith, Simon. *Performing Rites: On the Value Of Popular Music* (Oxford: Oxford University Press, 1996).

——. "Industrialization of Popular Music," *Popular Music and Communication* (Newbury Park, CA: Sage, 1992): 54.

—— and Howard Horne. *Art into Pop* (London: Methuen, 1988).

——. *The Sociology of Rock* (London: Constable, 1978).

Gardner, Elysa.. "A*Teens, *Pop 'Til You Drop.*" (record review) "Listen Up" *USA Today* (July 2, 2002): 3D.

——. "Traditional Pop Gets an Update." *USA Today* (February 13, 2001): 12D.

Giffney, Noreen and Myra J. Hird (eds.). *Queering the Non/Human* (Aldershot: Ashgate 2008).

Gilbert, Jeremy and Pearson, Ewan. "Discographies: Dance Music, Culture and the Politics of Sound (London and New York, 1999).

Gilmore, Mikal. "Don Henley" *Rolling Stone,* Issue 512 (November/December, 1987).

Gleason, R.J. "A cultural revolution." In Denisoff, R.S. and R.A. Peterson (eds.), *The sounds of social change: Studies in popular culture.* (Chicago: Rand McNally College Publishing Company, 1972): pp. 137–46. (Reprinted from *The Drama Review,* vol. 13, iss. 4, pp. 160–67, 1969.)

Golden-Perschbacker, Sarah. "'Not with You But of You': Unbearable Intimacy and Jeff Buckley's Transgender Vocality," in Jarmen-Ivens, Freya (ed.), *Oh Boy! Masculinities in Popular Music* (New York: Routledge, 2007): 213–33.

Gomart, E. and A. Hennion. "Actor Network Theory and After." In Hassard, J. and J. Law (eds.), *A Sociology of Attachment: Music Amateurs, Drug Users* (Malden, MA: Blackwell , 1999).

Gracyk, T. *I wanna be me: Rock music and the politics of identity* (Philadelphia: Temple University Press, 2001).

Griffith, Nanci. (Liner notes) *Other Voices, Other Rooms* (Elektra Records, 1993).

—— and Joe Jackson. *Other Voices: A Personal History of Folk Music* (New York: Three Rivers Press, 1998).

Gunderson, Edna. "Pop Raids the Recyclying Bin." *USA Today* (April, 2, 2004): 5D.

Guterman, Jimmy. (Liner notes) *Passion Is No Ordinary Word: The Graham Parker Anthology, 1976–1991* (Rhino Records, RCA Special Products, BMG Music, 1993).

Halberstam, Judith. *In a Queer Time and Place: Transgender Bodies, Subcultural Lives* (New York: New York University Press, 2005).

Hawkins, Stan. "On Male Queering in Mainstream Pop". In Whitely, Sheila and Jennifer Rycenga (eds.), *Queering the Popular Pitch* (London: Routledge 2007): 279–94

Haynes, Todd (Dir.). *I'm Not There.* The Weinstein Company (2007).

Headlam, Dave. "Does the Song Remain the Same? Questions of Authorship and Identification in the Music of Led Zeppelin." In Marvin, Elizabeth West and Richard Hermann (eds.), *Concert Music, Rock and Jazz Since 1945: Essays and Analytical Studies* (Rochester: University of Rochester Press, 1995): 313–63.

Healey, Jon and Richard Cromelin. "When Copyright Law Meets the 'Mash-Up'." *Los Angeles Times*. (March 21, 2004): 3F.

Hebdige, Dick. *Subcultures, The Meaning of Style* (New York: Methuen, 1979).

Hilburn, Robert. "Rock's enigmatic poet opens a long-private door." *Los Angeles Times*, April 4, 2004. Retrieved from http://www.calendarlive.com/music/pop/cl-ca-dylan04apr04,0,3583678

Hoggard, Stuart. *Bowie: Changes* (London: Omnibus Books, 1980).

Husserl, Edmund, *Ideas Pertaining to a Pure Phenomenology and to a Phenomenological Philosophy: First Book*, trans. F. Kirsten, Boston: Kluwer, 1982).

"Ice Cubes" (non-attributed column). *Ice Magazine* (September 2004): 8.

Inglis, Ian, "Covering the Market: Marketing the Cover," *Popular Music and Society*, vol. 28, no. 2 (May 2005): 163–70.

Jacobs, Dick and Harriet Jacobs. *Who Wrote That Song?* (2nd edn.). (Cincinnati, Ohio: Writer's Digest Books, 1994).

Jameson, Frederic. *Postmodernism, or, The Cultural Logic of Late Capitalism* (London and New York: Versa, 1991).

Jones, John Bush, *The Songs that Fought the War* (Lebanon, NH: Brandeis University Press, 2006): 4–8.

Johnson-Grau, Brenda. "Prodigal Sons on a Lost Highway: Records in Rock and Roll." *ONETWOTHREEFOUR*, Number 7 (Winter 1989): 21–36.

Kessler, Stephen. (Dir.). *Vegas Vacation.* (Warner Brothers, 2003).

Keyboard Magazine. "Imogen Speaks." vol. 32, no. 2 (February 2006): 32–6.

Klein, Larry. (Liner Notes) Joni Mitchell. *Both Sides Now* (Reprise Records 2000).

Klein, Joe. "Music: Bringing It All Back Home," *Time* (May 11, 2009): 151–2.

——. "Paying Musical Homage to the Greats" *CBS Sunday Morning* (September 9, 2007).

Kortes, Mary Lee. (Liner notes) *Blood on the Tracks* (Bar None Records, 2002).

Kot, Greg. "Bob Dylan proves unpredictable in concert at Allstate." *Chicago Tribune* (November 4, 2002): Section 5: 1 4.

Lanza, Joseph. *Elevator Music: A Surreal History of Muzak, Easy Listening and Other Moodsong* (London: Quartet 1995).

Laughey, Dan. *Music and Youth Culture* (Edinburgh: Edinburgh University Press, 2006).

Lawrence, Sharon. *Jimi Hendrix: The Man, The Magic, The Truth* (New York: Harper Collins, 2004).

Lax, Roger and Frederick Smith. *The Great Song Thesaurus* (2nd edn.). (New York: Oxford University Press, 1989).

Lazin, Lauren (Dir.). *Tupac: Resurrection* (Paramount, 2003).

Lebra, Takie. "*Migawari*: The Cultural Idiom of Self-Other Exchange in Japan." In Ames, Roger, Wimal Dissanayake and Thomas Kasulis (eds.), *Self as Person in Asian Theory and Practice* (Albany: SUNYP Press, 1994): 107–23.

Lee, Spike. (Dir.). *Clockers* (Universal, 1995).

Lemert, Charles. *Postmodernism is Not What You Think* (Oxford: Blackwell, 1997).

Lesser, Kira. *Personal communication with Joshua S. Duchan* (2008, 2009).

Leyland, P. "Cover songs: Or, as Jenny Lewis would say by way of the Traveling Wilburys, 'handle with care'" *Canadian Music, 29*, (2007): 1, 62.

Light, Alan. (Record liner notes) *Music from the Original Motion Picture: Masked and Anonymous*. (Columbia , 2003).

Linson, Art. (Dir.) *Where the Buffalo Roam* (Universal Pictures, 1980).

Lonergran, David. *Hit Records, 1950-1975* (Lanham, Maryland: Scarecrow Press, 2005).

Lord, Mary Lou. (Record liner notes) *Live City Sounds* (Rubric Records, 2002).

Lovesey, Oliver. "Anti-Orpheus: narrating the dream brother," *Popular Music* 23/3 (2004): 331–48.

Malkovich, John. (Dir.). *The Dancer Upstairs* (Fox Searchlight, 2003).

Mann, Michael. (Dir.). *Ali* (Columbia Pictures Corporation, 2001).

Manriki. "The History and Origin of Mashup" (2003) Retrieved October 15, 2008 from http://www.slurrymagazine.com/manriki.html

Manuel, Peter. "Cassette Culture: Popular Music and Technology in North India." *Chicago* Studies in Ethnomusicology (1993).

Marcus, Greil. "Old Songs in New Skins." In Guralnick, Peter and Douglas Wolk (eds.), *De Capo Best Music Writing 2000*. (New York: De Capo Press, 2000): 374–6. (Originally published in *Interview* (April 1999).)

——. "Real Life Rock: Greil Marcus's Top Ten." *ArtForum International* (December 1994): 14–15.

——. *Lipstick Traces* (Cambridge, MA: Harvard University Press, 1989): 57–60.

——. "A new awakening." In Denisoff, R.S. and R.A. Peterson (eds.), *The sounds of social change: Studies in popular culture*. (Chicago: Rand McNally College Publishing Company, 1972): pp. 127–36. (Reprinted from Marcus, G. (ed.). *Rock and Roll Will Stand*, Boston: Beacon Press, 1969).

Markert, J. "Sing a song of drug use-abuse: Four decades of drug lyrics in popular music—from the Sixties through the Nineties." *Sociological Inquiry*, 71, 2 (2001): 194–220.

Marrone, Mike (host/interviewer). *Songlines: Jackson Browne. The Loft, Sirius/ XM 50 Satellite radio* (September 27, 2008).

Marsh, Dave. *Louie, Louie.* (New York: Hyperion, 1993).

Marsh, Dave and Steve Propes. *Merry Christmas, Baby, From Bing to Sting.* (Boston: Little, Brown, 1993).

Martin, A. and Stenner, P. "Talking about drug use: What are we (and our participants) doing in qualitative research?" *International Journal of Drug Policy*, 15 (2004): 295–405.

Mashups. In Wikipedia. Retrieved November 22, 2008 from http://en.wikipedia. org/wiki/Mashups

Maslin, Janet. "So You Thought You Knew Dylan? Hah!" (October 5, 2004). Retrieved from http://www.nytimes.com/2004/10/05/books/05masl.html

——. "Bob Dylan at Budokan." *Rolling Stone* (July 12, 1979). Retrieved from http://uk.real.com/music/artist/Bob_Dylan/releases/At_Budokan

McDermott, John (with Eddie Kramer). *Hendrix: Setting the Record Straight* (New York: Warner, 1992).

McNair, Brian. *Striptease Culture: Sex, Media and the Democratisation of Desire* (London: Routledge 2002).

Mendes, Sam. (Dir.). *American Beauty* (Dream Works SKG, 1999).

Middleton, Richard. "Mum's the Word: Men Singing and Maternal Law." In Jarmen Ivens, Freya (ed.), *Oh Boy! Masculinities in Popular Music* (New York: Routledge, 2007): 103–24.

Milano, Brett. "How Many Tributes Does it Take to Exhaust a Fad?" *Pulse.* October 1991: 69.

Minamoto, R. *Kata to Nihon Bunka* (Patterned Form and Japanese Culture) (Tokyo: Soburisha, 1991).

Morgan, Glen Morgan and James Wong. (Scriptwriters). "Beyond the Sea." *The X Files.* Dir. David Nutter. Prod. Chris Carter. Fox Network (January 7, 1994).

Mosser, Kurt, "'Cover Songs': Ambiguity, Multivalence, Polysemy,", *Popular Music Online*, Issue 2: Identity and Performativity (2008): Last accessed: March 12, 2009, < http://www.popular-musicology-online.com/issues/02/ mosser.html>, "Section II: Species of Cover."

Murakami, Takao. "Mohouron Josetsu (An Introduction to Theories of Copying)." (Tokyo: Miraisha, 1998).

Nadel, Ira B. *Various Positions: A Life of Leonard Cohen* (Austin: University of Texas Press, 2007) (updated edn.).

"Nostalgia." *Sound & Spirit.* Public Radio International/ WGBH Radio Boston (January 1, 2000).

Osborne, Ben. *The A-Z of Club Culture* (London: Sceptre, 1999).

Osborne, Jerry. "'Covers' and 'Remakes'–They're Different Things." *DISCoveries.* No. 155 (April 2001): 10.

Pareles, Jon. "Plagiarism in Dylan, or a Cultural Collage?" *The New York Times* (July 12, 2003). Retrieved from http://www.nytimes.com/2003/07/12/arts/music/ 12/dyla.html

——. "In Pop, Whose Song is it, Anyway?" *New York Times* (August 27, 1989): Section 2:1.

Partridge, Eric, *Origins: A Short Etymological Dictionary of Modern English*. (New York: Macmillan, 1979): 249–50.

Pavlow, Big Al (comp.). *The R & B Files, 1940–49; & 1950–59*. (Providence, Rhode Island: Music House Publishing, 2001).

——. *The R & B Book: A Disc-History of Rhythm and Blues* (Providence, Rhode Island: Music House Publishing, 1983).

Pichaske, David. *A Generation in In Motion: Popular Music and Culture in the Sixties* (Dexter, MI: Ellis, 1989).

Plasketes, George (ed.). "Like a Version: Cover Songs in Popular Music" (Special Issue). *Popular Music and Society*. 28 (May 2005).

——. "Re-flections on the Cover Age: A Collage of Continuous Coverage in Popular Music." *Popular Music and Society*, vol. 28, no. 2 (2005): 137–61.

——. "Look What They've Done to My Song: Covers and Tributes, an Annotated Discography, 1980–95." *Popular Music and Society*. Volume 19.1 (Spring 1995): 79–106.

——. "Like A Version: Cover Songs and the Tribute Trend in Popular Music." *Studies in Popular Culture*, Volume XV:1 (1992): 1–18.

Posting by Staff. (2007, August 10). "The Infectious Spread of Mashup Music and Video." (August 10, 2007). *The World Time News Report*. Retrieved October 27, 2008 from http://www.wtnrradio.com/news/story.php?story=246

Powers, Genevieve. "Imogen Heap." *Remix Magazine*. vol. 8, no. 1 (January 2006): 20.

Proce, Michael. (Scriptwriter). "My Mother the Carjacker." *The Simpsons*. Nancy Kruse (Dir.). James L. Brooks, Matt Groening, Sam Simon (Prod.). Fox TV (November 9, 2003). (Episode: 315, EABF 18).

Proctor, David. "Anyone Can Sing An Elton John Song, But Why Cover What Originally Worked Well?" *Gannett News Service* (April 27, 1995).

Puterbaugh, Parke. "Building The Perfect Beast." *Rolling Stone* (January 31, 1985).

Rapkin, Mickey. *Pitch Perfect: The Quest for Collegiate A Cappella Glory* (New York: Gotham, 2008).

Reising, Russell. *Every Sound There Is: The Beatles' Revolver and the Transformation of Rock and Roll* (Aldershot, UK: Ashgate, 2003).

Reynolds, Simon. *Rip It Up And Start Again: Postpunk 1978-1984* (London: Faber and Faber, 2006).

R.G., (Review) *Pin-Ups The Music Scene* (December 1973) Retrieved January 8, 2008, from The Ziggie Stardust Companion, http://www.5years.com/pinupsreviewmsdec73.ht>

Rhino Records 1991–92 Music Catalog. (Santa Monica CA: 1991): 50.

Robinson, Bruce (Dir.). *Withnail and I*. (HandMade Films, 1987).

Robbins, Wayne. *Behind the Music: 1968*. (New York: Pocket Books, 2000).

Roby, Steven. *Black Gold: The Lost Archives of Jimi Hendrix*. (New York: Billboard Books, 2002).

Roberts, Sheila, "Todd Haynes Interview," Retrieved from http://www.moviesonline.ca/movienews_13495.html

Robertson, Pamela. *Guilty Pleasures: Feminist Camp From Mae West To Madonna* (London and New York: I.B. Taurus, 1996).

Robinson, J.P., Pilskaln, R. and Hirsch, P. "The rhetoric of revolt: Protest rock and drugs." *Journal of Communication*. 26, 4 (1976): 125–36.

Rosen, Jody. *White Christmas: The Story of an American Song* (New York: Scribner, 2002).

Rundgren, Todd. *Faithful* (Bearsville Records, 1976).

Sandford, Christopher. *Bowie: Loving the Alien* (London: De Capo, 1997).

Schaffner, Nicholas. *The British Invasion* (NY: McGraw-Hill, 1983).

Scorsese, Martin. (Dir.). *No Direction Home: Bob Dylan* Spitfire Pictures, Grey Water Park Productions,Thirteen/WNET, PBS and Sikelia Productions (2005).

Self, Joseph C. "The 'My Sweet Lord'/'He's So Fine' Plagiarism Suit," *910 Magazine* (reprinted at http://abbeyrd.best.vwh.net/stweet.htm) (1993).

Seward, Scott. "Why Baltimore House Music is the New Dylan," *Post Road Magazine*, Issue 3, Fall/Winter 2001, Retrieved from http://www.postroadmag.com/Issue_3/Criticism3/SewardCritic.htm

Sex Pistols. "God Save the Queen," *Kiss This* (Virgin, 1992) (a compilation album).

——. "Bodies," *Kiss This* (Virgin, 1992) (a compilation album).

Shapiro, H. (1988). *Waiting for the man: The story of drugs and popular music* (London: Quartet Books, 1988).

Shapiro, Harry and Caear Glebeck. *Jimi Hendrix: Electric Gypsy* (New York: St. Martins, 1992).

Shales, Tom. "The Re Decade." *Esquire* (March 1986): 67–72.

Shaw, Greg. "Pin-Ups Review." *Rolling Stone* (December 20, 1973). Retrieved from <http://www.rollingstone.com/artists/davidbowie/albums/album/177265/review/6212094/pin_ups>

Shepherd, J. (1991). *Music as social text* (Cambridge, UK: Polity Press, 1991).

Shih, Shu-mei. *Visuality and Identity; Sinophone Articulations across the Pacific*. (Berkeley, CA: University of California Press, 2007).

Sinagra, Laura. "With Her Synthesizer, She Mesmerizes." *The New York Times* (January 13, 2006): E3.

Smale, R. "Addiction and creativity: From laudanum to recreational drugs." *Journal of Psychiatric and Mental Health Nursing*, 8 (2001): 459–69.

Smith, Patti. (liner notes) *twelve* (Columbia, 2007).

Smith, Whit. Personal interview with Don Cusic (March 7, 2002).

Smith, Zadie. *On Beauty* (London: Penguin, 2006 (2005)).

——. *The Autograph Man* (New York: Vintage, 2003 (2002)).

Sontag, Susan. "Notes on Camp." *The Susan Sontag Reader* (NY: Vintage, 1982): 105–19.

Strinati, Dominic. "Postmodernism and Popular Culture." In Storey, John (ed.), *Cultural Theory and Popular Culture: A Reader* (Brighton: Harvester Wheatsheaf, 1994).

Taussig, Michael. *Mimesis and Alterity; A Particular History of the Senses* (New York: Routledge, 1991).

Taylor, Michael. (Scriptwriter). "Crossroads, Part 1." *Battlestar Gallactica*. Dir. Michael Rymer. Sci-Fi Network (March 18, 2007).

Thomas, Betty. (Dir.). *Private Parts* (Paramount, 1997).

Thompson, Ernest. (Dir.). *1969* (MGM, 2003).

Thornton, Sarah. *Club Culture: Music, Media and Subcultural Capital* (Cambridge, MA: Polity Press, 1995).

Turner, John Frayn, Frank Sinatra (Lanham, MD: First Taylor Trade, 2004): 154–5.

Verheiden, Mark (Scriptwriter). "Crossroads, Part 2" Episode # 320. Dir. Michael Rymer, *Battlestar Galactica*. SciFi Channel (March 25, 2007).

Von Ganrnier, Katja (Dir.). *Bandits* (Bavaria Film, 1997).

Von Gunden, Kenneth. *Postmodern Auteurs: Coppola, De Palma, Lucas, Spielberg and Scorsese.* (Jefferson and London: McFarland, 1991).

Warhol, Andy. *The Philosophy of Andy Warhol* (San Diego: Harvest, 1975).

Watney, Simon. "Cover Story," *Art Forum International* (October, 1994): 15–16.

Weekend Edition, "Faux French Rock with Les sans Celottes." Ben Shapiro (Prod.), National Public Radio (April 2, 2005).

Weinstein, Deena. "The history of rock's pasts through rock covers." In Swiss, Thomas, John Sloop, and Andrew. Herman (eds.), *Mapping the Beat: Popular Music and Contemporary Theory.* (Malden, MA: Blackwell Publishers, 1998): 137–52.

Wenders, Wim, (Dir.). *Alabama: 2000 Light Years From Home* (Hochschule für Fernsehen und Film, 1969).

Whitburn, Joel. *Top R & B/Hip-Hop Singles, 1942–2004* (Menomonee Falls, Wisconsin: Record Research, 2004).

——. *Top Pop Singles, 1955–2002* (Menomonee Falls, Wisconsin: Record Research, 2003).

——. *Billboard Pop Hits: Singles and Albums, 1940–1955* (Menomonee Falls, Wisconsin: Record Research, 2002).

——. *Pop Annual, 1955–1999* (Menomonee Falls, Wisconsin: Record Research, 2000).

——. *A Century of Pop Music: Year-By-Year Top 40 Rankings of the Songs and Artists that Shaped a Century.* (Menomonee Falls, Wisconsin: Record Research, 1999).

——. *Billboard Pop Charts, 1955–1959* (Menomonee Falls, Wisconsin: Record Research, 1990).

——. *Pop Memories, 1890–1954: The History of American Popular Music* (Menomonee Falls, Wisconsin: Record Research, 1986).

White, Hayden V. *Metahistory: The Historical Imagination in Nineteenth Century Europe* (Baltimore: Johns Hopkins Press, 1973): 45–6.

White, Timothy. (Liner Notes) John Mellencamp. *Rough Harvest* (Mercury Records, 1999).

Wicke, P. (1993). *Rock music: Culture, aesthetics and sociology* (R. Fogg, trans.) (Cambridge, UK: Cambridge University Press, 1993) (original work published 1987).

Wilder, Eliot. "Jules Shear: New Life to Old Tunes." *Paste* (October/November 2004): 33.

Wolf, Betty Jo. *Mashup Music* (April, 2008). Retrieved November 22, 2008 from www.meiea.org/Ezines/Vol5No2/mashup.htm

Wolf, P.L. (2005). *The effects of diseases, drugs, and chemicals on the creativity and productivity of famous sculptors, classic painters, classic music composers, and authors*. Archives of Pathology and Laboratory Medicine, 129, 11, (2005): 1457–64.

Wright, Christian. (Record review) "I'm Your Fan: The Songs of Leonard Cohen by ..." *Rolling Stone* (February 6, 1992): 80.

X. (Liner Notes) "Soul Kitchen" *Los Angeles* (Rhino Records, 2001).

Yano, Christine. "Covering Disclosures: Practices of Intimacy, Hierarchy, and Authenticity in a Japanese Popular Music Genre." *Popular Music and Society* 28(2) (2005): 193–205.

——. *Tears of Longing: Nostalgia and the Nation in Japanese Popular Song* (Cambridge: Harvard Asia Center, Harvard University Press, 2002).

Yamada, Shouji. *Mohou to Souzou no Dainamisumu* (Dynamism between Copying and Creation) (Tokyo: Bensei Shuppan, 2003).

Zak, Albin. *The Poetics of Rock: Cutting Tracks, Making Records* (Berkeley: University of California Press, 2001).

Zanuck, Lili Fini (Dir.). *Rush* (MGM, 1991).

Zemeckis, Robert. (Dir.). *Forrest Gump* (Paramount, 1994).

Index